HARD LABOUR

HARD LABOUR

THE FORGOTTEN VOICES OF LATVIAN MIGRANT 'VOLUNTEER' WORKERS

Linda McDowell

Routledge
Taylor & Francis Group
www.routledge.com

First published in Great Britain 2005 by UCL Press,

This edition published 2013 by Routledge
2 Park Square, Milton Park, Abingdon, Oxon, OX14 4RN
711 Third Avenue, New York, NY 10017

Published in Australia by Cavendish Publishing (Australia) Pty Ltd
45 Beach Street, Coogee, NSW 2034, Australia

Routledge is an imprint of The Taylor & Francis Group, an informa business

British Library Cataloguing in Publication Data
McDowell, Linda, 1949–
Hard Labour
1. Women refugees – Latvia – History – 20th century
2. Women refugees – Great Britain – History – 20th century
3. Latvians – Great Britain – History – 20th century
4. Alien labour – Great Britain – History – 20th century
5. World War, 1939–1945 – Refugees – Great Britain
6. World War, 1939–1945 – Great Britain – Women
7. Latvians – Great Britain – Social conditions – 20th century
8. Great Britain – Social conditions – 20th century
I. Title
305.4'89193041

Library of Congress cataloging in Publication Data
Data available

ISBN-10: 1-84472-020-9
ISBN-13: 978-1-844-72020-0

1 3 5 7 9 10 8 6 4 2

For Chris, Hugh and Sarah, with love

PREFACE

This is a book about the wartime plight and later working lives of a group of women migrants who left Latvia in 1944 as the Soviet army marched westwards. They came to Britain between 1946 and 1949 under government schemes to recruit foreign workers to fill post-war labour shortages in female-dominated sectors of the economy. Displaced by the huge disruptions of the Second World War, these women regarded themselves as refugees or exiles but were transformed by governmental decree from displaced persons, as they were known in the refugee camps in Germany, into labourers, designated economic migrants and recategorised as European Volunteer Workers (EVWs) on their entry to the UK. It is generally argued by theorists and empirical analysts of migration flows that women migrants tend to move as dependants of their male relatives – following their fathers, brothers, husbands or uncles who are seen as the main movers behind decisions to migrate. However, these women flout this generalisation. They came as young single women from parts of northern and eastern Europe with little or no connection to the UK, unlike the migrants from Ireland and the Caribbean whose migration to Britain in the post-war years is a more familiar story than that of the EVWs.

Neither geographical proximity nor the ties of Empire connected this latter group to the United Kingdom. Instead, these women came to Britain because of the dislocation of war. They had little knowledge of the UK before their migration and no reason, other than homelessness and economic necessity, to come to the UK. No common language or history led them to Britain and they assumed, at least initially, that their residence in this country would be a temporary one. This was not to be the case. Most of the women who came to the UK in the late 1940s still live here, despite the huge upheavals in the status of Latvia and the other Baltic States of Estonia and Lithuania in the last decade and a half. Independence in the early 1990s has been followed by European Union membership in 2004 as these small nation states reclaimed and then partially surrendered independence and turned their faces resolutely to the west. New flows of young migrants, many of them women, but moving voluntarily rather than in response to war and invasion, now reconnect Britain and Latvia.

The main focus of this book, however, is not on the Baltic States but on the lives of these women as they left and then settled in the UK. Its substantive focus is on work, both paid and unpaid, and on the connections between gender and work. These women came to the UK as workers at a time when many British women were being encouraged to go back to the home and when an idealised view of femininity based on domesticity and maternity was a dominant ideal. EVW women challenged these associations as they were recruited as paid workers. They had also been constructed and used as labour power, both free and bonded, during the years between leaving Latvia in 1944 and entering the UK, three and six years later. For most women, the type of work that they undertook in their early years in Britain placed them firmly in the working class and many of them were not to escape this location as the twentieth century progressed, despite their varied class origins. However, their working lives were also marked by gender as they took up firmly defined types of 'women's work' in the female-dominated occupational ghettos of the post-war British labour market. Their lives are, therefore, ones characterised by the connections between class and gender, by the particularities of place and time and by the vast dislocations of the Second World War in Europe. These events transformed these women's lives in ways that they had never expected as they grew up in the pre-war safety of urban and rural families in Latvia, often with a middle class standard of living and an expectation, at least until 1939, of settled lives.

While this story of the women who were recruited as EVWs by the British state is a particular one, it is also part of a larger and, until now, relatively unfamiliar one, at least in the west, about the great exodus of people, many of them of German extract, who fled from various eastern territories as the Soviet army moved westwards in the final stages of the Second World War. The fate of these migrants and their subsequent lives as displaced people in western Europe has remained largely uninvestigated and untold. In the face of the forced removals by the Nazis of Jews, gypsies and various 'decadents' and dissidents and the tragedy of the holocaust, the expulsion of peoples from German-occupied lands received relatively little attention from historians of the post-war period of reconstruction. It is, however, an exodus that more recently has begun to be documented. In 2002, the great German novelist Gunter Grass published a short but powerful novel *Im Krebsgang* (published in English the following year as *Crabwalk*) to a controversial reception. In this novel he re-examined the story of the sinking of the *Wilhelm Gustloff*, a German-owned former pleasure steamer that in the pre-war years took German workers on Baltic holidays but was later commandeered for war service. In January 1945, the ship was holed by a Soviet submarine and sank in the icy waters of the Baltic with the loss of more than 6,500 lives, the majority of them German women and children from East Prussia, as well as some troops, who were fleeing the advancing Soviet front. Grass's novel received a somewhat mixed reception in Germany when it first appeared as it seemed to be part of a hesitant but growing revisionist history advocating recognition of the suffering of Germans under the Nazi regime. About 15 million people of German ethnicity were driven from Eastern Europe in the closing stages of the war, from countries including the former Czechoslovakia, Romania and Poland and from the Baltic States. A German-based organisation – the Association of the Banished – has recently proposed the establishment of a museum in Berlin to commemorate these displacements. However, the proposal aroused fears of a revived nationalism among many intellectuals and politicians on the left, including Grass, who signed a petition against the museum (Cleaver 2003). It is clear, however, that the contested history of suffering and different forms of displacement during the Second World War deserves wider investigation as new sources continue to be uncovered.

The aim of this book is to contribute to the exploration of this contested history but also to add to knowledge about the variety of women's working lives in postwar Britain. In telling a small part of the story, through the voices of a particular group of women from Latvia, I have strayed across disciplinary boundaries, drawing on recent work in anthropology, history, social geography and women's studies. I have tried to bring together a number of different debates in a way which I hope raises new questions and adds to our understanding of post-war Britain as much as the contested events of the war and the aftermath of its disruption in continental Europe. The debates that I draw on include new research on work and employment, especially from a feminist perspective, that emphasises the connections between labour market participation and unpaid work in the home; debates in history and women's studies about the nature of the social construction of femininity in post-war Britain; and an expanding literature about migration, transnationalism, diasporic identities and citizenship in the context of the second half of the twentieth century as Britain became an increasingly multicultural nation. Finally, I have explored recent debates in both the social sciences and the humanities about social and collective memories. I hope that the book will interest scholars from all of these fields as well as those interested in multidisciplinary perspectives. However, I also want to interest a more general audience whose appetite for historical knowledge, especially relatively recent past events such as the Second World War in which their fathers and mothers, or perhaps grandparents, may have played a part, seems insatiable. Wanting to know more about my own parents' history was one of my own motivations for exploring the late 1940s and the 1950s.

In a sense that seems appropriate for a work about history and memory, this book has had a longer gestation than anything else I have written. Its antecedents lie in a piece of fieldwork I undertook years ago when I was an undergraduate student of geography at Cambridge University. In the early 1970s, as a dissertation project, I interviewed men from Latvia, Lithuania, Poland, the former Yugoslavia and from the Ukraine who were then working in the British Steel plant in Corby New Town. These men had come to Britain as what were initially known as DPs or displaced persons, people who during the Second World War had for various reasons left or been forced to leave their homelands. They came to Britain in the first few years after the end of the war to work as 'volunteer' labourers in heavy industries, short of labour and essential for the post-war reconstruction effort. In the years between the early 1970s and 1990s I seldom thought about Corby or the men whom I had interviewed until I rejoined the Cambridge University Geography Department and became the colleague of the late Graham Smith. Graham's passionate interest in the newly independent Baltic States rekindled my memories of the men from this region to whom I had talked more than two decades earlier. I began to wonder about how they had spent their working lives and what they thought about independence. However, I also realised that I had ignored their wives, sisters and daughters. How and why did young women from the Baltic States come to the UK and what sort of work had they undertaken? Did they come before, with or after the men to whom I had talked? And what sorts of lives had they led in those early years in Britain? In 1999, I made a grant application to the British Academy, whose support for this work I gratefully acknowledge, and began a new field project – to trace and talk to now elderly women from Latvia who also entered the UK as migrants and as workers in the post-war years.

Both the impetus to and the focus of this work, then, is memory: my own memories of an early study and of a much-missed colleague but, more importantly, the memories of women of wartime trauma and dislocation, of statelessness and of migration. It is also a book about migration and movement and the demands of strange cultures. These women left Latvia as young women and were unable to return to the country of their birth for almost 50 years. They came to the UK as volunteers and as exiles and, despite the expressed hopes of the British State, determinedly resisted assimilation. When I began to interview them in 2000, many of them had returned to Latvia during the 1990s for holidays but none of them had felt able to return on a permanent basis, tied to the country of their long exile by age, friends and family networks. However, all of them had enthusiastically accepted a Latvian passport. In all the quotations that I have included, I have transcribed the speakers' words as I recorded them, in an attempt to reproduce the tones and cadences of the interviewees. Many of these women continued to use, for example, sentence structures that reflected their origins. For ease of reading, Latvian first names appear without accents, although I have used them when referring to places. I have also used the common names of the time – and so Gdańsk is Danzig – when the women whom I interviewed did so.

Over the five or so years I have been working on this study I too have been a migrant, albeit on a tiny, less significant scale and by choice, rather than necessity. I began this project as I left the Cambridge Geography Department to move to London University and as I finished it I moved again – this time to the School of Geography and the Environment at Oxford University. All these departments have proved to be exceptionally interesting places, full of congenial colleagues interested in place, memory, migration and feminist theory. This is a better book because of the numerous exciting and productive discussions I have had with colleagues in all three locations. So, thank you. It almost goes without saying that I could not have written this book without the huge kindness of 25 women who welcomed me into their homes and allowed me to record their words as they shared their experiences of dislocation, loss and a new life in Britain. I feel honoured by the confidence they expressed in my ability to re-present their views. I hope this book lives up to these expectations. I have changed their names as we agreed but I am sure they will recognise their own words. I am also grateful to The British Academy for its financial support through the small grants scheme for the empirical work.

Parts of several chapters are based on revised versions of articles that I have written. I am extremely grateful to the editors and publishers of the respective journals for their permission to draw on the following papers: The particularities of place: Latvian migrant workers in 1950s Britain, *Transactions, Institute of British Geographers* 28, 2003, 19–34; Workers, migrants, aliens or citizens? *Political Geography* 22, 2003, 863–86; Narratives of family, community and waged work: Latvian European Volunteer Worker women in post-war Britain, *Women's History Review* 13, 2004, 23–55 and Cultural memory, gender and age: young Latvian women's narrative memories of wartime Europe, 1944–47 *Journal of Historical Geography* 2005. I should like to thank those individuals and organisations, including the Latvian National Council in Great Britain and the Latvian Welfare Fund, that gave permission to reprint tables, figures and photographs. While every effort was made to contact copyright holders before publication, any missing acknowledgment should be notified and will, of course, be added should the book be reprinted. Ailsa Allen drew the outline maps and Briar Towers was my guide through the editing and publication process: many thanks to them too. Finally, writing this book coincided with my own children leaving home – one as an economic migrant to Australia and then Japan, the other to become a university student. While their absence gave me a great deal more time to write, I continue to miss their lively presence and their inimitable ability to distract me from academic endeavours.

Linda McDowell
Oxford
February 2005

CONTENTS

LIST OF ILLUSTRATIONS

Tables, maps and figures

Photographs

CHAPTER 1

INTRODUCTION: LOOKING BACK TO THE 1940S AND 1950S

One of the great pleasures of being a feminist scholar writing about women's post-war lives in contemporary Britain is the freedom it allows to investigate a range of issues that have personal resonance. It is noticeable that as the generation of second wave feminist theorists who have been so influential in changing the nature of social science in the last three decades has aged so too has their empirical focus shifted from an interest in childbirth, housework and employment to an emphasis on ageing (see, for example, Greer 1985, 1992; Oakley 1974a, 1974b; Rowbotham 1989). A related feature of this shifting focus has been the recent interest among feminist scholars and others in their childhood memories of the early post-war period. One of the most vivid of the memoirs that has appeared in the last few years is Lorna Sage's (2000) moving story of her upbringing in rural Wales in the 1950s – *Bad Blood* – in which she explored some of the implications of her own spatial and social mobility as she moved to the north of England as a first generation university student and then into the middle classes as a university lecturer after a strange and lonely childhood. I too was a child in the 1950s and these various memoirs and reflections awoke only half-hidden memories. Alison Pressley's (1999) foreword to her book of personal reflections *The Best of Times: Growing up in Britain in the 1950s* took me straight back to those years:

> You remember Liberty bodices, suspender belts, nylons, roll-on girdles, paper-nylon petticoats, winkle-picker shoes, crisp packets with little blue waxed paper twists of salt inside, Duffel coats, black Bakelite telephones with exchange names and simple numbers …
>
> You are a Baby Boomer, born after World War II ended, just in time to enjoy the innocent, secure, never-had-it-so-good fifties.

I was born at the tail end of the 1940s and started school in 1954, growing up as post-war severity was gradually transformed into a more affluent society. I had already read with interest a whole series of recollections on the era, including Elizabeth Wilson's (1980) *Half way to Paradise*, Sara Maitland's (1988) *Very Heaven* and Liz Heron's (1985) *Truth, Dare or Promise* about girls growing up in the 1950s and 1960s. However, as well as my growing interest in the lives of women of my own age – the baby boomers – I found I was becoming increasingly curious about the lives of an earlier generation: those women, including my own mother, who were young adults in the late 1940s and 1950s, having their sons and daughters as part of the post-war baby boom and often perhaps moving into a life of domesticity after more active working lives during the war. I had long suspected that the stories about domesticity in the 1950s and women's supposed lack of political activity concealed more differences between women than they captured similarities. What about the women who remained in the labour market, combining domesticity, motherhood and employment in the immediately post-war era? How did they feel? Did their identity as workers conflict with their ideal of motherhood? And how were their home and working lives altered by new technology and growing affluence during the golden years of Fordist production, new consumer goods and more comfortable homes?

The publication in 1998 of Wendy Webster's study of the first two post-war decades – *Imagining Home: gender, 'race' and national identity, 1945–64* – revitalised my interest in these questions. Webster's main focus was a comparison of white 'native' women with in-migrants from the Caribbean, assessing the ways in which the social construction and regulation of motherhood excluded women of colour. I have a similar aim: reimagining those years from the perspective of women for whom paid work was a necessity and, in the early post-war years for the migrant women who are the focus on this book, a legal requirement. Instead of looking at the Irish and Caribbean women who met a significant part of the post-war demand for female workers, the focus here is on an earlier group of migrant women: women from the Baltic States who came to Britain as displaced persons. They entered the UK as 'European Volunteer Workers' (EVWs) at the end of the war and their presence and experiences are less well documented than those of other groups of migrants, despite the fact that about 20,000 women from the Baltic states and other parts of Eastern Europe entered Britain between 1946 and 1950.

The European Volunteer Workers scheme was introduced by the British government in 1946 to recruit single young women in displaced persons' camps in Germany to meet the labour shortages in female-dominated sectors in the UK economy. At the end of the war there were about seven million homeless people in Europe, many of them living in the camps in German and former German territories that the Department of Labour officials began to visit from late 1945. The camps housed a diverse group of people from many nations and former nations in eastern and northern Europe. Not all these displaced people were victims of the Nazi regime. Indeed, some of them had looked to the Nazis for assistance as they fled the approach of the Russian front westwards in the closing phases of the war. Among these people were several thousand former residents of the Baltic States – Estonia, Latvia and Lithuania – as well as people of German descent who had moved from what had been Polish territory back into the German heartland. Although many of these stateless refugees chose to return to the territories of their birth and others were forcibly repatriated at the close of hostilities, others decided to remain in the camps, hoping that the allies might allow them to enter one of the victorious countries as refugees and asylum seekers. While agreeing to their entry, in most cases, the allied nations took a strictly utilitarian view of their potential new citizens, seeing them not in humanitarian terms as deserving respect and recompense for wartime disruption but instead as labouring bodies, as potential workers to aid in the post-war efforts of reconstruction. Consequently, educational qualifications and employment skills, but above all, a fit and healthy body became an essential prerequisite for displaced persons hoping to continue to move westwards. The old, the unfit, the disabled and infirm were left behind. For women prospective migrants, an additional consideration was their suitability as potential wives and mothers of the new nation. The significance of a common European heritage and the physical suitability of the potential migrants were emphasised: stock and blood were common terms in Cabinet discussions, for example, and as Kathleen Paul (1987, p 88) has argued 'at a time of perceived demographic crisis, the United Kingdom could only benefit from an infusion of the right kind of stock, both male and female'. Male recruits might rectify labour shortages; women would also, it was argued, boost the general birth-rate..

This story of embodiment and labouring, of feminine respectability and purity, and the roles played by western governments in recruiting these women workers is not well known, and the opinions and later lives of the relatively fortunate camp occupants who were regarded as acceptable for employment in Britain has not been told, or at least not in their own words. In this book I begin to correct this lacuna, telling the stories of 25 women who came to Britain in the immediately post-war years as 'volunteer workers', at least in the eyes of the British government, if not in their own. Instead they regarded themselves as seeking refuge from the brutality of the Soviet regime that had, in their opinion, illegally seized their homeland. This was a view which they refused to modify over many decades of residence in Britain until, in 1991, Latvia once again became a nation state and their long belief in Latvia's right to self-determination was vindicated. By this time, however, it was too late for these women. Despite their long-held desire to go 'home', they found that age, family connections and relative poverty tied them to Britain, although some of them were able to return to Latvia as holiday makers and temporary visitors and one or two successfully reclaimed property that their families had owned in the inter-war period.

The women whose voices are heard in this book were recruited by officials from the British Ministry of Labour between 1946 and 1949. Under the auspices of two schemes, rather fancifully termed the Baltic Cygnet Scheme and Westward Ho!, fit, young and single women with no dependants were selected to fill job vacancies in Britain. At the end of the war, hit by labour shortages in many industries despite demobilisation, the British State decided, in the teeth of trade union opposition, to look outside the country for workers to replace the older workers and women who withdrew from employment in 1945. It was assumed by the government that women would perhaps be less unacceptable to the male-dominated union movement than male workers (although men were in fact recruited under the second scheme, Westward Ho!, and in larger numbers than women). As many women were initially recruited into forms of employment with tied housing, it was also argued that these migrant workers would not be in competition with British families for scarce accommodation, again reducing the potential resistance to the recruitment of foreign workers.

The women from the former Baltic republics and elsewhere who were recruited under these schemes were brought to Britain and allocated employment, in the main as domestic workers in institutions, especially hospitals, and in private homes, as well as industrial work in the textile industry. The history of these women's working lives in Britain has been left untold, despite the fact that it challenges the assumptions about women's withdrawal from the labour market in the early post-war years. The recruitment of the EVWs also more than doubled the foreign-born population of the UK at that time and preceded the more well known migrations from the Caribbean (Kay and Miles 1992, Paul 1997) and so is a significant element in the changing nature of the British population through in-migration in the post-war period.

Thus, while these women's lives and their wartime experiences as they fled the Soviet front advancing westwards are intrinsically interesting, adding a new dimension to our understanding of the position of women in the Second World War, their lives also provide an invaluable insight into contemporary attitudes, beliefs and behaviour about migrants in post-war Britain. A focus on the EVW schemes, therefore, provides a way into broader questions about both British immigration policy and the reconstruction of identity and community among diasporic peoples, as these 'volunteer workers' challenge many conventional assumptions and distinctions in the debates about migration into the UK. Their position as a hybrid or 'in-between' category in post-war Britain makes them unique, so providing a counter-focus to conventional assumptions about the post-war period.

Migration and identity: hybrid migrants

This 'betweenness' or uniqueness of the late 1940s European migrants to Britain lies in several areas. First, women were the initial migrants, entering the UK in advance of male recruits of the same nationalities and so reversing the common trend in migration flows. They also challenge conventional distinctions in both migration theories and policies between refugees and economic migrants, as in their own eyes the displaced people were refugees and asylum seekers, but in official policy they were designated as economic migrants or EVWs. Furthermore, these women were distinguishable from the other main categories of migrant workers into the UK, especially those from the Caribbean and from Eire, by their class, skin colour, religion and alien status. Thus, these women occupied an interesting hybrid location in post-war Britain, neither (or both) refugees nor migrant workers, women but not mothers, often middle class by origin but required to accept manual employment, alien and yet European, with no previous attachments to the UK, unlike Irish and Caribbean women, and unable to return to their homeland, which disappeared as an independent entity until the early 1990s when these former EVWs were, in the majority, too elderly to return. Unlike Irish and Caribbean migrants, with a history of attachment to and connections with the UK, these Baltic women had ended up in Britain through an accident of history and the trauma of wartime dislocation and yet, despite the disappearance of their homelands, they continued to wish for and organise around Baltic independence during their long 'exile'.

Their lives thus provide a fascinating comparison with other post-war migrants and an interesting study of how and why the British State chose to recruit them initially and how it constructed them as particularly desirable workers. Indeed, considerable efforts were made to present these women as suitable Britons in what might now be regarded as eugenicist terms. They were, for example, described in official documents as superior to rural Polish women and as potential marriage partners for British men. For this, and perhaps other reasons, Baltic refugees were treated comparatively leniently by the allies despite the Yalta Agreement in 1945 under which citizens of countries by then under Soviet domination were expected to be returned to the Soviet Union. These women, therefore, also occupied an ambivalent position as post-war survivors. They had lived in German-occupied territory during the war and sometimes they or their families had been active participants in German domination, albeit often on an involuntary basis. And there is a complex and contested history of Latvian collaboration with the Nazis, which has resulted in the post-war period in a number of expulsions from Britain of men originally from the Baltic States.

These women also provide a lens into the social construction of femininity in post-war Britain as, unlike many British women, especially those of a similar class background, they were required to participate in the labour market in the early post-war years. There is an interesting and expanding literature that is beginning to examine the diversity of women's lives in both the pre- and post-war decades, drawing both on historical records and on the testaments of elderly women (see, for example, Glucksmann 2000). This work documents the ways in which women's labour market participation is connected to and conflicts with their domestic responsibilities, a conflict that was largely unrecognised, or rather ignored, in the post-war rhetoric about women's dual roles. Focusing on migrant women in the post war period also allows us to question official ideologies of femininity in the 1940s and 1950s when the mark of a 'good woman' and of domestic respectability was, above all, motherhood and withdrawal from the labour market. The lives of migrant women challenged this association. Furthermore, these women's working lives provide an insight into the opportunities for and extent of social mobility as British society began to change from the 1950s onwards. For many of them, their lives were marked by downward social mobility, in contrast to the 'native' population, for whom, both women and men, the post-war decades seemed to be ones of increasing affluence and opportunity.

Leaving Latvia

The women whose voices and lives fill these pages are all from Latvia, a country that was occupied and incorporated into the Soviet Union in 1940, then occupied by Germany from June 1941 and reoccupied by the Soviet Union in the last stages of the war. It was, as Anthill (1958, p ix) noted, 'a small nation crushed between two leviathans'. During their short-lived initial occupation, the Soviet authorities arrested and deported or killed 15,000 Latvian citizens over a single night – 15 June 1941 – and were later to repeat the exercise in 1949 when 10% of the rural population of Latvia was deported to facilitate the collectivisation of farmland. During their occupation, Nazis had also arrested and exported thousands of Latvian citizens to forced labour camps in Germany, as well as conscripting many young men, ostensibly into a Latvian regiment but *de facto* into the German Army. When the German armed forces surrendered in the East in 1944–45, about 125,000 Latvians left for mainland Western Europe and the Scandinavian countries, fearful of their fate once the Soviet Union took over again, following their compatriots who had left, most of them for Sweden, in the early 1940s. Many of the second wave migrants ended up in Germany, fleeing the Soviet expansion westwards to find refuge, eventually, in the American and British occupation zones. Once there, these refugees were first placed in camps and later offered passages to other nation states, often with conditions attached, under a range of different schemes to recruit migrant workers as part of post-war reconstruction efforts. This flight and wartime dislocation, followed by obligatory participation as labourers for the by then faltering Nazi war effort, and then by life in the relative calm of the displaced persons camps is the subject matter of Chapters 3 and 4. In Nazi Germany these young women were directed to undertake a range of tasks, including sorting coal, manufacturing munitions, street cleaning and agricultural and domestic work. In the displaced persons' camps, the Allies also put some of them to work, although the youngest among these women attended school classes. Here too, those who worked undertook a range of manual jobs, as well as clerical labour: in all, hard tasks for teenaged girls and young women who were often from a middle class background.

Only a small number of books and articles about 'displaced' peoples have been published so far in English. In the 1950s, the main focus was on the Polish troops demobilised in the UK, although in 1958 JA Tannahill wrote a book about the European Voluntary Workers (EVWs) programme, outlining the origins of the participants and their early lives in Britain. After that date, nothing was published in Britain until 1992, when Diana Kay and Robert Miles published their re-evaluation of these schemes. However, almost nowhere in this tiny British literature do the distinctive voices of the workers themselves appear, apart from in a small number of archived interviews from the late 1970s, in the Bradford Sound Archives.

At the centre of this book, therefore, are the voices of elderly Baltic women, originally recruited as EVWs. During 2000 and 2001, I talked to and recorded oral narratives from 25 women, then in their 70s and 80s, who fled from Latvia in 1944 in the face of the advancing Russian front. Women from Latvia were the majority among the women from the Baltic who became EVWs and continue to be perhaps the most well organised as a community in the UK. Latvians who decided to leave escaped by ship, landing in Danzig (now Gdańsk in Poland) and journeyed westwards by train or on foot through the winter of 1944–45, one of the most severe winters of the century. As I noted in the preface, the story of one of these Baltic crossings has recently, and controversially become the subject of a novel by Gunter Grass but, in general, relatively little has been written about the 1944 migration from the Baltic States, and about the particular experiences of young women in this movement. Even less is known of their experiences as workers in the German war effort. In part my book helps to counter these absences.

Structure of the book

As women's work is the focus of this book, feminist scholarship has been a key influence. One of the great strengths of this work has been to question the key theoretical distinctions that have dominated our understanding of society, in particular the distinction between the public and the private spheres. Feminists have challenged the taken-for-granted associations of men with the former arena and women with the latter location, documenting not only the reasons for this association but its complexity in practice. One of the implications of this challenge was a rethinking of the definition of work, recognising the connections between work undertaken in different locations, especially unpaid work in the home and paid work in the workplace, its associations with women and with men respectively and so its differential value and, concomitantly, unequal financial rewards. Domestic labour was rescued from what might be termed the enormous condescension of history and instituted as a proper focus for academic attention. The British feminist scholar, Ann Oakley (1974a, 1974b) provided an invaluable spur to think again about the nature of women's unpaid work in the home. There has been a parallel and stimulating debate about women's position in the labour market, seeking explanations of their segregation in a limited range of occupation and their unequal financial rewards compared with the wages earned by men (see, for example, Bradley 1989; Walby 1986, 1997). Thus, the gendered attributes of different types of work have been examined, revealing the ways in which men and women have been employed in the post-war era under a range of different conditions and for different types of rewards that overall confirm women's inferior status in the labour market. Other more recent work has revealed how jobs and occupations themselves are imbued with gendered attributes, as well as investigating the ways in which gendered performances are constituted through everyday interactions and workplace cultures to construct women as 'out of place' in many workplaces. (For a summary of much of this work see Chapter 3 of McDowell 1999).

Other debates have also influenced this book. The growth of transnational migration in a globalised world, increasing the movements between national territories, has raised new questions about notions of belonging to a nation, about nationality and nationalism, as well as about the definition of citizenship. The collapse of the Soviet Union and the former Yugoslavia has seen the rise of new nation states, countering the movement towards a more cosmopolitan concept of citizenship. In these debates, contested notions of identity, culture and race have been central to the discussions about citizenship rights. In a sense, the language of rights has been transformed from a focus on universalism that often counterposed the terms culture and rights into a new insistence on the connections between culture and rights, on culture as a basis for establishing rights (Cowan *et al* 2001). In this conception, only people who are able to demonstrate an attachment to a particular territory and its myths and history are seen as legitimate and acceptable citizens. These debates, as well as the material changes with they are connected, have had a significant impact on the women in this book as their long belief in the case for re-establishing Latvia as an independent state was finally vindicated and they were able to go 'home': a return that raised difficult issues about belonging and identity after more than 50 years away and what is seen as their absence in the long struggle against the Soviet occupation. In May 2004, Latvia and the other Baltic States acceded to the European Union, raising new questions about the nature of European identity and its association with a shared cultural heritage. In Chapter 2, therefore, I assess some of these new questions.

I sketch in there the outlines of three connected debates that are too often discussed separately behind disciplinary boundaries. These include first, arguments from migration studies and the expanding literature about migration, transnationalism and diasporic identities, secondly, recent work about social and collective memories and, finally, feminist arguments about work and employment. Readers with less interest in theory might, without significant loss, I think, move straight into Chapter 3. However, I have endeavoured to make these debates accessible to the non-specialist. I see no need to pretend that theory is intrinsically complicated or that it must be expressed in complex prose. In my view, theory is more like a good map, allowing the reader to see the lie of the land, as it were, the connections between places or, in this case, sets of arguments that initially might not be obvious.

In the middle chapters of the book, the ways in which Latvian women coped with loss and with hard labour as displaced people in Nazi Germany during the final year of the war and then in camps established by the Allies in Germany after its defeat are the subject. I explore how these women came to Britain as economic migrants and how they managed the contradictions of employment and motherhood in the post-war decades. The negotiations between their residence in British working class neighbourhoods and their determination to reconstruct an imaginary version of a pre-war bucolic Latvian communal identity in Britain are also examined, desires that are explicable in part as a reaction to the loss of national identity and the dislocation of family life these women suffered in the last two years of the war. In Chapter 3, I examine the early lives of the 25 women and situate them within their families of origin that were, in the main, middle and lower middle class. I explore the types of expectations developed by these then young girls during the inter-war years – a period known retrospectively as 'the golden age' for Latvia – as well as the significance of a bucolic image of a rural Latvia, which as I show later (in Chapter 8) has been a key image in re-establishing Latvian myths and rituals in the UK. I deal with the circumstances in Latvia during the war, first in the early Russian occupation in 1940–41, then during the German occupation, looking at the political sympathies of their parents and older siblings and their varied experiences, some as German sympathisers and others as Latvian patriots and partisans, set in the context of the difficult and contested ethnic and cultural history of the Baltic States. I examine the decision to leave Latvia, the journey to the coast, the Baltic Sea voyage in late 1944 and early 1945 and arrival in German occupied territory.

In the second half of this chapter, the focus is on the survival tactics adopted by the young women and their companions on the journey, examining transport, food, personal safety and sexual danger, as well as the help they undoubtedly received from many different people, sometimes taking risks to help the refugees. I show how some women were drawn into the Nazi war effort as labourers, while others hid their identity through various strategies, including masquerading as Russians or Germans, or by dressing as boys for many months before arriving at camps for displaced persons in Germany where they gained a temporary respite – although often stretching into years – from wandering. In the next chapter, I explore the forms of voluntary and paid work in which these women were engaged in the camps, as well as showing how self-help and organisation was a key part of daily life there. For many young women, this period was a complex one in which their conflicting desires for greater independence and for close communal links struggled for dominance. I show how the theme of hard work under conditions of close bodily surveillance threads through their lives on the run, as forced labourers under the Nazis and as workers for the Allies unites these two chapters, and prefigures their future lives in Britain.

In Chapter 5, I begin to explore the continuities that developed in the working lives of these women as they moved from camp labouring to new work in Britain through the post-war 'volunteer' labour schemes, showing how these women became labouring bodies rather than individuals, part of a grand scheme to recruit 'good muscular working flesh' (Hulme 1954) as part of the wartime and reconstruction efforts by Germans and the Allies alike. The chapter is about the EVW schemes, volunteer worker schemes, introduced in Britain from 1946 onwards. I explore how and why young Latvian women were recruited by the British government, as well as their knowledge of the country before their arrival. I look at the rumours floating in the camps about slave trade and slave labour, at the procedures women were subjected to on recruitment – pregnancy tests etc – and at their arrival in transit camps in the UK, culminating with their initial allocation to employment. The chapter also examines the introduction of the EVW schemes from the perspective of the British government, as well as from the perspective of the participants, addressing the ways in which in state discourses Baltic women were constructed as superior, initially, to other displaced European women and, later within the UK, to women from the Caribbean. Here I shall show that, despite recruiting Baltic women primarily as units of labour, there was also a significant rhetoric about their suitability as potential Britons and an evident desire for these women to be assimilated into the British way of life, despite their exclusion from the then current ideal of domesticity for 'decent' women. In this chapter, I also address some of the comparisons between Caribbean and Irish women economic migrants and the EVWs, assessing the changing immigration policies of the post-war British State and the ways in which it differentially constructed migrant workers as more or less worthy.

In the next two chapters, Chapters 6 and 7, the focus is on the post-war lives of British women and the relationship established between their 'dual roles': as wives and typically and as participants in the labour market. The first and shorter of this pair of chapters is based primarily on secondary sources and provides the context for the following chapter which examines the types of paid work undertaken by Latvian women as they were released from the obligations of their initial allocation as EVWs. It looks in general at the position of women in post-war Britain, at the development of the ideology of domesticity but also at the gradual expansion of paid work for many women, especially part-time work that was regarded as unthreatening for women's primary role as wives and mothers. In Chapter 7, I explore in detail the working conditions experienced by the young Latvian women who were allocated jobs in hospitals and factories in the late 1940s, the ways in which these young women were regarded by the British population on their arrival and how they were treated by their co-workers. I show how their initial allocation, whether to domestic work in hospitals or in other locations or to manual labour in the textile industry, set the conditions for the rest of their lives. However, as well as occupational location, I argue that geography also mattered as not only did these women live different lives in different locations but the place in which they lived had real effects on the structure of opportunities facing them and the sort of communal ties that they were able to establish. I look at the labour process in the different sectors in which the EVW women were employed, at their tasks, hours and pay, adding to the empirical histories of women's work in the 1940s and 1950s.

In this chapter too, marriage and motherhood and the construction of a communal Latvian life in exile is described. Despite the early scheme – the Baltic Cygnet, recruiting solely women – in total 9,700 Latvian men compared with just over 2,000 Latvian women came to the UK as EVWs. This gender differential had a profound impact on the women's lives and was a central reason why they were able to reconstruct an imagined Latvian community in exile. Almost all the 25 women I interviewed married men from Latvia and lived within a community composed almost entirely of their compatriots until their children were born and, in particular, started school. I look at the ways in which communal self-help was significant in housing provision as well as at the organisation of a range of community activities based on Latvian folklore and rural traditions in which women were the key social cement in creating communal solidarity. I also examine the ways in which many of these migrants remained in the same type of work as that to which they had been allocated on entry to Britain. I think this is a reflection of their desire to be independent and relatively invisible to the host population. It became clear that their ambitions were not for themselves but for their children, many of whom have regained the educational, occupational and class status lost by their parents on fleeing Latvia. I look in particular at the ways in which migrant women negotiated the contradictions between being a mother and being a worker in 1950s Britain, the extent to which their location within working class towns and cities affected their construction of their sense of themselves as women and mothers and as aliens, assessing the extent of difference and diversity both within this group of Latvians and between Latvian women and other working class women who also combined paid and domestic labour.

In Chapter 8 I turn to the ways in which Latvians in Britain organised communal activities to construct an imagined version of Latvian nationality and community in exile, showing how their upbringing in the inter-war years influenced their sense of belonging to Latvia, even through the years of Soviet domination when few of them were able or willing to return 'home'. I end this chapter by addressing the implications of the re-establishment of Latvian independence for these by then elderly women.

All these chapters, with the exceptions of Chapters 2 and 6, draw on the oral histories that I collected from 25 now elderly Latvian women who came to Britain between 1946 and 1949. They follow a primarily chronological sequence, addressing the central issues in women's lives at different periods in the post-war era. Each chapter has a different location at its centre – whether a geographical location in the sense of a particular town or city, a sectoral location within a particular industry or the home and the neighbourhood – and mobility (or lack of it), both social and geographical, is a central theme in the ways in which these women reconstructed a Latvian identity in exile. Overall, the aim is both to shine new light on a now largely forgotten moment in history and raise a series of still significant questions about the nature of identity, belonging, memory and the treatment of 'others' in ways that reach into the past and the present.

CHAPTER 2

THINKING THROUGH GENDER: THEORISING MIGRATION, MEMORY AND IDENTITY

This exploration of migrant women's lives is through a dual lens: Latvian women's own experiential accounts of their lives, supported and contextualised by a study of contemporary records and documents of the period and other narratives of movement and loss. But it also draws on recent theoretical work in the social sciences and the humanities as a framework for analysing the changing position of Baltic women, albeit guarding against making assumptions that may have little resonance with these women's own view of the events at the time. I listened carefully to women's own voices, aware that contemporary theoretical debates may not reflect the lives and remembered realities of these women. Recent ideas about women's empowerment through participation in paid work, for example, may not be relevant to Latvian women's post-war lives in Britain, nor do they see their deep commitment to rebuilding a particular form of family life from the late 1940s onwards as necessarily oppressive: some may have found it so but many did not; others were more ambivalent in their reflections. However, it is also important to know how articulate and argumentative these women are. They were not prepared to leave the interpretation of their lives solely to me. Thus, in the process of research and writing, they offered useful feedback, added additional topics to the interviews, read some of my work and made it quite clear when they thought there were errors of interpretation and representation. First, then, before their voices suffuse the book, here is a critical survey of the theoretical propositions that informed the research process. For those of a less theoretical bent, this chapter may be read later. While its main aim is to position academic readers in the contemporary literatures that influenced the book, I hope it will also interest more general readers wanting to learn more about ways of rethinking these particular set of events in European history.

Three debates are juxtaposed in this chapter: first, a set of arguments about migration, nationalism and national identity, including recent work on the theorisation of diasporic and transnational identities, in large part but not entirely stimulated by postcolonial theory; secondly, a growing literature about social memory and oral narratives; and, thirdly, more established feminist arguments about work and employment. A common theme runs through the text, linking these three debates. All these arguments question and challenge what were once assumed by social scientists to be solid, unchanging concepts and categories: notions of the body, of individual identity, of memory, and definitions of masculinity and femininity. It is now widely accepted that social identity – whether as a woman or a man, as a migrant or a local, as black or white, as belonging or not belonging to particular nation – is more appropriately theorised as a fluid and mobile category, as a relational construct that is socially constructed in time and space through social interactions with others and in the institutional discourses and practices that regulate social relations. As the Latvian women were to find, their various identities as aliens, as outsiders, as white Europeans, as good mothers and/or transgressive women workers, depended on the context within which they were present or were being discussed and the nature of the comparisons with others that were drawn. Identity, in current social theory, is seen as multiple, and as hybrid. Thus, migrant women fall both within and outside the categories, boundaries and definitions of acceptability and legitimacy at different times and in particular contexts or places. For migrants, a shift in their identity is, of course, a key corollary of movement but, as Latvian women were to find, their various identities as workers, as potential Britons or as transmitters of Latvian heritage were all part of their sense of themselves as 'aliens' in post-war Britain. This notion of multiplicity informs all three debates – about migration, memory and work – that are now outlined in turn.

Theorising migration and transnational identities

Movement of people between places is a central dynamic in understanding the connections between nations, societies and individual and group identities. Throughout the twentieth century, international population movements, within Europe and beyond, have 'reforged states and societies ... in ways that affect bilateral and regional relations, security, national identity and sovereignty' (Castles and Miller 2003, p x) as well as people's own national and individual identities. Migration within Europe in the twentieth century has to be understood above all within the context of war and ideological contest. As Eric Hobsbawm (1994) argued in his magisterial history of this 'short' century, war and the rise and fall of two significant ideologies – national socialism and communism – transformed the meaning of Europe and restructured political relations between nations. In the second half of the century, the events of the Second World War and its aftermath, the rise and collapse of national socialism, the long years and spectacular collapse of communism in the East and, more recently, the establishment and expansion of the European Union and the circulation of people within and between the member states have all affected the nature of people's connections to the nation state in which they were born. Economic globalisation has also created new flows of capital and labour across national boundaries. At the same time, the growing significance of ethno-nationalist movements in the second half of the century has made clear the continuing importance of links between national identity and territory, exemplified in the disturbing rise of inter-ethnic genocide in Europe (in Kosovo (see Malcolm 1998), for example), by the widespread incidence of racist violence linked to migration and by growing ethnic diversity within national boundaries. For the women in this book, these great shifts in ideology and identity set the scene for their own transformation from citizens of an independent nation in 1939, to stateless aliens, then, for most of them, into British citizens and most recently as dual citizens in a greatly expanded European Union. Their lives, then, mirror the disruptions and restructurings of the relations between nation and identity that have marked the recent history of Europe.

Although the majority of the human population, even in this era of growing globalisation, remains in the place where they were born, migration has a significant impact not only on migrants themselves but also on the societies of the emigration and immigration countries. Those who leave their country of origin may be forced to do so or may have made a positive choice to move. In part this depends on the circumstances – involuntary or forced migration may be a consequence of war as populations are deported or flee to seek asylum. Others may move to improve their life chances and standard of living as economic and social inequalities between North and South widen. Theoretical approaches developed to explain migratory flows are, to some extent, related to the different reasons behind movement. Thus, neoclassical economic explanations based on the primacy of individual rational choices are typically developed to explain movement related to living standards, as for example in mathematical predictions based on relationships between the number of opportunities in the receiving area and the distance to be travelled. Alternative approaches place greater stress on structural inequalities in economic and political power as drivers of migration. Here, historical approaches based on large-scale structural explanations of events are more common. Often based on Marxist political economy, such explanations see migration as a response to capital's desire to mobilise cheap labour. Both approaches have their blind spots; the former focuses exclusively on the 'rational' individual, the latter on impersonal forces to the neglect of individual attitudes, hope and beliefs and the social networks that develop between groups of migrants and their families. More recently writers such as Margaret Grieco and Sally Boyd (1998) (and see Massey *et al* 1993) have adopted a multidisciplinary and multiscale approach or integrative perspective. Here, the focus is on family and group decisions, as well as on institutional agents who act as intermediaries, facilitating migratory paths between particular nations. Clearly, in the unique conditions of flight from an invader, neither of the first two perspectives has a great deal of purchase, although the emphasis in the integrationist perspective on individual and group decisions and on the role of intermediaries, especially during the journey, is a useful one.

In most cases, people tend to move as a group rather than as individuals, especially during wars when huge numbers of people may move across the landscape. The consequences for the places that they leave vary. Sometimes it is the most energetic members of a community who migrate, affecting the extent of entrepreneurial skills and often the overall prosperity in the places left behind. Remittances home, however, often reduce the impact of the loss and may enhance the standards of living of those left behind. During a war, it is often members of a persecuted minority, whether religious or ethnic, who may be forced to leave. In the case of the Baltic States, the people who fled in the 1940s were often, but not always, members of the professional middle classes, and their departure meant a loss of skills and knowledge. In the countries of immigration, the areas in which migrants settle are usually in the larger cities where job opportunities are available or where compatriots are already settled and able to provide assistance or advice. In many western cities these patterns of in-migration result in identifiable neighbourhoods, associated and sometimes named after the ethnicity of their occupants. For the European Volunteer Workers (EVWs), however, there was no choice of where to settle, at least until they were released from their contracts of employment.

The official status of in-migrants also varies. Migrants may enter illegally or legally, and in some cases under special, typically state-run or sponsored, schemes, often for economic migrants, such as the early post-war schemes addressed here. Until relatively recently, around the 1980s in most industrial nations, migrants tended to be divided into distinctive, legally defined categories such as permanent settlers, foreign workers or refugees, admitted under particular schemes by different agencies, such as the immigration department or the ministry of labour. Their residency and behaviour was regulated accordingly, by aliens' police or by welfare authorities, for example. This was the way in which early post-war migration from Germany to Britain was managed. A further consequence of in-migration is to increase the extent of ethnic diversity in the immigration societies. The affects of this growing ethnic diversity in part depend on the significance attributed to the differences between migrants and the population of the receiving society and the rights accorded to the incomers. The difference between varying legal statuses – between a citizen or a foreign worker, for example – is crucial in the impact it has on entitlements to legal and social rights. But attributes such as age and family status, religion, language and skin colour also affect the reception and status of in-migrants. Potential immigrants are often ranked, whether officially or unofficially, in a complex hierarchy of acceptability. Foreign workers without citizenship are typically constructed as temporary migrants with few rights, whereas those who are officially designated as permanent migrants usually enter under more preferable terms and conditions. This was an important distinction between Latvian in-migrants and those from Ireland and the Caribbean. But in Britain skin colour is a particularly significant axis of hierarchical discrimination, in which a black/white binary division parallels that of lesser or greater eligibility, so disrupting the distinction between foreign workers and citizens. However, there are also complex hierarchies within the 'white' population and new theoretical work on white identities by scholars such as Alistair Bonnet (2000), Richard Dyer (1988, 1997) and Ruth Frankenberg (1997) is helpful in thinking through the particular location of Baltic immigrants in late 1940s Britain.

The official policies that both regulate the position and affect the social construction of incomers' identities change over time as circumstances merit – in relation to economic cycles, for example, and as 'incomers' become more established members of their communities. As Stephen Castles and Mark Miller (2003) have documented, in countries where the permanent settlement of migrants has been recognised and encouraged, there has been a shift over time from policies of individual assimilation based on an idealised notion of a good citizen to the acceptance, at least in official discourse, of some degree of long-term cultural difference. Since the 1970s, in some advanced industrial societies, Canada and Sweden for example, and to a lesser extent in Australia and the United Kingdom, this acceptance has resulted in the granting of minority and cultural rights in particular social arenas and to a wider acceptance of a politics based on the concept of multiculturalism. The mirror image of multiculturalism – assimilation as a condition for citizenship and social rights – often tends to position visibly different migrants as marginalised ethnic minorities, as in France where the secularisation of the state has led to severe conflicts between, for example, the French notion of human rights and religious identities especially among the minority Muslim population, seen most recently in arguments about wearing the headscarf among Muslim schoolgirls.

Conflicts between in-migrants and the local population lie, in large part, in the challenge that migration poses to myths of national identity. As Anthony Smith (1986, 1991), Benedict Anderson (1983) and many others have argued, the ideal of the nation state that developed in the modern era is based on the notion of cultural as well as political unity within the boundaries of an identifiable territory. As Anderson (1983) has so clearly demonstrated, the construction of a series of myths of unity between strangers who are nevertheless co-residents of a nation state is the basis of the establishment of a discourse of national identity. These myths emphasise common history, culture and traditions, often based on language or religion, and typically a version of ethnic homogeneity. As critics have argued, these myths, rites and rituals are based not only on fictional representations of the nation but typically on a particularistic, usually masculinist and elitist, version of history that excludes not only the new migrants but also large sections of the 'native' population, whether women, the working class, or others excluded from the central locations of power. A more optimistic view of the consequences of migration that insists that the identities of both in-migrants and the local population are altered, often for the better, is found in recent work on the concept of diasporic identities – a concept that has largely influenced the politics of multiculturalism mentioned above. The main arguments of this school of work are outlined in the following section.

Diasporic identities

Although the word diaspora is an ancient one, it has recently regained currency in a range of research. In its broadest sense, the term captures the consequences of migration, displacement, immigration and exile for all peoples who have become dislocated from their homelands. Its derivation is Greek – from dia *across* and sperien *to scatter* – but it is a term most commonly used to describe Jewish communities living in exile. As Avtar Brah (1996, p 181) has noted, this association with the dispersion of the Jews has a particular resonance in European studies of displacement where the Jewish diaspora is 'emblematically situated within Western iconography as the diaspora *par excellence*'. But the term has become used far more widely in current work on migrant identities to refer to numerous migrations, from enforced movements such as the slave trade between Africa and the Americas to more recent transnational movements from the Asian subcontinent to the west. Indeed, as well as embodying the notion of dispersal from a homeland, the term has been extended almost infinitely to encompass a wide range of forms of movement, including travel for pleasure and even to forms of symbolic displacement not involving movement across geographic space. This stretches the term too far, in my view, but it remains an extremely helpful way to capture the links between a migrant population spread across several nation states. Thus, the connections between Latvians now living in the UK, Sweden, Australia, the US and Canada are usefully summarised by the term.

Trying to bring greater specificity to the term Braziel and Mannur (2003, p 3) 'suggest that theorising diaspora offers critical spaces for thinking about the discordant movements of modernity, the massive migrations that have defined this (the twentieth) century – from the late colonial period through the decolonisation era into the twenty-first century'. They argue that the second half of the twentieth century is distinguished by the changing significance of the nation state as mass migration movements and the waves of political refugees seeking asylum in other countries have reconfigured nation states, especially in Central and Eastern Europe. As this book focuses on the time period between the abolition and re-establishment of the Baltic States, Braziel and Mannur's delimitation of diaspora is particularly useful. It allows the connections between individual and group identities and national and international political movements to be emphasised, building on the multiscale approach to migration outlined above. Where the concept of diaspora is particularly helpful, however, is its focus not only on movement but also on the regrouping and shifts in identity that occur among different populations in their exile. It invites questions about the socio-economic, political and cultural conditions that surrounded movement, the different reasons and the relations of power that inscribe a specific diaspora and distinguish one set of movements from another, as well as drawing attention to a further set of questions about the circumstances of arrival and settling down.

There is, inevitability, a debate about these questions: about the meaning of common terms, about the commonalities or differences in the circumstances of leaving, about the consequences of exile, the extent to which diasporic communities are united by common or a varying histories and the impact of migration on both diasporic and indigenous communities. Questions such as how a group comes to be situated in official discourses about 'one' and the 'other', about the nature and impact of state policies and how social and institutional structures of regulation affect different groups and their position within economies and societies have been addressed. Here, the work of Stuart Hall (1990, 1992) has been extremely influential. Hall has argued strongly against an essentialist view of 'home' among both migrant and indigenous groups, suggesting instead that both groups are affected by migration. He insists on the positive as well as negative, or perhaps more accurately the ambiguous, impacts of migration and settlement, for both migrants and the communities among which they live. Terms such as hybridity and creolisation, or the more neutral term heterogeneity, have been used to capture the continuous process of change amongst diverse communities, creating a new, albeit often contested, cultural construction of nationality and belonging to a nation that challenges taken-for-granted associations between place and identity (Gupta 1992, Low and Lawrence-Zuniga 2003, Ong, 1999). In similar vein, Paul Gilroy (1987, 1993) has criticised those forms of ethnic absolutism that insist that common histories, heritage and racial descent hold together diasporic peoples such as Black African communities, for example, or the Jewish diaspora. He too argues that diaspora entails hybridity and heterogeneity as the lived experiences of both peoples who have moved and those they now live among are altered and changed, marked by both positive and negative changes, and by ambivalence and contradiction.

These notions of hybridity and ambiguity are, in part, a satisfying way to understand the circumstances of Baltic migrants who not only came from a 'mongrel' land, subjected to successive waves of invasion, but who through the dislocations of war and exile found themselves in post-war Britain on the eve of the post-war transformations of national identity in part created by in-migration, and not only of Europeans but also by Caribbean and later Asian in-migrants. However, as I shall also demonstrate later, a more conservative and static notion of an essentialised Latvian identity was a key part of the construction of an idealised version of Latvian community in the UK.

The new research on diaspora challenges fixed and static notions of home and identity based on geographical foundations – usually a nation state – and undermines the claims of belonging to a particular place that are so important in uniting migrants. But is also clear that whether claims to an authentic identity or more optimistic notions of travelling, hybrid or translated identities are held by theorists and by migrants themselves, there remain significant axes of differentiation within migrant communities. Differences based on class, gender, age or sexual identity, for example, continue to divide and structure the lives of migrants. The images and myths of homeland and national identity that are so significant in constructing versions of solidarity in migration/exile often depend on ignoring differentials of power based on gender, sexuality or class position. To unpick these inequalities, scholars of diaspora are now developing more complex notions of identity based on multiple forms of identification, in which the intersections of nationality, dislocation, race, and gender, as well as age and generation are recognised. Some Latvian migrants in post-war Britain struggled to construct new hybrid identities, but others attempted to create a community identity based on their idea of an authentic Latvia, a notion of belonging to a nation state formed during the brief flowering of national self-consciousness in the inter-war years, the very time when the women whose lives are at the centre of this book were growing up.

Transnational theory

More recently, a new variant of this vein of theorising about migration and its consequences – transnational theory – has become influential (Glick Schiller *et al* 1999; Vertovec 1999). Here the emphasis is even more explicitly on both ends of the migration chain – the countries of origin and of (re)settlement. Transnational theory reflects a wider recognition that in an increasingly globalised world, contacts and travel between places have become immeasurably more common. Rapid changes in communication technologies mean that migrants are able to maintain contacts between distant places in ways that previously were not possible. Sending money, making visits and temporary return are now easier. Indeed, as Aiwa Ong (1999) has documented in her work on Chinese entrepreneurs, repeated or circulatory migration, especially among the rich and footloose, is now common, resulting in migrants who maintain economic and social links, through investment, business network and social contacts, in at least two societies and economies. Alejandro Portes (1999, p 464) has suggested that these types of activities are best described as transnational, that is 'those that take place on a recurrent basis across national boundaries and that require a regular and significant commitment of time by participants' who might range from employees or owners of transnational businesses (transnationalism from above (Portes *et al* 1999)) to individual migrants who maintain a range of cultural or religious contacts with 'home' (transnationalism from below). For Latvian migrants, transnational contacts did grow over the later post-war decades, but the opportunity to establish links with those who remained or to return 'home' was significantly affected by the political circumstances of those years.

The development of transnational theory has been valuable as it stresses links between places in late modernity, what Ong (1999, p 4) defined as 'the condition of cultural interconnectedness and mobility across space'. Further, this approach encourages the integration of political economy and situated ethnography, the structural circumstances and individual behaviours identified earlier, creating what Michael Burawoy (2001) has termed the practice of 'global ethnography'. This approach usefully challenges conventional distinctions between structure and agency, between political economy and forms of individualist explanation, as well as the binary division between global processes and local lives, which tends to be mapped onto these binary distinctions. It emphasises instead the connections that bind people together across widely separated spaces and is an important development in theorising migrant identities. It is as useful in the exploration of earlier twentieth century migrations such as that between Latvia and the UK, and in explaining Latvians' lives in Britain as it is for understanding more recent migratory flows. Despite the notable absence of transnational flows and linkages, at least in the early Cold War years when travel to the Soviet Union was forbidden or extremely difficult and the maintenance of transnational cultural and social links often dangerous for the Baltic people who remained *in situ*, the nation of a transnational identity is a helpful way to understand the double attachment – to Latvia and to Britain – that was reported by the women whom I interviewed and which sometimes troubled them.

However, the idea of living across borders also raises complex issues. This complexity is problematic for individuals, who are often torn by ambivalent ideas of belonging or not belonging, as Anne-Marie Fortier (2000) has explored among post-war Italian migrants to London. It also challenges conventional concepts of citizenship, traditionally tied to the rights and obligations of individuals within a single nation state. The rise of transnational identities, or even the acknowledgment of dual citizenship rights, challenges this model of political obedience to a single nation state. But so too does the acceptance of forms of cultural and political multiculturalism: a contradiction not yet resolved by the current British government whose recent statements on national identity veer between the two poles of traditional citizenship and multiculturalism.

Although the widespread discussion of ideas of transnational identities and multiculturalism has come to the fore with the increasingly diverse origins of migrants into the industrial west in recent years, it is clear that the reconsideration of that relatively small, homogeneous group of Baltic in-migrants to the UK between 1946 and 1949, especially when their position is contrasted with that of the workers who came from the Caribbean at much the same time, has a great deal to say about transnational identities and about belonging and attachment. The Baltic migrants came to the UK not as citizens with legal entitlement, but instead bound in complex relations of obligation to a country that rescued them and gave them work, and of betrayal, as the Yalta agreement recognising the right of the Soviet Union to absorb Latvia, in their view gave away their homeland.

Body, blood and nation – gender relations and national identity

The group of migrants who are the focus of this book are women and women play a particularly significant part in the construction and reconstruction of ideas about national identity and belonging. A series of new theoretical debates, in the main among feminist scholars, about the connections between gender, identity and nationality in the context of migration and transnational communities are helpful in understanding the position of Baltic women migrants. In their innovative work, Floya Anthias and Nira Yuval-Davis (1989) have outlined three areas in which gender matters. First, women are the biological reproducers of an ethnic group. For many men from the Baltic States, who eventually outnumbered women by something like four to one in the post-war migration to the UK, a continuing commitment to an exclusive version of national identity based in blood ties entailed a long bachelorhood or less typically marriage 'out', whereas most Latvian women were able, if they so chose, to marry within their own group. However, secondly, women are more than biological reproducers: typically they are also the primary cultural reproducers, playing an essential role in the transmission of language, myths, stories and other cultural symbols to the young whose links to 'home' are based on the imagined community constructed in exile. Thirdly, images of femininity, womanhood and maternity are embodied in nationalist discourses, where femininity is variously equated with suffering and forbearance, with humility or bounty and fertility, but almost always with a passive dependence that is counterposed to an active masculine dominance.

These images of gendered identities are often entangled with a sense of national identity based on ethnicity and on the cult of blood or racial superiority (Anthias and Yuval-Davies 1992; Linke 1999; McClintock 1995; Nash 2002; Walter 2001). Such ideas of ethnicity differ from conventional notions of national identity in the UK, or more accurately England, where the dominant version of sense of Englishness is based on class and residence, rather than on blood ties, and is what Cowley (2004, p 27) has termed 'one of resolute pragmatism, respectful of tradition and the accumulated wisdom of past generations'. In Latvia, however, as I show later, more Germanic notions of blood lines and racial purity were part of the traditions under which the then-young women in this book grew up and which also affected why and where they fled in 1944. Although most of these women spent only about two decades in the land of their birth, deeply embedded ideas about the nation and their national identity have proved to be a significant element in their reconstruction in Britain of an imagined and imaginary version of

Latvian identity based on memories, story telling and other oral and written sources such as poetry and music.

Social memory, oral testimonies and gender identities

The second set of contemporary debates that provides a framework for this book includes work on social memory and oral testimony. Most of the second generation Latvians in the UK were born in 'exile' and with their parents, part of the wartime diaspora of peoples escaping the Soviet Union, they were, in the main, unable to visit their 'homeland', except in exceptional, and highly regulated circumstances, at least until 1991. Social memories, therefore, play a crucial part in their reconstruction of a sense of national identity during their years in 'exile' in the UK. The idea of social or cultural memory is dependent on an 'act of transfer' (Connerton 1989, p 39) in which 'images of the past and recollected knowledge of the past are conveyed and sustained by (more or less ritual) performances' (Connerton, p 4). Cultural memories therefore are not only stories, images, documents and artefacts from the past, but they are also constructed and reconstructed in the act of passing the memories on to others. Thus, memory is a fluid and mutable concept, and it is the function of what Deborah McDowell (1989, p 147) has termed 'a continuous present and its discourses' rather than a singular and unchanging discourse. Memories vary over time as circumstances change or as new knowledge is assimilated into the stories of the past.

For diasporic populations acts of transfer through embodied performances, such as story telling, are a central part of remembering and recreating images of the past. Thus, 'performative memory is bodily' (Connerton 1989, p 4). It is also specific to a particular place or location: 'situated' or 'located' are the terms commonly used by theorists. As Maurice Halbwachs (1925) argued decades ago in innovative work on memory, collective memory cannot exist without reference to a socially-specific geographical framework, to 'the mental and material spaces of the group' (Connerton 1989, p 37). Material spaces take two geographical forms: first, the recreation of memories of a particular place and, secondly, reconstruction in a place. For diasporic populations, these two locations do not coincide. There is a disjuncture between the locations that alters the creation of memories. In part this is because the acts of transfer necessary for social memory are also contested and bound by the various power relations in the two locations: power relations that precluded almost all contacts between the UK and Latvia for EVWs.

In totalitarian regimes such as the post-war USSR a particular version of collective memory is officially sanctioned through mechanisms to ensure what might be termed 'organised forgetting' through official histories that omit key events, through the abolition of minority languages and by other acts of oppression such as, for example, enforced migration from the country or of another minority into the country. For Latvians, with their contested history and direct Soviet rule between 1945 and 1990, official versions of collective memory were influenced both by deportations of the 'local' population and by in-migration of people from other parts of the USSR, especially Russia, to dilute nationalist sentiments. As well as deportations by the occupying Soviet power during the war years, the Soviet regime continued to treat Latvia harshly after the end of the war and russified Latvians held power for several decades. The ethnic Russian population in all three of the Baltic Soviet Socialist Republics grew largely by in-migration associated with industrialisation. Net immigration between 1951 and 1989, for example, into Latvia has been estimated as more than 400,000 and by 1989 the percentage of the population that was 'Latvian' in origin had fallen to 52 per cent out of a total population of 2.5 million. Russian also replaced Latvian as the national language until the re-establishment of independence.

Fears of becoming a minority in their own land led to a revival of resistance movements in Latvia in which collective memories of earlier decades, especially the brief flowering of independence in the 1920s and 1930s, were influential. For the voluntary migrants – those who left the country in the war years – collective memories were also transformed by their migration, by a largely unspoken history of their relationship with the Nazi regime and by their long exile from Latvia. These multiple versions of a shared past may therefore lead to conflicts both within and between the generations, and especially between those who remained in the country during the post-war decades and those who had left. Each group had very different sets of experiences and different sets of memories, as well as a different interpretation of their actions during the war which, as I shall show later, sometimes led to feelings of guilt and regret among Latvians in Britain and to resentment amongst those who stayed behind.

Migrants also have to be able to communicate a version of their past to the inhabitants of the country to which they move to reinforce the legitimacy of their own identity. Latvians moving to the UK found that there was little sense of a shared past with the British population, indeed even of the existence of Latvia. The British population was as likely to confuse the Baltics with the Balkans (Skultans 2003) as to be able to locate Latvia on a map. In the early post-war years, the incoming Latvian population was regarded as having been on the 'wrong side' in the Second World War. The Soviet Union had been on the winning side and the British population found it hard to understand why Latvians had fled. The Nazi war crimes loomed far larger in the British imagination than Soviet mistreatment of Latvians. The extent to which Latvians had been Nazi collaborators was a live and contested issue whereas Soviet crimes were unacknowledged or, indeed, not widely known about in the early post-war years. It was hard, therefore, for the Latvian exiles to construct a story of their past that resonated with the British interpretation of recent historical events.

It is evident, then, that cultural memory is imbued with political power in which recollections of a shared past are often contested. Cultural memories, as Hirsch and Smith (2002, p 5) have noted, 'emerge out of a complex dynamic between past and present, individual and collective, public and private, recall and forgetting, power and powerlessness, history and myth, trauma and nostalgia, conscious and unconscious fears and desires' and so are 'acts of performance, representation and interpretation' in which fragmentary personal and collective experiences are connected, negotiated and continuously recreated. As Penny Summerfield (1998, p 15) has argued:

> local and particular accounts cannot escape the conceptual definitional effects of powerful public representations ... thus personal narratives draw on the

generalised subject available in discourse to construct the particular personal subject.

These 'official narratives' or hegemonic cultural memories and myths are, however, often essentialist and monolithic, writing out the ambiguity and ambivalence that marks traumatic events during war-time for example. The individuals who experienced the trauma and dislocation of occupation and flight from Latvia in 1944 were of different classes, ages and genders, as well as of different ethnicity and religions, and so their memories are located within specific sets of circumstances and contexts. As feminist historians and cultural theorists have demonstrated, the construction of the dominant version of cultural memory is a reflection of the negotiation of contested claims and consequence of power relations in which the voices of women, especially young women, tend not to be heard.

Oral histories and testimonies

Work drawing on oral histories and other biographical sources has begun to uncover alternative memories, insisting on the redrafting of a singular public memory, challenging the singularity of 'public memory' and its denial of diversity and difference. This work, not all of it explicitly feminist in its perspective, challenges the typical or conventional rhetoric of progress and achievement to construct a more provisional story, writing in previously ignored figures and events (Charlesworth 1994; Chivallon 2001; Graham 1998; Holcomb 1998; Landzelius 2003; Tunbridge and Ashworth 1996; Uzzell and Ballantyne 1998).

The greater recognition that memories and accounts of past events are always partial, that knowledge is contextual and situated and that multiple versions of the past are continuously being created as events of the past are reinterpreted through the circumstances of the present, has had a enormously productive impact on historical scholarship on memory, especially in the turn to new sources and methods. It has been argued in recent post-structuralist analyses that new hybrid, migrant, performative and marginalised identities emerged in these and the succeeding transnational movements related to decolonisation and post-imperialism. In this work, new theorisations of the relationships between identity and place and conceptualisations of the self during and after transnational migration have become dominant (Braidotti 1994; Brah 1997; Clifford 1997; Walter 2001), bringing together the debates on memory and transnationalism.

Drawing on new sources including literary and cultural texts and oral histories has transformed work on memory and provided new insights into the complex relations between memory, nostalgia and identity. In these new studies, the notion of the authenticity of both personal and common histories has been destabilised, and identity is retheorised as a site of textualised constructions and reconstructions in which the complex, multiple and fluid hybrid identity of migrants has been a central theme. There has also been a growing insistence that the histories of the 'receiving' nations, peoples and cities are also textualised narratives. Thus, a new focus of research is on the ways in which First World places are also transformed by migration in a network of inter-relationships at multiple spatial scales. While these studies have undoubtedly had a huge influence of the theorisation of migration and identity, and in anthropology and geography on reconceptualisations of place, I want to sound a cautionary note. It is important to counterpose the more optimistic versions of hybridity and translation found in new work on transnationalism to an alternative theorisation that insists on the continuing significance of nostalgia and a turn to an essentialist version of national identity. Nostalgic and conservative constructions of identity are also common reactions to movement and change (Hall 1990), and to discrimination in the new location. In these constructions, diasporic communities draw on imagined historical narratives of tradition.

The traumas and dislocation experienced during wars have become the subjects of a great deal of recent research in which there is a noticeable emphasis on the testimony of witnesses and on the recollection of events through the individual voices and bodies of participants. Whilst accepting that these memories are socially constructed and organised within dominant discourses, it has also become clear that a focus on the narratives or testimonies of individuals is an important way to uncover both the diversity and particularity of experiences of such hardships. As Hirsch and Smith (2002, p 7) commented in their introduction to a collection of feminist work on cultural narrative:

> Cultural memory can best be understood at the juncture where the individual and the social come together, where the person is called on to illustrate the social formation in its heterogeneity and complexity. The individual story, whether told through oral narrative, fiction, film, testimony or performance also serves as a challenge and a countermemory to official hegemonic history.

This work encouraged me to turn to oral narratives as a method to investigate the explicitly gendered experience of flight and loss of national identity. My interviews were with women who had left Latvia in 1944 and so their current age raises questions about the loss of memory as well as the implications of repeated tellings of the same story. It is also important to remember that the relationship between the participant in these events and her interrogator affects the terms of the story. For just as cultural memories are a negotiation between past and present, so too is historical scholarship and the contemporary analysis of past events. The ways in which questions are asked, the theoretical framework within which they are constructed and the answers analysed are set within contemporary debates – thus many of the terms introduced here – identity, subjectivity, diaspora, sexuality, femininity, which are key concepts in current feminist work on memory – are derived from current debates and conceptualisations which in all probability would have been unfamiliar, and perhaps are still unfamiliar now, to the women caught up in the events more than half a century ago. Further, the particular ways in which questions are phrased and the prior knowledge and assumptions of the interviewer affects the way in which a life history is recalled and retold. There are as well the inevitable slips of memory, the collapse of events and a focus on particular aspects of a story, that become part of the telling and retelling on the flight from Latvia. Thus, the parameters of oral testimony are set by both researchers and participants. The skills and emphases of researchers are influenced by their own trajectories as a scholar, by previous experiences of research, by knowledge of and sympathy for different approaches and methods and by political perspectives and moral beliefs.

But the agency and interests of the narrators also shape the interaction. My initial interest in and emphasis on these women's lives in Britain in the late 1940s and 1950s and in the debates about paid employment outlined in the succeeding section of this chapter was countered by their own insistence of the greater significance of the events between 1944 – leaving Latvia – and some time at the end of the decade when they arrived in Britain. Thus, the focus of the work shifted in recognition of the differential importance placed on the events of their lives by the narrators. Miriam Glucksmann (2000, p 34), whose own studies of the histories of women's employment have influenced my work, has pointed out: 'What the interviewees have to say and how they say it may well refine or redefine the project, altering it from its original course.' This was definitely the case here as the women whom I interviewed insisted on the significance of the immediate post-war years and to a lesser extent events since 1991 as the key periods in their testimonies, while regulating the long decades of 'exile' to a less significant place.

While the recent focus on individual testimony in studies of social memory may have shifted the balance of contemporary research, I also want to insist, with Connerton (1989, p 14), that 'historical reconstruction is still necessary even when social memory provides direct testimony of an event'. Historians and social scientists interested in social memory always need to question the status of their evidence. This is not because they believe people lie or deceive but because if statements are accepted at face value 'that would amount to abandoning their autonomy as practising historians' (*ibid*). Historians, biographers, anthropologists, geographers and many others interested in people's recollections of their own lives, often lived in extraordinary circumstances, need to make up their own minds on the basis of weighing the evidence from a range of sources and of witnesses, and thus in their research accept the theoretical arguments about the intersections of private and public memories. Personal recollections cannot be taken at face value, as it were, and analysed as if there were no necessary connections to the events experienced. Thus, I remain committed to a modernist version of memory as rooted in material events, despite accepting the fragmentary and transitory nature of memories and their continuous construction and reconstruction over time. As a consequence, during the research process, I compared and counterposed the oral narratives to other sources, including official documents, newspaper reports and personal testimonies by people from the Baltic States who left displaced persons' camps and migrated to countries other than the UK (see, for example, Eksteins 2000; Nesaule 1995; Whittaker 1995; Wyman 1998).

Recollecting the past

For the women whom I interviewed, too, the recollection of these events, especially the loss and dislocation of the 1940s, is in part based on these official sources, investigated and read after the events, as it were, which at the time were unclear to them. An important and complex issue, then, raised by these oral histories is that of retrospective reanalysis of events about which at the time of their unfolding the participant had no knowledge: Latvian women did not know where the Russian front was as they escaped through German occupied territories, for example, nor later on, when they agreed to move to Britain as economic migrants, did they know where they would live nor, in many cases, what sort of work they had agreed to undertake. More significantly of course, they had no idea that their exile in the UK would become permanent but their recollections are filtered through these later knowledges. Many of the women to whom I talked longed to return to a more innocent time, a time when they did not know what was going to happen to them during the war and its aftermath: consequently their memories of their Latvian girlhoods are often suffused with nostalgic longings. Indeed, their attempts to reconstruct an identity based on the self who existed before 1944 – as a Latvian woman – were also often based both on written and oral memories and other sources as well as on their relatively limited range of personal experiences. In this sense, then they combined personal and collective memories with national myths and stories of belonging (see Bell (2003) for a discussion of the distinction between memory and myth), constructed and transmitted through a range of sources including written histories, poetry, folksongs and other forms of representations as well as through story telling. As many of these women were still in their teens when they left their country, their sense of national identity is largely dependent on retellings of folk memories, myths and histories from written records and later, in exile in the UK, the reconstruction of an imaginary rural Utopia, a golden inter-war age when Latvia had a brief period of independence. Thus their own memories are located within a cultural and historiographical discourse of national Latvian identity. Freud wrote discussing the connections between early individual memories and the construction of national identity is a significant part of cultural identity. 'We must above all remember that people's "childhood memories" are only consolidated at a later period ... and that this involves a complicated process of remodelling, analogous in every way to the process by which a nation constructs legends about its own history'(Freud 1909).

When disrupted by exile, these connections become particularly complex. For women such as these, who have experienced a huge rupture between a past and a present through war, trauma and exile, telling stories to bridge this rupture is a key part of identity. It is clear that experiences such as war, migration, abuse, assault, capture and imprisonment make the relationships between the self before these events and the self after much more problematic than for individuals for whom the division of life into stages of before and after may depend on more widely experienced life events such as the birth of a child or death of a parent. In this particular case, there are also interesting and complex issues about how this discourse is now being recreated not only among Latvian exiles but those Latvians who lived through the decades of Soviet domination until the early 1990s (Skultans 1998, 1999), as well as the relations between the two groups, which remain to be investigated in depth. It seems clear, however, that the re-establishment of independence in 1991 transformed understandings of national identity. Had I collected the narratives say 20 years earlier, then it seems probable that a different story of Latvian identity may have emerged. Interestingly, in 1998 Mark Wyman reissued his book about the experiences of former displaced persons who emigrated to Canada and the USA, originally published in 1989, with a new preface reflecting on the significance of independence. Thus, for historians, especially those who rely on oral narratives, the idea of retranscription or retranslations raises complex methodological issues about the status of the texts/data/interview material collected at a particular point in time. Indeed, the recognition of retranslations destabilises the notion of 'the past' itself. All memory is a continuous process of retranslation – it is impossible to recover the past 'as it really was'.

The nature of this complex relationship between past and present selves and the significance of memory is, however, neither simple nor uncontested. It is, for example, a central issue in psychoanalysis as well as in historical work on cultural memories. Recent studies of the psychology of forgetting, fantasy, and false memory have also added to the recognition that identity and self is much more provisional and fluid than may have been previously believed. As Nicola King (2000, p 12) notes, this recognition 'unsettles the belief that we can recover the past as it was and unproblematically reunite our past and present selves', although, as she adds, 'the assumption that memory can give us direct access to the preserved or buried past retains a powerful hold on our culture'. The Latvian women to whom I talked were quite clear that the version of events that they told me accurately reflected their past experiences. Their recollection and retelling of the events between 1944 and 1947 was a dominant feature of their lives and had become part of the history of the Latvian community in Britain, told and retold among families and at the Saturday schools and other communal activities that were important particularly in the early years in Britain. Inevitably, over time, these stories have altered in their focus and detail. Yet, in everyday social discourse as well as in a great deal of autobiographical writing, narratives, such as those told to me and repeated within the community, 'tend to elide memory as a process: the content is presented as if it were uniformly and objectively available to the remembering subject, as if the narrating 'I' and the subject of the narration were identical' (King 2000, p 3) which is not so, in part because story telling follows certain conventions that structure the narrative. Vieda Skultans (1998, p 3) makes the same point in her discussion of the narrative histories she collected from Latvians, in this case from those who had lived in Latvia throughout the years of Soviet domination. 'The narrative I is ambiguous – referring as it does to both the teller of the tale and the earlier self – victim or hero of the story. The precise nature of the narrative I varies: author and hero coexist more happily than author or victim. After all, western literary conventions stipulate that plots should have heroes'. In addition, as Hayden White (1973) has suggested, historical narratives tend to be organised according to one of the tropes of tragedy, comedy, romance or irony, and events may be consciously or unconsciously embroidered or exaggerated to make these stories more interesting.

In her work on Jewish women's memories of migration, Ruth Swirsky (1999) has suggested that migrant women may have difficulty in articulating the trauma and loss of migration and so retell their histories as a story of moving forward, as a journey to a better life for economic migrants or to greater safety for political migrants. Thus, she notes 'such narratives tend to be cast within an archetypal autobiographical form which gives them an "heroic" quality'. White (1980, p 26) has also emphasised the moral purpose of narrative: where 'narrativity is present, we can be sure that morality or a moralising impulse is present too'. Thus, in a commentary on the Baltic odyssey of a German Estonian woman and her family, Whittaker (1995, p 289) noted that the tale was one of 'courage against all odds, of hapless innocence confronting massive evil ... the story is one of paradise lost and regained'. However, transforming experiences of loss and violence into a heroic narrative is not easy, perhaps especially for young women whose conventional narrative position is not usually that of the active hero but more typically the dependent heroine whose dominant role is as a passive spectator. In exceptional circumstances, these Latvian women did become agents of their own lives, albeit often forced rather than choosing to relinquish their protected position of daughter. Their independence culminated in migration to Britain as single adults without dependants and yet they seldom told a tale of heroism or of odds overcome. Instead, their narratives were infused with loss and regret and with yearning for a different life. However, they did place themselves at the centre of their story about escape. Thus, the circumstances between leaving Latvia and their arrival in Britain remained uppermost in their narratives of self and so, as I noted above, the years between 1944 and 1949 played the major role in the interviews that I undertook. Most of the 25 women were able to recall in detail when and where these events took place, including place names and dates in many cases. As Wyman (1998, p.x) noted in the preface to his own work with former displaced persons now living in the USA and Canada: 'I know that memory can become dimmed, that tales of what occurred can become burdened with nostalgia, that unpleasant incidents can be forgotten.'

However, dramatic, crucial events are usually recalled in vivid detail and as contemporary accounts and records provide a way to measure the accuracy of 'recollections', it is possible to substantiate the details of the women's accounts of the war and early post-war years from official records of patterns of movement, of ships used and the locations of displaced persons camps, for example, as well as from Tannahill's (1958) survey of EVWs entry to the UK and their early post-war jobs and from Kathleen Paul's (1997) excellent survey of British post-war immigration policies. By contrast, the events of the years in England were less vividly recalled, in part as their stories were less dramatic and despite my encouragement, it was hard for some women to accept that I really was interested in the details of their post-war years of domesticity. But through such conventional markers of time passing such as anniversaries and birthdays as well as exceptional events such as visits abroad or large purchases – a first car perhaps – these women were also able to provide a remarkable amount of detail about their daily lives over the past 60 years, the paid work that they undertook, the houses they bought, the children they raised and eventually their plans in retirement. While not denying the complexity of memories and their continuous reinscription, then, I believe that it is possible for researchers to construct a version of the 'truth' that is most satisfactory at a particular point in time. By searching for continuities and similarities in what each woman told me and comparing their stories with official records, I have constructed an account of their lives that is as accurate as I was able to make it while not denying the impact of the particular interactions that took place between me and these elderly women, the effects of time, of new knowledge and *post hoc* rationalisations on their memories.

Theorising work and gender divisions of labour

Finally, before turning to the women themselves, debates about the connection between work and home need a brief introduction. As well as a story about migration, dislocation, memory and diasporic identities, this book is about work and labour, work not only undertaken for money but also the voluntary unpaid labour that millions of individual women undertake in their own homes and in the community. The unpaid work of Latvian women in Britain from about 1950 onwards not only reproduced family relations and kept the household functioning but was also an important part of the reproduction of a sense of belonging to Latvia, albeit in exile.

The focus on paid work needs little justification. For these 25 women – many of them middle class by origin and some well educated – the experiences of manual labour in Germany, in the camps and in the UK, transformed their expectations of their future lives and for many resulted in permanent downward social mobility. Work – labouring – like memory, is essentially an embodied act of performance and the regulation and control of these women's labouring bodies looms large in this story. In addition, entering the labour market is for many young women the first time they move outside – at least temporarily – patriarchal familial relations of social control. For these Latvian women, caught up in the trauma of flight when many of them were little more than children, recruitment into various forms of involuntary labour was a key challenge to their identity as a daughter and/or as a dependant of familiar adult authority figures. For these women, involuntary or forced work was a consistent feature of their lives – while waiting to leave the ports in occupied Poland, during their journey across Europe and in the camps in Germany. It was also their ticket to a new life in England. Later in their lives, paid work remained a constant part of the struggle to adapt to life in the United Kingdom. Many of the EVW women continued to work in the types of jobs to which they had initially been allocated by the British Ministry of Labour in the late 1940s.

Paid work is, of course, a key element in migration. Whether migrants flee persecution or disaster or move explicitly to seek employment, once they are resettled, whether on a temporary or a permanent basis, the search for work is usually driven by economic need. Whether manual workers, highly educated professionals or entrepreneurs, most migrants are forced into the labour market as they are usually ineligible for the forms of social support that exist for the permanent population. The structure of the labour market in the receiving country, especially in the towns and cities where most migrants live, has a key impact on the types of jobs and occupations open to migrants, as does the regulation and recognition of previously acquired skills. Too often migrants, whatever their educational and occupational qualifications, find that only jobs in the least-skilled and most poorly-paid parts of the economy are open to them. As a consequence, downward social mobility is not infrequently associated with international migration. In directed labour schemes such as the post-war recruitment of displaced people by the British government, where individuals are allocated to slots in the labour market irrespective of their previous qualifications or experience, downward mobility is inevitable as migrants usually are allocated the jobs and occupations that are hardest to fill and that the local population prefer not to do.

As well as work in the labour market, Latvian women who came to Britain in the late 1940s also worked hard at home and in their local communities to construct and recreate a version of domestic and communal life that reflected some of the customs of home, and so providing a haven from a harsh world of exile. These two spheres of work are connected as the conditions in each affect the other, both in the availability of time and in the assumptions made about the worth of women workers. In the main, it has been through the efforts of feminist theorists that the theoretical and empirical connections between these two forms of labour – paid work in the market and unpaid work in the home – have become part of the analyses of working lives and gender inequalities in different parts of the world.

Gender inequality is largely enacted through the gendered divisions of labour in paid and domestic work (Pateman 1988), as men and women typically are allocated to and undertake different types of work. Different jobs in the labour market and their associated monetary rewards embody widespread assumptions about the attributes of masculinity and femininity, as well influencing the social construction of gendered identities and the moral responsibilities attached to these identities. Despite temporal and geographical variations in gender divisions of labour, an ideology of separate spheres for men and women has a long history. Such a distinction was crucial, for example, in the post-war development of the welfare state in 1940s Britain and in the re-establishment of the home sphere as women's primary responsibility after the war. While women's moral responsibility and role in life was assumed to be the care of others in the private domain of the household, increasingly associated with the nuclear family, men were to fulfil their moral obligations towards the care of others by sharing the rewards of their independent work achievements. These assumptions are reflected not only in individual lives but also in the institutional structure and regulation of society, in the tax system and the law as well as in the welfare state. Thus, one of the key assumptions behind these institutional structures was that after the war childcare and care for other dependants should be provided primarily by family members – almost always an individual woman – within the home without financial compensation. A woman's participation in the labour market was constructed as a secondary role, one where she laboured for what was somewhat derogatorily termed in the post-war period 'pin money' but typically and more realistically, often paid not only for luxuries, as consumption expenditure increased from the 1950s onwards, but also for some of the essential items for household survival.

The consequences of this construction of women's work as secondary, however, and the association of the 'natural' attributes of femininity such as domesticity, docility and self-evident interest in caring for others resulted in a gender-segregated labour market in post-war industrial societies in which women are concentrated in a limited range of 'feminised' jobs. A whole set of jobs, including 'caring' work, such as nursing, teaching and social work, and 'servicing' jobs such as secretarial work, as well as unskilled manufacturing tasks that apparently demand the manual dexterity of women's 'nimble fingers' (Elson and Pearson 1981) are constructed as 'women's work' and, accordingly, are low paid. If these tasks draw on the 'natural' attributes of femininity, the argument goes, then they require little training and so are, by definition, unskilled and so the women performing them do not deserve high rates of pay. So that women might continue to have time to carry out their primary roles within the home, a new category of employee – the part-time woman worker – became increasingly common in the post-war British labour market. This form of participation was seen as an ideal way for women to combine what was often referred to as their two roles (Myrdal and Klein 1956) as both wives and mothers and as workers. As Anne Phillips (1987, p 63) noted in her history of women's work in the UK in the twentieth century, the post-war era is characterised by a 'growing army of part-time workers, disproportionately concentrated in "women-only" jobs in sales work and cleaning and canteens, earning wages that even hour for hour are appallingly low'. Even educated women who, in growing numbers, benefited from the expansion of higher education in the post-war era and who were able to enter the ranks of the professions and other expanding middle class occupations from the 1950s onwards but especially post-1970 found themselves restricted to the lower ranks of these jobs, held back under a 'glass ceiling' that operated to limit women's promotion prospects. Thus, the post-war labour market in the UK, and in other industrial nations, developed strong patterns of horizontal and vertical gender segregation, where most women worked either in female-dominated sectors and occupations (horizontal segregation) or were clustered in the bottom ranks of middle class occupations (vertical segregation).

Clearly, the war years – 1939–45 – were something of an exception to these generalisations. Labour shortages provided a challenge to the ideology of domesticity that had characterised earlier decades of the twentieth century and which was to be strongly re-established the immediate post Second World War years. During both the First and Second World Wars, women left their homes in large numbers in response to government pleas to them to fill the jobs left vacant by men entering military service, but not at 'male' rates of pay of course. It is also instructive to recall that in these wars, different types of industrial labour were compared with domestic tasks in government propaganda in an effort to encourage women's participation. Welding, for example, was compared to knitting. It seemed unimaginable to the governments of the time that women might have an intrinsic interest in industrial work, as well as the aptitude to undertake it, or be motivated by patriotism to enter the labour market. At the end of the war, women's invaluable wartime work was rewarded solely by the re-establishment of an ideology of domestic maternity. Thus, their peacetime contribution was to be in the arena of reproduction rather than industrial production as they were encouraged to return to the private sphere of the home, to produce children in larger numbers and re-establish the traditional ideal of the home and household as a sphere for the rest and recreation for their menfolk and children, who were to be tenderly cared for by their womenfolk. The ways in which this ideology became a dominant norm in post-war Britain and its consequent impact on the status and the ways in which the populous viewed women economic migrants forms the background to this book. Clearly, the Latvian women who came to Britain fell outside this dominant notion of women's role, at least in the sense that they had no option but to take employment. How they managed their 'dual roles' and thought about their employment is therefore a central part of the story.

The connections between paid and domestic labour and the necessity of each for the maintenance of a capitalist mode of production have been described in many terms. Among them, Miriam Glucksmann's (1995, 2000) concept of the 'total social organisation of labour' is perhaps most comprehensive. It is useful as it captures both the variety of different forms of work, the often fuzzy distinction between them and they ways in which their relationship changes. As she argues, it is important for understanding gender relations to explore the different ways in which labour in distributed 'between different kinds of function: production, services, welfare, education and so on ... [t]he market and the household might be conceptualised as two sectors, but not the only two, of a larger structure of production and reproduction in industrial societies. At any given time a particular form of structural division and connection exists between them such that they are articulated in a particular manner. They are interdependent ... distinct but not autonomous [and] it is possible to conceptualise links between hierarchies of inequalities in each' (2000, p 19). So in different societies, in different places at specific times, those tasks that are essential to ensure that social and economic relations continue to function, all sorts of work are done and families and children are looked after and reproduced, are divided between men and women, between the market, the state, the home and the local community in different ways. Some tasks are paid and some are not, some forms of work bring high status and generous rewards and others do not and, typically, it is women who undertake the voluntary and family work of caring and nurturing. An alternative way of describing these patterns of hierarchical inequalities is to use the term 'division of labour'. Depending on the adjective used to qualify the concept, the division of labour might refer to the 'technical division' of tasks into component parts, the 'social division' of jobs and occupations between people, the 'gender division' between men and women and the 'spatial division' which refers to the distribution of different types of work and employment between places. In this book, I tend to use the term the division of labour to refer to particular aspects of work and its differential allocation, preferring to reserve the term the total social organisation of labour (TSOL) for the total distribution and allocation of all forms of production and reproduction.

As more research on the conditions within what Margery Spring Rice (1939) called the 'small dark workshops' of the home was produced the diversity in women's working lives began to be documented. It became clear that the boundaries between waged and unwaged work are not pre-given, unvarying or unregulated by the state but are instead negotiated and struggled over both by individual men and women in their homes and by employees in their workplaces and in workers' associations such as trades unions, as well as established in state institutions and policies such as the benefit system and minimum wage legislation. What seems to be a private matter – who does what within the home –

is in fact a distinctly public issue, of concern to employers and the state as well as to individuals. In Great Britain and other industrial societies the second half of the twentieth century, especially more recent decades, has been marked by a transformation in the nature of the TSOL and so in the connections between paid and domestic work and its gendered allocation. The earlier post-war model of the male breadwinner wage and women's primary commitment to domesticity has been largely replaced by a new 'post-Fordist' regime, distinguished by a new gender order or gender contract (Connell 1987; McDowell 1991; Walby 1997) in which both men and women are expected to engage in paid work as individuals. In general, in these post-Fordist regimes, support for the social institutions that buttressed a traditional gender division of labour has increasingly been withdrawn (McDowell 2001), although differences remain between the EU states for example.

Within the EU states considerable differences also remain between regional and local economies and their spatial divisions of labour, differences that are connected to their past histories of work, to class and ethnic divisions, for example and to cultural assumptions about appropriate gender roles and behaviour. These inter-national, national and local differences are interconnected as economic cycles and national regulatory frameworks influence both economic and social policies, affecting the structure of incentives to enter the labour market, as well as the forms of social support for those who are economically inactive. In turn, the particularities of local labour market opportunities and the range of options that are available for women to combine paid and unpaid work in different ways affect the decisions made by both individuals and households within the home about how to distribute the various tasks between different household members. I am particularly interested in the extent of these geographical variations between women's lives in Britain, in the difference made by the places where women labour and care for others and in the ways in which men and women negotiate ways of dividing the total labour of social reproduction that is necessary for them to maintain a particular way of living, within particular and changing national welfare regimes and diverse local cultures. In analyses based on national census data and other sources, Duncan and Smith (2002) have revealed deep-seated and long-standing differences between the North West and Yorkshire and the South East of England. They compared, for example, the textile towns of Lancashire and Yorkshire and Manchester itself with the smaller towns and suburbia in the South East where there were marked differences in the traditions in different industries and in patterns of work. As a consequence, a national ideology about women's place – that traditional and dominant set of assumptions about the significance of women's domesticity during the 1950s, for example – is filtered through geographical differentiation at the local level and different patterns of economic expansion or contraction, resulting in different 'gender bargains' in different localities.

For the Latvian women, the type of work to which they were allocated as they entered the UK – limited to domestic service in private households, domestic work in tuberculosis sanatoria and mental hospitals or manual work in the textile industry – and the locations within which they were employed had a significant impact on their future lives. The women who became private domestic servants, or cleaners in isolated hospitals, for example, were less likely to be surrounded by fellow country folk than women who entered either the cotton or woollen textiles industries. This group of women was not only more likely to be working with other Latvian women but also found themselves reasonably close to areas where Latvian men had been directed to work in the iron and steel industries, for example, or in coal mining in labour markets not too far from the textile towns. Further, in the textile districts, especially in Lancashire, with their tradition of women's full-time work, local working class women had long been workers as well as home-makers and mothers (Liddington and Norris 1978; McDowell and Massey 1984). At the time that the Latvian women first entered Britain, these textile towns had not yet begun to experience the rapid rates of deindustrialisation of more recent decades and so employment opportunities for women were plentiful, attracting both local and Irish working class women into the mills as well as the EVW 'volunteers'. In these areas, then, Latvian women may have felt less out of place as working women. Thus, where Latvian women were first sent to work was important for their later experiences, both within and outside the labour market.

Almost all the women to whom I talked eventually married, often to men who were also refugees, and usually from within the Latvian community in Britain. Some of them became mothers but almost all of them were also paid workers throughout the 1950s and 1960s. Many of these women were employed until they reached the official retirement age, typically re-entering the labour market on a more full-time basis after a period of lower involvement or withdrawal for a few years to raise children. Indeed, one of the most noticeable features of these women's lives is how hard they have always worked, both in the home where many of them supported and looked after their parents as well as their children and in the labour market. In an era when domesticity was the ideal and idealised option for married women, these Latvian women were exceptional in their participation in paid work. The particular ways in which they combined their 'dual roles' were, in part, affected by the social and material circumstances in which they found themselves in different localities that structured the opportunities and constraints on their paid work and so had an impact on how they organised their domestic lives. As well as the availability of different forms of work and childcare provision, locally and regionally-specific beliefs about the whether women should take up paid work or primarily be home-makers influenced the ways in which Latvian women were seen to conform to or transgress local cultural expectations.

It is clear, then, that the lives of the Latvian women who came to Britain after the war raise challenging and wide-ranging questions about the nature of modernity, the rise of the nation state, about the dislocations of war, about how young women were treated in the camps that housed the millions of displaced peoples after the defeat of Nazi Germany in 1945, about the connections between transnational migration and national identity, about the rights and obligations of citizenship, and about women's work and the transformations of their social and economic position in post-war British society. The 25 women whom I interviewed might be seen as a sort of tracer element in British society, revealing the extent of its relative openness as well as the ways which a group of in-migrants who were less visible than the larger number of Caribbean people whose arrival in Britain overlapped with that of the economic migrants, who were also refugees, from the Baltic. But their stories also have an absorbing intrinsic interest: they are inspiring tales of fortitude in the face of adversity, deeply moving and humbling as well as complex and ambiguous. Latvia had a vexed history of involvement in the Nazi war efforts, as well as one of heroic resistance, which these women made little attempt to deny, although their personal involvement was limited by their youth. While one or two women told tales of secret trips to visit partisans in the woods, the predominant emphasis in the narratives is one of passive endurance, stories of attempts to rebuild a community and to adhere to strongly imbued values of hard work and individual responsibility in the face of catastrophic world events that reshaped their lives in ways that they had never imagined in their youth. I believe that my admiration for these women has not clouded my academic judgment but I also strongly hope that it infuses the chapters that follow.

CHAPTER 3

DISCIPLINING BODIES: EXILE AND INVOLUNTARY LABOUR

This chapter and the next are about loss, dislocation and labour. In this one I explore the reasons why almost 200,000 Latvians decided to leave their country between the middle of 1944 and the spring of 1945, examining the immediate economic consequences of their decision, including their involuntary recruitment as workers in the Nazi war effort and their later employment in displaced persons' camps. Following a brief look at the complex history of Latvia as it was occupied and reoccupied by, amongst others, Germans, Swedes and Russians – a history that helps to explain the diverse and complex ethnic loyalties of Latvians - the chapter is divided into two main parts. The first part tells the story of lives lived on the run, as young and elderly Latvians, children, teenagers, women and some men fled westwards to the coast as the Russian front advanced across Latvia. I look at how they managed to secure a sea-passage, usually just to a port on the coast of occupied Poland, from where others were attempting to flee, and then at how they travelled by various means across Europe, eventually to arrive in the allied zones in Germany. This journey was hazardous and dangerous, undertaken during one of the harshest winters of the century and, for many, basic survival could not be taken for granted. Cold, hunger, hostile local people, fear of the advancing Soviet army as well as of the retreating Germans, fear of separation from relatives and friends, of attack, of rape, and even of death was a constant accompaniment to the journey west.

Some of the women whom I interviewed were recruited into the Nazi war effort during this period and worked, often under conditions of severe hardship, for periods of varying lengths in different branches of industry or in the agriculture sector. It is here that their long lives of hard labour began. I look at the work that they undertook, the ways in which they were regulated and controlled as units of labour and at the racial distinctions embedded in the National Socialist ideology that meant that Latvian women were constructed as superior to other women workers and so treated marginally more favourably.

The second part of this story of hard work in Germany is the subject of Chapter 4, where the same themes are important. It deals with life in the refugee camps set up by the Allied forces at the end of the war where, for young women, some semblance of a more normal life was re-established under abnormal conditions and where for some study, instead of or as well as employment, was part of everyday life. The second of this pair of chapters closes as camp occupants considered the options open to them to move west once again to establish new lives in the UK, France, Belgium, the USA and Canada and in Australia. For Latvians moving westwards (actually or metaphorically) was a preferable alternative to repatriation in their homelands which had, by then, become part of the Soviet Union. As those who had fled from Latvia, and from the other Baltic States in 1944, were regarded by the Soviet Union as traitors, it was hardly surprising that these people were keen to accept the offers from various western powers to move there as paid workers. As I shall demonstrate here, however, these offers were seldom based on disinterested humanitarian principles but rather on hard-headed economic necessity that involved discrimination against all but the most able-bodied and physically-fit camp dwellers. Governments and employers were able to pick and choose from amongst some of the most desperate victims of the war, abandoning those who were least eligible as potential workers in the economic reconstruction efforts of the late 1940s to their fate. Indeed, in a speech in 1948, a US Congressman, John W Gibson, noted that the plight of the displaced people and reactions to it by the Allies was 'a venomous postscript to World War II' (quoted in Hulme 1954, p 174).

A brief history of Latvia: occupation and its consequences

To understand the bitter resentment felt by Latvian exiles in Britain towards the Soviet Union and, amongst some, an equal dislike of Germany, it is important to know a little of the modern history of Latvia. Latvia is a northern European country on the eastern shore of the Baltic Sea, opposite Sweden, and west of Russia (see map, Figure 3.1). Geographically, it is about the same size as the Republic of Ireland and it currently has a population of just over two million. The country is basically a flat plain crossed by the River Daugava which drains into the Gulf of Riga, open to conquest by raiding and trading nations over its history. While both Poland and Sweden have at different times held lands in what is now Latvia, German and Russian occupations were more common and long-lasting in their impact. Thus, many Latvians have both German and Russian ancestors. A long period of German control during the early modern era was brought to an end by the Russian conquest of Latvia under Tsar Peter I which began in 1710 and was finally completed 85 years later. For 200 years from that date, Latvian society and culture, as well as the polity, was dominated by a mixture of foreign elites. The German nobility remained dominant in economic, cultural, social and local political life, for example, whereas the Russian bureaucracy was in charge of higher politics and administration.

The relative stability of this period of co-existence was disrupted by industrial urbanisation between 1880 and the outbreak of the First World War as Russia strengthened its hold on the territory. Riga, for example, became the third largest port in Russia and many factories were built in this period, attracting not only Latvians from the countryside but also Russians from the interior. Discontent grew among the expanding working class as standards of living remained low and political controls heavy. The growing discontent was exacerbated by the shooting of 70 peaceful demonstrators in Riga in January 1905. Strikes followed, supported by peasant uprisings. In savage reprisals, 3,000 people were shot and many others were exiled to Siberia. In addition, others fled abroad. These events led to anger against both Russian authorities and German barons and landowners and set the scene for the repetition of similar events over the next half of the

Figure 3.1 Latvia in its region

twentieth century, despite an intervening 20-year period of independence in the inter-war years.

Latvian independence was proclaimed on 18 November 1918 but its real advent was in 1920 after the withdrawal of all foreign armies from Latvian territory. Soviet Russia recognised independence on 11 August 1920 and Latvia became a member of the League of Nations in 1921. These 20 years of Latvian independence are embedded in Latvian consciousness as a golden era of progress and achievement, now referred to as the second awakening. The women whom I interviewed grew up in these years and so their notions of Latvian national identity were formed by atypical political circumstances. Until the 1990s, the history of Latvia was determined by the shifting balance of power between Germany and Russia. In the First World War, for example, Latvians fled east to escape the German invaders. In the Second World War the direction of flight largely was reversed, although during the war Latvia was invaded by both the German and the Soviet armies, as I explain in more detail below. The post-war fate of Latvia was sealed in August 1939, when the foreign ministers of the Soviet Union and Nazi Germany – Molotov and von Ribbentrop – signed a secret protocol giving Estonia and Latvia to the Soviet Union and Lithuania to Germany. Five weeks later Lithuania was also added to Soviet possessions in exchange for other territories and gold. In September 1939, Hitler proposed a resettlement scheme for ethnic Germans from the Baltic States. They were to be resettled in western Polish territories incorporated into the Third Reich. Himmler was placed in charge of the repatriation and resettlement of these ethnic Germans (a decision apparently only reached between Hitler and Himmler on 27 September (Aly 1995, p 39). The first settlers from the Baltic arrived in Danzig on 15 October 1939 (Browning 2000, p 7). In this Baltic settlement programme, space was made both by brutally clearing half the population of Gdynia (then Gotenhafen) and by murdering the patients of mental hospitals (Aly 1995), thus 'making room' (*Platzschaffung*) for ethnic Germans.

A vivid insight into the consequences of war and this resettlement programme for a single Baltic German family – living in Estonia, rather than in Latvia – is to be found in the diary of Martha von Rosen (Whittaker 1995). Martha and her husband Jurgen were among the Baltic Germans who believed that they had been summoned by Hitler to Germany. They abandoned their farm and possessions and set off for, as they believed Germany, only to be resettled on an estate confiscated from farmers in central west Poland near Posen. In 1942 Martha's husband was drafted into the Afrika Corps, stationed in Italy, while the rest of the family moved to another position in estate management nearby. Here, with other Baltic Germans, the middle years of the war passed in relative peace and almost complete ignorance of events further east. In the last year of the war, however, Martha and her children became part of the more general exodus west, desperate to escape the Russian advance. I have drawn on the diary that she kept during the flight west for comparative purposes, as her route across Europe and her experiences were similar to those of many of the 25 women whose journeys are described later in this chapter. For the Von Rosens, their ethnic identity and support for Hitler made it essential that they were not trapped behind the Soviet line. For others who left the Baltic States, identification with the German war effort was ambiguous and their ethnic origins more mixed. While some had German, others had Russian ancestors, but all of them had left, actual or potential victims of the Soviet occupation of Latvia in 1940 and 1941 and Latvia's absorption into the Soviet Union at the end of the war. For these exiles, however, their voluntary movement to German-occupied lands associated them with the Nazi regime and at the end of the war they found themselves ineligible for displaced person status and excluded from the allied nations' resettlement schemes that form the final part of this chapter.

At the beginning of October 1939, the Soviet Union coerced Latvia into signing the Pact of Defence and Mutual Assistance under which 30,000 Soviet troops were moved into the country. A 'people's government' was assembled and elections were held to legitimate this but there was only a communist slate of candidates. On 21 July 1940, the Latvian Soviet Socialist Republic was proclaimed. This process of Sovietisation was disrupted, however, when Hitler attacked the Soviet Union on 22 June 1941. The week before this attack, the Soviet regime had arrested and deported to Siberia in sealed cattle trucks about 15,000 of the former Latvian elite – intellectuals (what one of my respondents termed 'all the thinking people'), businessmen, property owners, members of the armed forces and the police – as well as suspected anti-Communists, including 5,154 women and 3,225 children. At the same time there were deportations from Estonia and Lithuania. In all, during the first year of occupation, Latvia lost 35,000 people to deportations or executions. Most deportees died in Siberia. These deportations touched the families of some of the women whom I interviewed, including the deportation of the fiancé of one of the oldest of the 25 women, and were an ever more present memory as Soviet troops once again occupied Latvia in 1944.

The German occupation 1941–44

The brutal German government occupation of Latvia that replaced the Soviet occupation in 1941 officially lasted until Germany's final capitulation on 8 May 1945, although from the autumn of 1944, Latvia was partially reoccupied by the Red Army. In 1941, Germany immediately began to implement its plan to turn the Baltic into an area of German settlement. Its policies in the invasion were to starve the local populations to feed the occupying forces, to exterminate Jews, gypsies and Russian prisoners of war and to deport Slavs to inhospitable Siberia. Three different types of resettlement/extermination plans were implemented by the Germans: for ethnic Germans in other territories; for Slavs; and for Jews, gypsies and other 'riff-raff'. Latvia's Jews and gypsies were almost annihilated and only a small number survived this holocaust period. Between 70,000 and 80,000 Jews were killed or deported to Siberia between 1941 and 1944, the majority by the end of 1941 (Browning 2000; Ezergailis 1996). Jews from other territories had been deported to Latvia where concentration camps were set up, the largest in Salspils. It was also in Latvia, in Riga, where 'modern' methods of mass extermination – the gas chambers – were first tested. A gas van prototype, for example, was tested at Riga (Browning 2000, p 46). This was a dreadful feasibility study for the 'final solution': the total extermination of all Soviet Jews and those in the Greater German Reich. In addition, there were a number of vicious pogroms in the occupation years, in which some of the Latvian population was undoubtedly involved, in part it seems because the Latvian Jewish population was identified with the Soviet regime in the eyes of many Latvians. Hiden and Salmon (1991, pp 118–19) are generous in their discussion of this shameful period in Latvian history, arguing that 'there is little in their previous record to suggest that it would have taken place without German instigation. All the three Baltic governments had a good record for their treatment of Jews between the wars'. New archival material made available since 1990, however, has meant that the role of regional and local authorities on the one hand, and Hitler and the central authorities on the other, as well as Germans and non-Germans, is beginning to be explored, raising complex moral questions about the extent of collaboration by the Latvian population and necessitating the revision of official histories of this period (Cesarini 1992; Commission of the Historians of Latvia 2000).

As well as the brutal repression of the population in general, the occupying Germans also treated partisans ruthlessly – communists and others were rounded up and shot, often after digging their own graves. Bodies were left hanging as 'deterrents' and houses were burnt down in areas where opposition was suspected to deny lodgings to partisans. A small number of the women whom I interviewed took huge risks to assist partisans, although initially many Latvians had hoped that the German occupation would be less oppressive than the Russian one. Class background, occupation, property ownership, religion and place of residence, as well as ethnic background, all had an impact on whether the Russians or Germans were regarded as foes, friends or with indifference. There is little doubt, however, that for many Latvians, living in both the towns and the countryside, the German reoccupation in 1941 was seen as something of a relief after the brutality of the Russian period. As Liza, one of the women whom I interviewed, commented: 'During the first the Russian invasion, the regime was very cruel. Something I just don't want to remember.' But her ambivalence about the succeeding years is clear in her next statement:

> And then came the Germans, the German occupation, which again was very bad for the Jews. But for us it was a relief, we felt surer; we didn't look over our shoulders anymore. During the German occupation, our family lived a more or less normal life.

Ida was more prepared to recognise the worst features of the German reoccupation:

> The Germans did not persecute us because of our race, politically yes but not because of our race. They could marry Latvian girls but not Poles, or Finns, they are Slavs you see. The Poles had to walk in the road [in Riga and other cities] and wear a P on their backs, like the Jews.

But as Elvira made clear, for all the population, occupation was oppressive:

> In a way, at first, we were glad the Germans came. We did not know that they would kill us too and take people away. I am often angry that people these days that have no idea of what it was like accuse people of doing this or doing that. We had no real say in our lives when the Germans came. They made the rules and we had to obey. We were occupied and we had to obey.

And as Pauline makes clear, whether Russian or German occupation the consequences for Latvia were hard:

> War is terrible. What the Russians began, Germans finished. They used to send the young ones to Germany for work and they took people who had not even done anything to a concentration camp. Russian mostly send you to Siberia but Germans had in Latvia and in Poland concentration camps.

One of the consequences and part of the obedience mentioned by Elvira was particularly problematic for young men. The occupying Nazi regime drafted young men into the armed forces on the basis of an order from Hitler in February 1943 – an action that is illegal in occupied territories under international law. Although the Hague Convention prohibited the induction of men into occupation military forces, it permitted the use of men and women as labourers, and so men were drafted into a 'voluntary' legion under Rosenberg's labour law of 19 December 1941 under which workers were drafted into the Nazi war effort as I explore below. The young Latvian men who were drafted into the occupying army fought in two SS divisions – the Latvian SS Voluntary Legion – against the Red Army and suffered high casualties. The legion comprised the 15th Division with 14,446 men initially and the 19th Division with 12,298 men, although later construction and border-guard battalions were added to it. Whether or not these young men, recruited by force and often against their will, were strictly speaking Nazi collaborators is a matter for moral judgment. Among them, drafted into German-organised regiments, were the fathers, brothers, cousins and friends of some the women whom I interviewed and in their comments they capture some of the ambiguity of their status. This is Agnese, whose father, as a high ranking Latvian Army officer, had been deported to Siberia in 1941 where he later died, and whose brother was conscripted:

> My brother was taken in the German army to help with the occupation. He was the age of 15. Well, he went as a volunteer but there was a Latvian Legion formed which was supposedly volunteer but the Germans called up the young man. But they were quite happy to go and fight the communists and the army officers who were the Latvian higher army officers only agreed with this that they wouldn't fight in the west but only in the Eastern part.

For other young men, their ambiguous loyalties were even more of a problem. According to Jelena, for example, her brother 'ran away several times when he was about 14 to Riga to join the army to fight the Russians. My father had to fetch him back. But then when the Germans wanted to conscript him when he was 16, he wouldn't go'.

In a fascinating assessment of whether these men were heroes, Nazis or victims, based on a series of documents originally submitted to the OSS (Office of Strategic Services) war crimes investigation between 1945 and 1590, Ezergailis (1997) concluded that most of them had little choice. But further, he suggested that they saw their decision as a way of fighting against the Soviet Army that had so cruelly repressed the Latvian population between 1939 and 1941 rather than as part of the Nazi war effort. For these men too, like the Baltic resettlers, their status and affiliation became a crucial issue as it determined their right to emigrate (or not) to the United States and other allied nations at end of the war. The OSS, for example, placed undercover agents in Latvian displaced persons' (DP) camps in Germany, looking for collaborators; as Ezergailis (1997, p 11) notes, 'the Latvian DP population, especially its political leadership, was subjected to scrupulous surveillance'. And yet it also seems clear, as Ezergailis admits, that 'the OSS failed to apprehend the real Latvian war criminals. It was their inattentiveness that allowed numerous Latvians who had committed atrocities to join the legion's veterans and enjoy their "denazified' privileges"' (1997, p 11).

As well as drafting young men into the army, in all the German-occupied territories, compulsory labour service was promptly instituted. Inhabitants, including in the early years of the war some of the Jewish population of Latvia, were conscripted and compelled to work in local occupations to assist the German war economy. Some of the women I interviewed, for example, recalled the edict to send all school children to farms during the summer to undertake agricultural work. There were also orders to restrict the number of agricultural workers to a maximum on each farm, as Pauline recalled:

> On our own farm only three people were allowed to work on the acres we had, so I had to go. I was all the time in Kurland. I lived with other people, they were very nice to me, they weren't nasty to me because I always used to do my work, on the farm, do the cows and the milking.

But as she also noted: 'During the occupation it was slave labour for next to nothing – directed labour under the Germans; you had to go where you were sent and you were paid only a few marks.'

As local supplies of raw material and the production of industrial goods became inadequate to meet the ever-expanding demands of the Nazi war machine, an order to permit the compulsory deportation of workers to Germany was issued and so large numbers of inhabitants of German-occupied territories were pressed into participation as involuntary and slave labourers. As well as the predominantly Jewish slave labour in concentration camps (Bloxham 2001) and elsewhere (the German publishing conglomerate Bertelsmann AG, for example, used Jewish slave labour from the Riga ghetto in its printing house (Index on Censorship 2002)), civilian forced labourers were deported from many of the occupied eastern territories, especially Russians, Poles and Ukrainians as the initial intention of using Soviet prisoners of war was stymied by their poor condition and high mortality rates (Herbert 1990, 1997). Enormous numbers of foreign workers were pressed into service to replace the 11 million German workers conscripted for military service. Committees were set up to 'encourage' recruitment in all countries invaded by Germany and, in addition, labour was obtained from 'friendly' countries such as Italy and Spain. The inducements included both promises – to return a prisoner of war, for example, for every labourer who volunteered – and threats, including the withdrawal of ration cards from those who refused to go, sackings from jobs and the denial of unemployment benefits. In the occupied territories, the police and the army rounded up thousands of young men and women within weeks of invasion and by the end of the war there were 7.5 million foreign workers in the Reich, of whom less than two million were prisoners of war (Dohse 1981). It has been estimated that by 1944 foreign workers produced about a quarter of the total industrial output (Pfahlmann 1968, p 232).

On 17 December 1941 the occupying German power in Latvia introduced the duty of obligatory labour (*arbeitspflicht*) under which it had total freedom to dispose of inhabitants as it wished. Young men aged 16 and over were called for compulsory labour service in Germany under the RAD (*Reichsarbeitsdienst*), the paramilitary State Work Service. As well as providing valuable labour power, the secondary aim of this service was to teach Nazi ideology and select potential soldiers. Other young men, from the age of 15 and upwards, had to act as anti-aircraft aides. Still others, including thousands of women, were transported for military construction work or for work in the militarised industries (Ezergailis

1997). In total, about 12,000 Latvian citizens were deported to work in Germany in 1942 and several more thousands of young people were drafted for voluntary labour service, to work in agriculture and in munitions factories, for example. Pauline seems to have received several letters drafting her as 'voluntary' labour, finally agreeing to go in the closing stages of the war:

> In 1945 in early January I left for Germany ... They sent me three letters and said I had to leave for Germany and one day I got fed up and packed my bags and said I'm going, there won't be no trouble. Go to Germany or leave everything behind, mother and sister to go in the woods with other partisans. I didn't want to go in the woods 'cos that is not a life.

It is calculated that by 1944 the numbers of Latvians deported had reached 20,000 (Nollendorfs 2002). When acute labour shortages developed in Latvia, compulsory labour service also had to be performed locally (Grunts 1980). Furthermore, as I explore later in this chapter, many of those who left as refugees rather than as deported workers in both the 1941 and 1944 waves of migration, ended up working alongside the civilian forced labourers in the German Reich, where it seems that they received preferential treatment compared with, for example, the Polish and Ukrainian civilian workers. This preferential treatment depended on a racial categorisation. Latvians were classified as Aryans rather than Slavs. As I shall show later, this distinction was made by many EVWs themselves, as well as, perhaps implicitly, lying behind the British government's preference for Baltic rather than Polish women in the first scheme for women economic migrants. In Germany it played a part in the allocation of Latvian women to particular types of work, as well as in their own attitudes towards their co-workers. In the last few days of the German occupation of Latvia in 1944, the German military police was apparently ordered to round up every able-bodied person and transport them to Germany. People were detained in the streets, in their homes and places of work, without regard to their family status and their health (Landsmanis 1967, p 245). In this way, several thousand Latvians were taken to Germany on an involuntary basis, joining the voluntary exodus of many thousands more.

This brief history of occupation by both Germany and the Soviet Union and of wartime enforced recruitment, into work and the army, sets the scene for the exodus in 1944. It also provides some context for the complex issues raised by the diverse ethnic mix in Latvia as a consequence of its long history of exploitation by its neighbours: issues that continued to dog the country during the long Soviet era and indeed remain significant in these post-independence years. The horrific events of war, occupation and flight pose ethical dilemmas that are seldom amenable to simple historical reconstruction, let alone easy judgment. In late 1944 and into the early spring of 1945, as the Red Army advanced into Latvia, about between 200,000 and 300,000 Latvian refugees (the numbers are disputed) decided to flee to the west, fearing Soviet occupation as in many cases their relatives had been amongst those killed or deported to Siberia in 1941. Many refugees lost their lives in the Baltic Sea, their transport ships sunk by Soviet naval patrols and others were bombed on land. A sizeable group was captured and turned back to be punished for their 'disloyalty'. However, about 150,000 eventually settled in the west where they continued a long struggle for Latvian independence as well as for recognition of the inhumanity of the Soviet treatment of Latvia during the war and after. As The Soviet Union had been an ally of the western powers during the war, the crimes they committed in occupied territories were not recognised or made public for many years – even decades – after the war (see also Adamczyk 2004). Among the escapees from Latvia were the 25 then young women whose voices inform the rest of this and the succeeding chapters. Table 3.1 shows their date and place of birth and the occupation of their parents. Before turning to their testimonies, I want to draw on secondary sources to fill out the details of the flight from German-occupied territories in the face of the advancing Red Army front.

Leaving Latvia: the Baltic odyssey and life on the run

The story of escape and flight outlined here is based not only on the oral narratives of the 25 women but on a number of different types of published sources which supplement, reinforce and validate the information I collected. These sources – three of them records of similar contemporaneous journeys, one based on the experiences of an official in a displaced persons camps and the final one a recent semi-fictional record of the flight from the German-occupied eastern territories – help to confirm the details told to me by women whose recollections now straddle several decades but nevertheless remain vivid. The first three of these written sources are all accounts by individuals who were part of the exodus. The first is a personal account of the traumas of war and exile by Agate Nesaule (1995) who left Latvia as a child aged seven and so has fewer personal memories than the women I interviewed who were several years older when they left. Nesaule's account was published in 1995, by which time she was an academic in a US university. The second account is somewhat similar: it is also a personal memoir by a Latvian, Morris Eksteins (2000) now working as an academic in North America, in Canada in this case. Eksteins, who was born to Latvian parents in 1943, just before their decision to leave, reconstructed his parents' and grandparents' lives as part of a more general account of the great displacements of people during and at the end of the Second World War. The third memoir, also published in the 1990s, is rather different as it is based on the reconstruction of the contemporary diaries of Martha von Rosen (Whittaker 1995) that I have already mentioned. The von Rosens were ethnic Germans from Estonia rather than Latvia, part of the land-owning aristocracy who had lived in the Baltic States for centuries. Some members of this class had been dispossessed by the first Latvian state after 1918 but others retained their lands until they were transplanted to Germany or German-occupied territories in the early 1940s (Plakans 1995). Martha von Rosen, her elderly parents and her children plus assorted relatives and servants travelled west to German-occupied Poland in the early years of the war, while her husband was fighting for the Germans in Italy. Later, like many other ethnic Germans, she had to flee further west in 1944 as the Soviet front advanced.

The fourth source is different, written from the perspective not of a displaced person but of a camp official. It is a book, first published in the 1950s, based on one

Table 3.1: Latvian women's place of birth and parents' occupations

Name	Born	Place of birth	Father's job	Mother's job
Agata	1927	countryside, on a farm	small farmer and district official (like a mayor)	housewife, and casual farmwork
Agnese	1926	Daugavpils	army officer (shot by Russians)	housewife, after 1940, bookkeeper
Anya	1930	countryside	headteacher	schoolteacher and
Anyuta	1929	Riga	electrician	then factory charge hand
Beate	1927	Riga	army officer (shot by Germans)	housewife
Brigita	1930	Saldus	farmhand	farmworker
Dagnija	1919	Riga	engineer	concert singer (before marriage)
Diana	1920	Riga	Ministry of Agriculture official	housewife
Elvira	1920	countryside	army officer	housewife
Eva	1928	Riga	artist, toymaker	housewife
Grieta	1918	countryside	blacksmith and small farmer	housekeeper and farmhand for relatives
Helena	1927	Tukums	train driver	hospital nurse
Ida	1914	Stende	station master and bar-keeper	teacher
Ilona	1926	Batish	miller	worked in mill
Jelena	1931	Belden	forester and smallholder	housewife
Lina	1931	rural area, central	deceased	farm and house helper
Lize	1928	farm in South	small farmer	farm helper
Lizina	1928	Riga	electrician	school catering
Mara	1916	Russia	builder	ran small shop
Monika	1930	Riga	civil servant	bookkeeper
Natalija	1926	Riga	policeman	housewife
Pauline	1924	rural Courland	small farmer (died in 1927)	ran farm
Valda	1919	Wolke	hotel owner	helped in hotel
Velta	1926	small regimental town	army officer	'lady of leisure'
Vieda	1930	small village	died when v young	peripatetic housekeeper

US woman's work in a DP camp and the stories she collected there (Hulme 1954). The woman is Katherine Hulme, perhaps far better known to a British audience for her later publication *The Nun's Story* (1956) which was made into a popular film in 1959. At the end of the war Hulme worked as the deputy director of a displaced persons' camp, Wildflicken – the wild place – built originally as an SS camp, although when she worked there it housed mainly Polish refugees. Her book entitled *The Wild Place* was first published in the US in 1953, and in the UK in 1954. The final source that deals with the same events is also a recent publication, Gunter Grass's latest novel *Crabwalk* (2003), mentioned earlier, in which he controversially reopened an event that both the Russian and the Nazi wartime propaganda machines had successfully kept hidden at the time and which has remained relatively unexplored since then. This was the sinking by a Russian submarine of the German liner *Wilhelm Gustloff* in the Baltic in 1945 with a loss of somewhere between 6,000 and 10,000 people who were fleeing the advancing Russian front. Originally published in German, this book had a far more significant impact on public opinion, in Germany in particular, than any of the other four sources, which remain little known. In Germany, there was a fear that Grass's work would support a right wing revisionist version of the history of the Second World War, focusing on the suffering of Germans and that it might lead to new claims to return property abandoned at the end of the war. However, Grass disassociated himself from these views, while not denying the traumas experienced by the millions of refugees who left the Baltic States, Poland and Czechoslovakia after 1944. All these sources provide useful information to substantiate the narratives I recorded.

The impetus to leave: the Soviet advance

During the winter of 1944–45 as the Nazi dominance in the east waned, there was a fierce Bolshevik winter offensive along the River Vistula. Heavy artillery bombardments throughout Poland and the German eastern territories of East Prussia and Silesia unsettled the population and, in the face of German defeat, hundreds of thousands of people began to move west, fleeing towards the Oder in trains, carts and on foot. In the Baltic too, the Russian front was advancing. Elvira, who was then living near to the eastern border of the Latvia explains:

> We could hear the bombing and see the lights. We knew we had to go. The Germans wanted people to stay where they are, not to move away but there were so many people who wanted to go from Vizimmer which was near Russia and so the roads were crowded. But on the other hand the Germans needed people to work in their factories at home in Germany and so there was a chance to go as a worker. That was what we understood. But from our point of view it was to save our lives, the Russians were coming back and the front was collapsing. We knew the Germans were losing the war but we hoped the Americans and the Allies would help. We never thought they would let the Russians go into Berlin. So we hoped. We thought we were leaving for a few months and then we would come back.

Thus, a large-scale movement of people westwards began from the early autumn of 1944. By the late summer Riga was full of refugees from the countryside to the east and as Eksteins (2000) records 'panic was in the air'. His father was a Baptist clergyman who preached his last sermon in Riga on 13 August 1944. Riga fell into Soviet hands on 13 October. Eksteins retells the story that must have been told and retold during his childhood to become part of his family's store of memories – he himself was only a year old in 1944: 'A week later my parents locked the door to their apartment leaving everything in place, beds made, table set on the assumption that they would be back shortly. They never returned' (p 190). A similar story was repeated by some of the 25 women; others left with a little more preparation, although none on them realised how long it would be before they saw Latvia again.

Although the official line from the Wehrmacht staff running the country was for civilians not to leave at this time – in part as it would suggest defeat but also as traffic congestion would impede the movement of troops and supplies, unofficially the occupation authorities encouraged people to leave. Food was in scarce supply in Latvia and there were labour shortages in the Reich that might be met by recruiting the Balts who planned to leave. Over that autumn, through the winter and into the next spring, it seems that almost 300,000 Latvians alone left, as well as several thousand Estonians and Lithuanians, some of them hoping to escape to neutral Sweden, others to Germany. In a far-sighted comment at the time, a British Foreign Office official, GM Wilson, recognised that their flight might result in problems for the Allies at the end of the war, which was now in sight. He wrote in a memorandum in October 1944[1] that 'anybody who makes a getaway from Soviet-occupied territory will automatically be dubbed a fascist. So will those who try to help them or even express any sympathy with them'. He continued: 'The more we keep out of it the better. We shall have plenty of trouble on our hands here in course of time from the Balts'. His comments did not augur well for the future reception of Latvians by the Western Allies, although as we shall see, his fears were only partially justified.

The weather was extremely bad that winter with biting east winds, hard frosts and snowstorms, making the plight of the refugees perilous. Travel on the roads was extremely difficult, as well as dangerous because of the Soviet advance. Mud, deep potholes and great ruts from the frost, full of icy water, impeded progress and the roads were jammed with people, lame horses and broken-down wagons and carts. In January 1945, for example, Martha von Rosen started on her long journey west from German-occupied Poland on roads glazed with ice in a column of six horses and three wagons: one a covered coach, the other two open work carts in a party consisting mainly of women but also including an elderly neighbour then in his 80s and her own son who was aged five. She initially planned to catch a train from a nearby town but thousands were crowding the platform when they arrived and anyway no trains appeared while they waited. Thus, they continued by road, in the company of a huge mass of people including 'children, crying from hunger and cold, whining and complaining mothers,

---

1 Memorandum, 23 October 1944, FO 371/43533, Public Record Office, and quoted by Eksteins 2000, p 192 and p 244.

frightened men trying in vain to keep their horses at a trot, before they too died like so many others whose remains were evident on the side of the road' (Whittaker 1995, p 19). And not only horses were the victims of the cold which also claimed the lives of the weakest and the most ill-prepared among the refugees:

> Beside the low stone walls, lay many little, cold bundles, now unsuffering. The ground was frozen to an impenetrable depth and no-one had time to dig graves. Someone counted thirty-five bodies. These unfortunate people had not been prepared, having taken neither the warm clothing nor the provisions needed for survival. The agonies and miseries of those who found no shelter were indescribable, and I thought of the countless children who had already frozen and starved to death.

Those fleeing Latvia in 1944 also often started their journeys by horse and cart, some of them taking with them supplies of food as well as a few portable valuables to exchange for food or for safe passage later in their journeys. Ida told me: 'I had butter and bacon in a small case and we put something under the papers when we had to show them – it helped us.' But all the refugees in that winter suffered from the appallingly cold weather, like Martha von Rösen's party. While some people were able to catch a train – Ekstein's family, for example, fled north to Tallinn in Estonia by train from Riga, and from there on by sea – most refugees travelled west across Latvia, on foot, in carts, to the ports on the Baltic coast. This passage from a Latvian refugee's narrative – Lina – describes her slow journey across the country to the coast and the strategies for survival adopted by her foster parents and the friends and relatives with whom they were travelling:

> We left home on 4 August and moved through Latvia bit by bit until 4 December. We had a horse and cart with our belongings and even cattle. [We] had brought flour along and barley and meat, what there was and up to the time we left Latvia we managed. The sheep were killed one by one and the heifers. We sold the last two cows just before we got on the boat to go to Germany and the horses as well.
>
> I was 13 when I left home. First of all we left with our neighbours and they stayed with us only up to the first place because the father of the family was blind and the mother became ill so they stayed behind. And then later the daughter of my foster parents and her family joined us later on and there was three of them, so six of us together and then later still their son joined us and that was five more people. So we travelled like a group together throughout Latvia.
>
> We stayed for a month in a forest and my foster father made huts with branches. The rain did go through when it rained but fortunately it didn't rain a lot because it was August and very warm and there was a little stream for water that you could drink out of with no worry so we stayed there for a month but we could hear noises and bombing coming nearer so we just moved on. And then after that we moved bit by bit by bit . . . When we got to the area nearest the sea we stayed in two places for about a month. One was a deserted dairy house, then we left that place and moved on and then we stayed at a farmhouse which was one on three in the middle of a huge forest. This was now close to Liepāja where we left from and those people were very very generous. They said they had enough food for us and our cattle and they said 'don't go away. Stay with us to Spring and you will be able to go back home again and you will be OK'. But again the frontier came nearer and we had to

> leave that place and then we got to Liepāja and nowhere else to go, so then on a boat and so to Germany.
>
> There were hundreds of people there. At Liepāja we were put up in a deserted museum place. So we stayed about a week until we got onto a boat and we had to leave in the evening because during the day the boats could be bombed from the air. So we left about 4 or 5 in the evening when it was just about getting dark and then we went to Germany. Where we arrived in Germany, at that time it belonged to Germany but it is now in Poland and I can't remember its name. In German it is Gotenhafen [now Gdynia].

The initial destination for those who planned to leave Latvia was one of the coastal ports, in the hope of securing a passage across the Baltic to Sweden or to the ports in occupied Poland. Because of the great uncertainties of the time, decisions about whether to leave or not had to be made in haste and often led to families being separated as some members of families decided to postpone the decision. Here, Elvira explains the circumstances in which she became separated from her sister and the rest of her family:

> My sister was at my grandparents' farm, a little way away and she was pregnant and her husband was in the army. And we all decided we would go to Germany but later on my parents changed their mind. They didn't want to leave my sister. I didn't want to leave my parents but I decided to go with the friends. My mother said 'go with them and then perhaps later on you can get us out if the worse happens'. So I went with those farmer friends and I stayed with them for a little while until I found some of my own family. But that was in Germany.
>
> I sailed from Liepāja, that's one of the ports, one of the main ports in Latvia, to Danzig, near Poland and Lithuania. There was a sort of camp there. You see in a way I wanted to persuade my parents to come as well but also perhaps I shouldn't because the boats were being bombed and perhaps we would all go down in the Baltic Sea and then there was my sister. So it was such uncertainty. If my mother had said don't go I wouldn't have gone. I never saw them again.

Jelena, describing the first stage of her journey across Europe, also remembered the dangers of the journey, both by train and by sea:

> Neighbours took us to the nearest railway station and loaded us into a goods truck. Father had made some wooden boxes. We went on the train to Liepāja. It was bombed; there were air raids and we spent about two weeks there. There was a Latvian committee there under German supervision that organised things. We were loaded onto a big ship in the beginning of December 1944. We landed at Gdańsk, which is now in Poland. We went into mine fields on the ship. Then we went to Gotenhafen on the train.

Agata also left by sea. 'We went as part of a convoy from the Bay of Riga up into the Baltic Sea. There were Russian boats and planes and one of the convoy boats went down. It was terrifying. We were lying on the floor of a cargo ship.'

All these women clearly realised and recalled the dangers to shipping in the Baltic. This danger and the consequent loss of life among the refugees fleeing at the end of the war was the impetus for Grass's novel *Crabwalk* (2003). In vivid prose, he documented the plight of ethnic Germans fleeing westwards from East Prussia and their search for a sea passage:

> It (Grass's generation) should have found the words for the hardships endured by the Germans fleeing East Prussia: the westward treks in the depths of winter, people dying in blinding snow storms, expiring by the side of the road or in holes in the ice when the frozen bay ... began to break up under the weight of horse-drawn carts after being hit by bombs, and still, ... more and more people streaming across the endless snowy waste, terrified of Russian reprisal ... fleeing ... white death ... (p 103)

Some of the refugees reached the ports of Pillau, Danzig (now Gdańsk) and Gotenhafen (now Gdynia), the very same ports where the Latvians were arriving: 'My mother, brother and I, we went, we landed in Danzig, what was called the Polish corridor' (Helena). Several women recalled their terror as bombs fell on the ports and the ships and as ships around them were torpedoed.

From these coastal towns where the Latvians were disembarked, German migrants and soldiers were queuing to leave on board a motley collection of former cruise ships, including the *Wilhelm Gustloff* whose sinking dominates *Crabwalk*. As Grass notes:

> Hundreds of thousands tried to escape by ship from the horror closing in on them. Hundreds of thousands – the statistics tell us over two million made it safely to the West – crowded into airships, passenger liners, and freighters. (p 107)

On the *Wilhelm Gustloff*, the ship that was torpedoed, there were apparently 1,000 u-boat sailors, 370 members of the naval women's auxiliary, crew members of dismantled flak batteries, wounded soldiers from the Kurland front and several thousand refugees. The *Gustloff* was then both a troop transporter, and a refugee and hospital ship. It was painted grey and so offered an ambiguous target to Russian submarines. Grass suggests that it was an armed passenger liner under the command of the navy, not just a refugee ship, although it seems that of the 6,600 passengers recorded, 5,000 were refugees on a ship that was originally a holiday cruiser for 1,600. Of these 5,000, Grass estimates (2002, p 110) that close to 4,500 were infants, children and youths as, even in January 1945, fitter looking men were being pulled out of the crowds by the military police as suitable for military service. It is clear that there were also large numbers of unrecorded passengers: estimates of the total number of people on board range from 6,600 to 10,600. The ship was so overcrowded that Grass describes it as a 'mattressed encampment' (p 114). The ship left on 30 January 1945 in extremely cold weather, leaving thousands behind on the pier. Icebreakers had to clear a channel in the Bay of Danzig and heavy seas and squalls were predicted. The lifeboats on board were probably iced over. The ship was hit by a torpedo from a Russian submarine and, in the icy conditions, there was little hope for the overcrowded passengers. The total number of survivors was only 1,230, making it one of the worst, and probably the least known, maritime disasters of the twentieth century.

For those unable to flee further west by sea, most of the Latvians among them, the long journey across Europe had to be undertaken by whatever means of transport were still available, including journeys in freight trains to often unknown destinations, in carts and coaches and on foot, often in adverse circumstances. 'Father got a hand-cart and so we walked. There were streams and streams of refugees, the roads were full, mainly Germans' (Jelena). Elvira, on the other hand, managed to board a train in occupied Poland. Here she describes this part of her journey:

> [We went] to the railway station to see if there were any trains to go somewhere west. By the time we got back to the little village to arrange some farmers to get some carts and so on, there was almost no one left. So we had to leave all our things there. So we started going on the train, not really a train just a goods train with only two wagons. It was all open flat trucks and two closed, one for mothers and children. There were bales of straw to sit on and it was March. We just went and went and stopped somewhere and people had to jump off to do their business and there were some soup kitchens but we never stopped at any towns. I was about three days on the train and in the end I was so cold, feeling awful. I decided at the next stop I'll get off and I don't know what I'll do but ...

Fear of the advancing Soviet front was ever-present. At the time, horror tales of Russian atrocities were circulating in newspaper reports, radio commentaries and by word of mouth among the refugees. A common story about Russians, for example, reported by Hulme (1954) was their desire for watches – shouting *uri! uri*! as they searched the columns of refugees. This story was repeated to me by several of the Latvian women. Here is Elvira again, describing a later part of her journey, this time by cart:

> The front came nearer and nearer ... [and] we were stuck in the traffic of Germans fleeing west. For three or four days and nights we just kept going and on the coast, near the coast, in northern Germany, there was a big field and we decided to catch a few hours sleep. And my cousin said she heard people shouting 'don't sleep, you don't know the danger coming up'. I never heard them. We did stop and about six the next morning with a nice sun coming up, we boiled some water for tea and all of a sudden, just like mushrooms out of the ground there were Russians with the red star and they said 'uri, uri', watches. I had this ring, my godmother gave it me on confirmation day and I put it in my boot and I said I had nothing. The German lady thought they were asking the time and they just ripped off her watch. And we were all turned back.

Diana confirms this story: 'They took wedding rings, they took watches, they took everything that they could'.

It was clear, too, that physical abuse was common, including rape. As Hulme records from the stories circulating among Polish refugees in Wildflicken camp:

> Along with the looting went rape. In that unprecedented Spring, the victors went on the rampage. Women protected themselves as best they could. Faces streaked grey with ashes or dotted with red to suggest spotted fever, black kerchiefs tied low over their forehead, they would hobble along like arthritic old crones. Sometimes it helped, usually it did not. (Hulme 1954, p 70)

The women to whom I talked also recalled adopting forms of disguise, usually as boys rather than crones as most of them were still teenagers, as well as their fears of rape.

Jelena describes the reason for her disguise:

> We lived there for nine months under the Russians (on a German occupied farm in what is now Slovakia) and the soldiers didn't bother us. Though one night the windows were broken and four soldiers came in and tried to rape the daughters (of

> the tenant farmers). They were only 16 and 18 and my father went over because he could speak Russian and he talked them out of it. The Russians said to him 'you are one of us and they are the enemy. We can do what we like with them'. And the next day I had my hair cut short and my brother's clothes on. I spent those nine months dressed a boy.

For Elvira, a witness to the rape of a travelling companion, the memory of her own narrow escape persists to the present in a vivid recollection of that day, captured in the often remembered image of a bright blouse:

> One morning the sun was shining and though we were all anxious it seemed quite bright in a way and I thought 'I'll put a summery blouse on' and it was bright yellow. We had a big cart with a cover on that was more on less our home. And I needed to go into the bushes. There I was squatting there, the sun shining on my bright yellow blouse and I heard some Russians talking. They had found us. I slide down and crawled further into the bushes and thought 'why did I put this blouse on? It is so bright'. And one of the girls was just standing there and they took her to the bushes and they raped her. If I had been there it would have been my turn.

Like Jeleņa, many of the Latvian women whose stories I recorded told me that their ability to speak Russian (Russian had been the language of instruction in schools during 1940 and in addition many of their parents spoke good Russian) often protected them. As Diana said:

> They (Russian soldiers) were like animals. I am not lying, believe me. They were terrible and they raped the German women. Even the girls, 13 and 14. My three sisters, we were hiding in lofts and everywhere, where we could and I think what saved us was that we all could speak Russian.

It is clear from the narratives that anti-Russian (Russian and not Soviet was the term typically used) feeling was extremely strong among the women to whom I talked, based on these experiences as young women in 1944. As I shall show later, it remained a potent force in their political identification throughout the post-war years. Their claims about the brutal behaviour of the Red Army are supported by Naimark's (1995) work on the history of the Soviet zone of occupation in Germany between 1945 and 1949. As he shows, German women in the occupied zone suffered particularly badly. Drawing on analyses of Soviet propaganda, Naimark suggests that a sustained campaign of humiliation of the civilian population was mounted from 1945 onwards. In East Prussia, for example 'it was not untypical for Soviet troops to rape every female over the age of 12 or 13, killing many in the process; to pillage the homes for food, alcohol and loot; and to leave the village in flames. The reports of women subjected to gang rape and ghastly night rapes are far too numerous to be considered isolated incidents' (pp 72–73). Beevor (2001) has recently documented the savage treatment of German women in Berlin by the victorious Soviet occupiers. Ida was in Berlin as it fell to the Russians but she only recalls the dreadful bombardment 'the bombs, the shooting as we hid in cellars'. Numerous analysts have shown that rape is a common occurrence during wars and other conflicts. As feminist theorists have argued, women are typically considered as property, part of the booty taken by victorious armies, so that wartime rape is perhaps the ultimate metaphor for military victory (Ball 1986; Brownmiller 1975; Card 1996; Vickers 1993) or indeed revenge for defeat. Thus, it might be argued that 'the conquest of females complements or, in some cases, substitutes for the defeat of an army' (Gray 1970, pp 66–67). However, as historical research has made clear, the retreating Germans were also raping and looting as they fled. Further, rape by members of the victorious allied armies was not unknown, even in the comparative safety of DP camp accommodation, as one of the Latvian women I interviewed discovered. While it is clear that German women were the main victims of the rapists, the ambiguous position of Latvian women, neither ally nor enemy, did not protect them from harassment and attack.

Exile and bodily memories of involuntary labour

The reception, status and treatment of Latvians and other refugees by the occupying authorities and by the local people as they moved westwards in the final months of the Third Reich remains murky. It seems that many of the individuals involved were themselves unsure about their status; whether, for example, they were or were not prisoners, paid or unremunerated workers, and if in this latter category, whether their labour was undertaken freely or was involuntary. In part this is because memories have faded but also because of the uncertainty of those months. The confusion of the times is documented in the oral narratives I collected and also reflected in written memoirs. Here is Agate Nesaule (1995), for example, reporting the initial reception of her family as they arrived in Germany by ship from Liepāja:

> The adults had assumed that once we disembarked in Germany, we would be allowed to contact friends, find a place to live and move about freely. Instead, uniformed guards with swastika armbands and guns kept us waiting on platforms for days and then ordered us into a train which crossed Germany, took us into Poland, and then back into Germany again. After about a week we were taken to a place called Lehrte (a camp for west-bound refugees).
>
> A high barbed-wire fence surrounded the dilapidated great barracks. Iron bars covered the dirty windows, chains and more bars secured the doors. The countryside outside the camp was flat and grey. No trees or houses broke the monotony of the deserted field. (pp 42–43)

The family lived there for three months sharing a hut with others, uncertain whether they were prisoners or not. Nesaule recalls that later when she asked her sister, who was older than her, about the camp she replied that it 'was a place where people the Nazis did not trust were concentrated, that it was *like* a concentration camp, but was not one in actuality' (p 47). The family's release from the camp came when they received work orders to go to an institution for the mentally ill where her father and his brother worked in the fields alongside the inmates and her mother and aunt in the kitchens. In an as yet unknown parallel this was to be the very type of work allocated to many migrants as their ticket to the UK, the USA, Canada or Australia.

It seems clear then that the great streams of people heading west were perceived as useful labouring bodies to prop up the faltering German war effort. Through strategies of control and depersonalisation, the men, women and children who moved through the camps, from German to allied control and then onto western nations as imported labour were transformed from individuals, from refugees with names and histories, into units of labour, whose bodily strength was their sole advantage in their passage to 'freedom'. Nesaule (1995) noted, for example, that at Lehrte the occupants 'were issued with tags with numbers on them. These were to be sewn onto our clothes ... [and] from now on we would be called by numbers rather than by our names' (p 43). This depersonalisation and embodied transformation of the DPs into units of labour is the subject not only of the rest of this chapter which focuses on exile in Germany but also of the next chapter where the Latvian women whose story this is were transformed into labouring bodies as 'volunteer' workers in the UK.

Space, bodies, biopower and forced labour

In Michel Foucault's (1994) influential analyses of the epochal shift characterised by the rise of modern forms of the nation state, the establishment of social control through the organisation of space and the regulation of the body – both the social body of the state at large and the individual bodies of the population – is the focus. He argued that the connections between spatial arrangements and social power enabled the creation of a 'docile body', in large part through the enclosure and organisation of individuals in space. Foucault drew a parallel between Jeremy Bentham's 1787 plan for the Panopticon, which was an ideal spatial arrangement for a prison in which the individual cells could be seen only by the supervisor and without the knowledge of each occupant's social arrangements. In the Panopticon, each inmate must behave as if under surveillance at all times, thus becoming his/her own guard, behaving as if subject to regulation at all times. Foucault suggested that other examples of such spatial control included military and civilian hospitals, factories and new towns (and see Rabinow 1989) but also argued that this analysis was a way to understand the relationship between spatial arrangements and relations of knowledge and power, both analytically and politically at a range of different scales. Thus, Foucault distinguished three regimes of space and power: the sovereign, in which the basic unit is territory, specifically the modern nation state; the disciplinary, where the problem is the spatial control of bodies by spatial ordering so that efficiency, docility and an accepted hierarchy are simultaneously achieved and maintained; and biopower, in which power is exercised on a population existing in a particular location or milieu. All three sets of spatial tactics operate simultaneously, although their significance varies by location but biopower has become increasingly significant in the modern era. At its most general, biopower includes the management of welfare, life and death in which the problems presented to government by a group of people living as a population are rationalised and controlled, both through the establishment of large scale institutions of welfare and by the micro-management of individual bodies and the circuits of control between them. Disciplinary power over these bodies is, as in the Panopticon, is maintained not only by regulation but by self-surveillance by individuals.

As a number of scholars have pointed out, at a smaller spatial scale, as well as the locations or institutions identified by Foucault, various forms of forced labour camps, from the nineteenth century establishment of plantations in tropical colonies to the mines and farms of apartheid South Africa, as well as the Nazi extermination camps and other forms of involuntary labour of the mid-twentieth century, are laboratories of modernity in which extreme forms of disciplinary and biopower are used to control the incarcerated or indentured populations in carefully confined and regulated spaces. Thus, James Duncan (2002, p 317) has argued, drawing on his work on British tea plantations in what was then Ceylon (and is now Sri Lanka), 'plantations can be conceived of as modern technologies for the reconfiguration of space ... bringing together culturally heterogeneous populations, stripping them of their former social attachments and reconstituting them as workers through the use of space–time strategies of monitoring and control'. In these plantations and in other forms of involuntary labour camps, individuals are stripped of their individuality and reduced to units of production or 'abstract bodies' through rigid adherence to notions of rational planning, direct surveillance and, commonly, through the threat and use of physical force to discipline the bodies of the labourers. As Henri Lefebvre (1991) has argued, the dominance of instruments of rational planning and the commodification and bureaucratisation of everyday life that characterises modern societies results in a form of abstract space, occupied by idealised abstract bodies that are, as Foucault argued, made docile and useful, disciplined, normalised and sexually regulated and so constructed as exploitable economic resources.

I want to suggest that this set of theoretical arguments is a useful way to conceptualise the experiences of forced labour endured by young Latvian women, both in their exile in Germany, as labourers for the Reich and for the Allies, and later in their initial years in the UK. In each of these three cases, their physical attributes – their embodiment as young, strong, clean women – were significant elements in their construction as desirable workers and subject to surveillance. Their spaces of both residence and employment were also regulated, controlled and clearly delimited.

This rest of this chapter focuses on the early years after leaving Latvia in 1944 and examines the work that Latvian women undertook in farms, factories and camps regulated by the Germans and then their labours in the displaced persons' camps established by the Allies at the end of hostilities. It is important to remember, however, that these young women were treated very differently from other groups of involuntary workers used in the Nazi war effort. Their status in Germany, as it was to be in the UK, was an ambiguous one. They were not Jews nor Slavs, not Catholics, not peasants, not part of that enormous number of people seized in German-occupied territories and forced to labour and, above all, not occupants of the extermination camps and so slave labourers. Rather, they were Protestants, some of German ethnic origin, fleeing from the advancing Soviet front and so in some ways guests of the German government and, as I shall show, treated with some leniency by the Nazi regime. Nevertheless, many of the people who had fled from the Baltic territories in 1944 were recruited into a range of occupations and laboured alongside involuntary workers, some taken from Latvia in the earlier years of the German occupation, often enduring abysmal conditions.

As Schmidt (2001, p 7) has argued, 'forced and slave labourers constituted a complex ambivalent reality which was shaped by economic and racial objectives; this led to tensions – as well as to compromises'. Thus, Baltic women were set to work alongside a range of less eligible refugees and captives – Polish and Ukrainian peasant women, allied soldiers and prisoners of war – as directed labour, subject to the same disciplinary and regulatory structures and to the same conditions of work. In this sense, these women might be classified as a type of indentured or 'unfree' migrant labour rather than categorised as fixed slave labour, as the occupants of the extermination camps were. Indeed, this distinction was embedded within the labour laws of the Third Reich enacted in 1939. Originally referring to Poles aged between 18 and 60, rounded up as involuntary workers, 'compulsory labour' (*arbeitspflicht*) was imposed by a directive issued in October 1939. On the same day, another edict imposed 'forced labour' (*arbeitszwang*) on the Jewish population aged 14 to 60. This second edict, unlike the first, contained no details about types of work, payment or social benefits. The lives of this first group, while indubitably hard, cannot be compared with the fate of Jewish labourers. Indeed, as Karay (1996, p xvii) argues, the purpose of Jewish labour was quite different. 'The Nazi authorities did not regard the actual work performed by Jews as particularly important but were rather concerned with destroying the Jewish economic bases as the first step towards their final extermination.'

Amongst the compulsory labourers, among whom it seems accurate to classify the young Latvian women who found themselves employed in the last months of the Third Reich in 1944 and 1945, 'racial' categorisation continued to affect their treatment. The foreign female labourers were predominantly from the East (87% compared with 62% of the men) and the lower a group was in the Nazi political and racial pecking order, the higher the proportion of women. However, women from different backgrounds were treated differently. While the lives of women from the Baltic were indubitably difficult, especially compared with their earlier years, many of the Latvian women also experienced some kindness, as well as found ways to resist the worst excesses of disciplinary control and dehumanising treatment. In several cases, as I shall explore, families were able to stay together and sometimes work together and in others, young women from similar backgrounds drew comfort from their shared experiences in the past.

The women to whom I talked worked both in labour camps and as workers in German factories and plants, on farms and in individual homes. They were recruited in the main from refugee camps in the occupied territories in the final months of the war. Thus, they entered the labour force at the tail end of a massive period of recruitment of foreign workers by the Reich during 1943 and 1944. By 1944, the proportion of foreign workers in the total labour force of the greater German Reich had risen to approximately 25%. It was substantially higher, however, in the armaments industry and in agriculture, as little foreign labour was employed in sectors such as administration or in the consumer goods industries. Thus, in late 1944, as the Latvian refugees were beginning to be recruited, almost every other worker in German agriculture was of foreign origin and about one in three in mining, metals and chemicals. The table below shows the distribution of civilian foreign workers (almost six million in total, including

Table 3.2: Male and female civilian foreign workers in the Third Reich, September 1944

Nationality	*Men*	*Women*	*% female*	*% of all Foreign workers*
Belgium	170,058	29,379	14.7	3.4
France	603,767	42,654	6.6	10.8
Italy	265,030	22,317	7.7	4.8
Yug and Croatia	294,222	30,768	9.5	5.6
Netherlands	233,591	20,953	8.2	4.3
Slovakia	20,857	16,693	44.4	0.6
Hungary	17,206	7,057	30.0	0.4
Soviet Union	1,062,507	1,112,137	51.1	36.4
Poland	1,115,321	586,091	34.4	18.5
Total	3,986,306	1,990,367	33.3	100

Source: *Der Arbeitseinsatz im Grossdeutschen Reich,* No 11/12 December 30, 1944 and Herbert, 1997, p 462

forced labourers but excluding the POWs, of whom there were almost two million employed in 1944) by gender and by nationality in September 1944. Herbert (1997, p 462) suggests that the figures of workers from the Soviet Union are too low. Furthermore, as the definition of 'nationality' is based on a National Socialist definition, it is unclear how Latvian workers would have been classified during the period of German occupation. The numbers of Latvian workers by this date are similar to those from Hungary, although from a much smaller total population. It is also clear that at the time when Latvian women were recruited, conditions had become difficult for conscripted labourers: food was short, urban premises often damaged by constant bombing raids and the organisation of the workers was slipping out of control in some areas. Indeed, by the summer of 1944, thousands of foreign workers were homeless and were left to wander in industrial towns and cities in the west of Germany, where ruthless measures to suppress riots and looting by deserting workers were introduced in the autumn of 1944. And yet at the same time, Balts escaping the Russian advance were being recruited as workers, in the main, in the occupied Eastern territories.

The women to whom I talked worked in a range of different sectors, including munitions and agriculture. Many of them told me of the hardships they had suffered, forced to undertake forms of manual labour of which they had no previous experience. 'The Germans came round the camps and all the young people were asked to go, like, in the army or to work in the factories. We had to go and we had to leave our parents. I was only 16 then' (Eva). It was probably in the forced labour camps that the Latvian women found conditions at their worst. Three distinct types of camps seemed to have existed in 1944. The first category included camps where forced labourers and sometimes prisoners of war worked either as voluntary recruits or as the victims of intimidation and terror tactics. The second were camps where prisoners of war worked for limited periods as required by the task for which they were established and the final category was the concentration camps (Karay 1996). As well as working within these camps, forced/slave labourers were hired out by the SS to private employers. Workers who were inmates of the first two categories were usually released when the task was finished and the camp dismantled. This was not the fate of workers in Jewish labour camps. They were destined for obliteration through the extermination of the entire population: the chief purpose of the camps, rather than to meet economic goals. Even in the first two categories of camp, however, workers were treated differently 'in accordance with ideological-racist and political criteria, that is in line with the German attitude to each of the enslaved nations' (Karay 1996, p xvi).

The differences in how women from different ethnic backgrounds were treated had been apparent to the Latvian women I interviewed. Although some Latvians – in the main Jews and Gypsies – had been forcibly deported and used as slave labour earlier in the war, the women who were part of the 1944 voluntary exodus, despite having no choice about working, were treated as a superior sort of worker. They were regarded as Aryans by the Nazis (although not all of them were ethnic Germans by any means) rather than Slavs. Vieda remembered that when she collected her rations 'there were two queues for bread. Germans and Balts went first and the Poles had to wait'. Agnese also commented on the differential treatment of particular categories of workers. She explained that Latvian women, despite being forced to work in munitions factories, were treated more favourably than other Slavic women, as typically they were regarded by the Germans as asylum seekers rather than as prisoners:

> We worked in munitions factories and it was five kilometres to walk ... part of the factory was in forest, half underground and we walked five kilometres in the morning. We got up a four o'clock, had some breakfast, walked to the factory started work at six am and, well in the evening the same journey back [to the camp]. We were 40 Latvians, 13 Estonians and three Lithuanians, all women and there were some German girls as well. And there were French and Italian prisoners of war, soldiers and Belgians and they worked beside us, even though they were men. But they took no notice of us.
>
> They were quite good to Latvian women really, you know, to us. At first we weren't very well treated but some of the women, if husbands were officers in the Latvian legion and they wrote to Berlin that we were not treated very good, you know. And so we were left alone but they were very cruel to Polish and Ukrainian women, they were really, you know.

Agnese's comment about the 'pull' that might be exerted by male relatives in the Latvian Legion perhaps challenges the extent to which the legion was a conscripted and unwilling group of men with little influence in the Reich. It is also important to remember that these women were 'conscripted' in the closing months of the war when fears about the approaching Soviet front and of foreigner workers from the East within the Third Reich were intensifying. The Latvian refugees and their German employers were, then, united in their anxieties and fears of rebellious and vindictive Eastern workers, as well as Soviet reprisals.

Ilona, in her comments about the first months in Germany as a forced labourer, also remarked on the differential treatment accorded to workers from different ethnic backgrounds but in this case complaining of her association with Polish women:

> Then in Germany … a kind of a committee came round and all young girls, I was 18 then, this was 1944, and all the young girls were called up to help in the war. So we couldn't stay with our parents, we were sort of mobilised. And we were all collected and sent to a special kind of work camp and we had a German woman in charge of us. And then they didn't decide what to do with us and we were too many to feed, so they put us out to the farmers. I was with a farm, harvesting the vegetables on the fields, rain or shine, and then they found out that I could milk a cow and I was milking cows. ... On this farm in Germany when I first went, there were two Latvian girls and the Germans had us in their room for a meal and when they found out that we were refugees, so they put us in a room where the Poles were sitting and eating, not the Germans, so we were degraded.

This comment by Ilona reflects widespread beliefs among ethnic Germans and others about the nature of Slav women, who were regarded as less civilised by their employers and, as Ilona's remarks reveal, by some of their co-workers. In part, this is based on the different class origins of the Baltic workers, who often were from middle class and urban backgrounds whereas Polish, Ukrainian and Russian women were more usually from rural backgrounds. Courses were provided in factories and in camps to discipline the unruly bodies of Eastern women who were perceived as dirty, unfamiliar with 'even the simplest hygienic product, such as sanitary napkins' (quoted in Herbert 1997, p 303). This association of cleanliness, and its absence, with women from different national backgrounds found an echo in later recruitment strategies adopted by the Allies, that differentiated female occupants of the DP camps, ranking them in a hierarchy of desirability reflecting not only their suitability as future workers but also as future mothers.

After her experience of agricultural labour, Ilona moved into the manufacturing sector. Later that year she explained, 'the order came to the farms that the girls got to be back [in work camps] again because the front is nearing and the bombarding and so on. So they called us together and they moved us out to the middle of Germany'. Like Agnese, she was then sent to work in a munitions factory: 'there we were taught how to mix tar with oxygen, then you could produce a fog to guard the factories when the aeroplanes came'. Factory work typically was monotonous, often heavy and back-breaking. Shifts were long, night work common, and workers were closely monitored, even during short toilet breaks which were strictly limited. In addition, the overseers and guards were usually men, reinforcing gender divisions of power and status and insuring little collusion between the workers and their guards or resistance among the women workers. Perhaps the hardest conditions of all were those endured by Velta, who was sent as a surface worker in a coal mine. From a privileged background, she was pitched into a temporary working life which she could hardly have imagined would be her lot. Her memory of the hardships she had to survive is constructed through the image of an item of clothing – a pair of white gloves – that became a reminder of the lost innocence of her childhood. Velta had carried these gloves with her for months during her journey across Europe but eventually she wore them to sort coal and ruined them in a single day. Here she reflects on the memories encapsulated in the gloves that stand as a symbol for her own lost opportunities. The gloves could not protect her hands, just as her class privileges had failed to protect her against exile and forced labour:

> I was the daughter of an army officer and my mother was a lady of leisure. I remember the life they lived, above their means really but she had wonderful clothes. I remember the balls. They used to come and collect my mother in a carriage and my mother was in a long dress and white gloves. She ordered her ball gowns from Paris. ... I had a protected life until the war. During the German occupation, all students had to work on a farm in the summer, to replace the men who'd been sent into the army. It was such hard work but nothing to what I had to do afterwards. It turned out to be good grounding for me. In Germany, I worked in a mine, sorting coal on the surface. My hands were torn to pieces. I still had a pair of mother's little white gloves but they were no use; they were ruined in less than a day.

Velta spent eight months there. The coal passed on a conveyor belt in front of the standing women workers, who were employed on a shift basis. They stood under the roof of what Velta referred to as 'a half building', sorting clinker from the coal and by the end of the day they all had bleeding fingers. As well as this task, Velta sometimes had to change the nets that caught the coal dust from the conveyor belts and while this was a filthy job too, it was some relief from the pain of standing at the conveyor belt for hours on end.

It seems probable that Latvian women received some form of payment for their work, unlike the forced labourers in the camps and the prisoners of war, although most of the 25 women to whom I talked could not recall whether they were paid or not. Helena, however, in describing the work that she was allocated in 1944, did mention payment in passing:

> I was in a camp near Thüringen that was more or less south Germany. I was sent on my own and put in a house, house cleaning. That wasn't too bad. Then we were sent working in a munitions factory with a few other Latvian girls, just for a few months. ... I think we did get paid.

As these recollections reveal, as well as work directly related to the war effort, Latvian women were recruited for a range of other tasks, including domestic work of various types, outside as well as in homes and institutions. Pauline, for example, recalls that in January 1945, she 'arrived in Gotenhafen in Germany. We were living in the camps and as I was a refugee they just send you on the street, to clean the street. You had to go and clean the snow and the ice, like chipped ice, on the streets'. Those weeks of arduous physical work were etched in her memory as a period of gnawing hunger: 'in the morning they gave us a coffee, we had cups, half a pint something like that, and one piece of bread and I think they gave us a slice of cheese or something to put on that bread. And that was it, finish, you had to wait til the night'. For Anya, too, and her mother and sister, life as involuntary workers was hard and memories of hunger and humiliating treatment, but also small acts of kindness, remained vivid. They worked in a cigarette factory, 120 miles from Stuttgart near the border that employed as well as 13 Latvian women and 2 men, German and Polish, Armenian and Ukrainian women and children, who were regulated and ethnically divided: 'We all had armbands in national colours'. (This was a widespread system. Overseers, usually German nationals, who enforced strict discipline, typically wore white armbands). Anya's mother and sister were sent to make screws for machines for weapons. This work blistered their hands and Anya recalled the small kindness of German co-workers who brought old socks and gloves for her sister and mother to wear on their hands. All three of them lived in a small room with two other women in what Anya described as a guest house where as she recalled 'they took our ration cards from us as breakfast and the main meals was provided, but the food was very poor. Mother went round farms at the weekend and begged for food – it was terrible and very humiliating'.

Food shortages were widely experienced: it was not just Latvian women who were hungry. Indeed, as Herbert (1997) documents, food was used by firms employing foreign workers as an incentive. He draws on a contemporary study of the conditions under which Eastern workers laboured in the metal industry in the last two years of the war. At Deutsche Edelstahlwerke (DEW: German High-Grade Steel Works) in Krefeld in the Ruhr, the management reported that 'these people were chiefly interested in good food. So they were amenable to influence in this connection and we made sure they would get good meals'. The strategy was clearly successful as he noted that 'as a whole, Eastern workers are performing better than their Western workmates. Their desire to work is greater. The performance of Eastern workers and their motivation to work depend crucially on provision of good food rations' (quoted in Herbert 1997, p 300; original source DEW nd). Like Anya's mother, other workers also searched for food locally to supplement their rations. A report on the conditions at the Bochumer Verein metal factory in 1944 recorded that Russian women working there often purchased turnips and other vegetables locally without ration stamps (Herbert 1997, p 302). The huge significance of food at the time and in structuring memory is captured in Vieda's vivid image, still recalled with a sense of wonder, of her reception at an allied camp later in 1945: 'We arrived in the American zone and I remember, I remember seeing for the first time the white bread, it was white bread and oranges they were giving us'. Jelena also remembered how escaping across Europe in a slow train, she and her companions countered hunger and delay by recounting in exact detail their favourite meals made by their mothers before the war.

But this is to get ahead of the story of flight and arrival. First, the refugees had to move westwards as best as they were able to seek refuge with the Allies. For the Latvians, the journey across Europe to the west through occupied Poland was by train, cart and foot, involving numerous detours, considerable hardships and sometimes acts of kindness from local people who fed, hid or employed the escapees. Memories of the loss of belongings, as well as of food and its inadequacy that had dominated the lives of young women forced into forms of hard physical work, were a common feature of the narratives. As Vieda said:

> At first we arrived in Stettin (Szczecin) at the mouth of the Oder by ship, and it was all, there was only rubbish, nothing. The whole placed was bombed. ... Then we had to walk ... and after a few weeks we arrived by the River Oder ... and you had to go on a sort of wooden boat across and the water was seeping and you weren't allowed to carry anything so a German just grabbed away my bundle and chucked it away and so went my photographs. And then we crossed the thing and then we

> started to walk, hundreds of us ... and so we walked and walked and walked, sleeping in the woods, in some sheds. That is how everyone did it.

During the few months that these women were workers for the Third Reich their treatment varied. They were to some extent the beneficiaries of a system of compulsory labour organised on racial and racist principles, in which Jews in concentration camps and the huge numbers of Poles recruited from 1939 and from 1941 onwards Soviet workers, were the recipients of the most inhumane treatment based on National Socialist racial precepts. As Herbert notes (1997, p 389), foreign labour deployment 'instituted a functional national hierarchy based on racial criteria: Germans on top, foreigners underneath, graded from the French above all down to the Russians at the bottom. Here was a Nazi vision of the future, a foretaste of a German-dominated, racially stratified Europe'. In practice, however, local and regional differences, based on considerations of economic efficiency, on productivity or on security issues, and on the attitudes and behaviour of officials and overseers, as well as shifts in national policy during the war years, also affected how different groups of workers were treated. The camp workers lived in, the sector in which they were employed and the type of job they had all influenced the conditions under which workers in general, and Latvian women in particular, worked and lived. As I argued above, Latvian women were sometimes treated well by their overseers, co-workers and by those who housed them, but in other cases they were not. In general, women deployed as domestic servants and agricultural workers found conditions less onerous than those working in munitions factories or in mining. In these months during the final stages of the war, it seems that their ambiguous status, as refugees rather than forced labourers, perceived perhaps as Nazi sympathisers, whether they were or not, and as part of the huge movement westwards of ethic Germans, whether they were or not, saved them from the worst forms of oppression in the labour force. It may be also that their gender protected them from the worst treatment. Not all women undertook forced labour, although it seems that most of them did. Ida, for example, who had relatives in Germany, was able to find work as a clerk in a brewery run by her uncle, even though she had to endure the same sort of hardships on the journey from Latvia to Germany, walking across occupied territories from Danzig. But she was unable to stay with her uncle. His children were Nazis and unsympathetic to her views (and those of their father) and her uncle helped her leave as the Russian front approached.

The ambiguous status of Latvian women – not slaves, but forced workers, Aryans but not Nazis, refugees rather than or as well as workers – was to follow them and define them as they moved into the camps run by the Allies on liberation and later, as I document in Chapter 5, into Great Britain.

CHAPTER 4

LIFE IN THE CAMPS: FROM FOREIGN WORKERS TO DISPLACED PERSONS

The focus of this chapter is the transformations that began to occur in the uncertain lives of the Latvians who fled their country in 1944 as refugees and as asylum seekers. In Germany many of them were forcibly recruited as foreign workers but, at the end of the war, they were again categorised as refugees, as homeless displaced persons (DPs), housed by the Allies in hastily established 'assembly centres'. In these camps, barracks and requisitioned houses and flats, young Latvian women and their families, friends and other compatriots were able to establish a greater degree of permanency, to achieve some security and to re-establish a semblance of a normal life, even resuming their interrupted education as schools and universities were established. Despite this, life in the camps was also riven by uncertainty as Latvians and other Baltic people, at least initially, feared repatriation. Once this fear had receded somewhat, uncertainty still remained about their future status. In the camps too, strict regulation of bodies and of social relations and economic participation remained constant, and hard work remains as much a theme of this chapter as the previous one.

Becoming a DP

The enormity of the task facing the Allies in 1945 is hard to imagine. Estimates by the Allied Supreme Council suggested that there were just over 6.3 million displaced, stateless and homeless persons in the three western zones and a further five million elsewhere (Herbert 1997, pp 376–77). As Herbert notes: 'The blanket label "displaced persons" was applied indiscriminately by the Allies to former concentration camp inmates, French civilian workers, soldiers of General Vlasov, Soviet POWs, Italian military internees and female Polish agrarian labourers'. In fact, these groups often had little in common; worse, there were serious differences between them. They were united only because of their status as foreigners in German territory. As Marrus (1985, p 299) noted, among the displaced persons:

> were every possible kind of individual – Nazi collaborators and resistance sympathisers, hardened criminals and teenage innocents, entire family groups, clusters of political dissidents, shell-shocked wanders, ex-Storm Troopers on the run, Communists, concentration camp guards, farm labourers, citizens of destroyed countries and gangs of marauders. Every European nationality was present in both the East and the West.

The history of the transformation of huge numbers of people from forced labourers into displaced persons is a complex one, and as Herbert notes, 'it remains largely unresearched' (Herbert 1997, p 377). However, it is clear that serious differences and difficulties soon became evident among this diverse population of DPs. Herbert also suggests that 'it is disturbing to realise that, even after 1945, those who had suffered the worst fate were often the very same persons who had suffered most in Germany during the war' (Herbert 1997, pp 376–77). As Latvians were perhaps amongst the most fortunate, it might be expected that their post-war treatment by the Allies was favourable and, indeed, in some ways it was. Despite the agreement at the Yalta summit meeting (1945) under which inhabitants of lands then under Soviet control were to be returned, it is clear that Latvians received preferential treatment, compared with Ukrainians for example, and were in the main allowed to remain in the West rather than be forcibly repatriated. Nevertheless, the majority view among Latvian DPs was one of Allied betrayal of the hope for Latvian independence (Nollendorfs 2002, p 83). As Elvira explained in her unemphatic way: 'After the Yalta conference there was such a disappointment that we were abandoned'. Livija was more forthright: 'We hoped that at last the English and Americans would have understood communism. We never thought they'd let Russians into Berlin. We thought they'd understand we wanted to be free'.

In the attempt to bring some degree of order to the vast population of refugees and stateless people, the Allies grouped DPs into 'assembly centres' (trying but failing to avoid the term 'camp' and its Nazi connotations), typically organised by nationality. Thousands were housed in vast camps, previously occupied by foreign workers and by German troops. Warehouses, schools, cinemas, barracks, barns, stables, even ships in harbour were used to house the refugees. In Lübeck, for example, where both Pauline and Lizina, as well as Modris Eksteins, spent some time, more than 100 different locations were eventually used as what Eksteins satirically terms 'camping facilities' (Eksteins 2000, p 155) and in total there were 28 separate centres. Elsewhere, vast single camps were established, often on the site of former forced labour camps. At Wildflicken in the US zone, for example, the camp where Katherine Hulme was deputy director, there were 20,000 occupants by the end of 1945, most of them Poles but also Ukrainians registered as Poles to evade repatriation. The camp covered about 15 square miles and an average of 350 people living in cramped conditions were accommodated in one of 60 large block houses. There were 12 kitchens, each providing meals for about 1,500 DPs, as well as a huge bakery, a central supply area consisting of 12 large warehouses and 5 hospitals, one of which was a maternity hospital. Despite the uncertainty, the atrocious living conditions and lack of privacy, and limited rations, babies were born. Food was commandeered from German sources by order of the military government, creating envy and distrust between the DPs and the local German population. Although neither group had enough to eat, the DPs had larger rations – in 1947 the German population received an average of 1,700 calories compared with 2,300 for DPs (Hulme 1954, p 107). Housing was also a source of further conflict, as not all DPs were housed within camps. Many were accommodated in houses and apartments, requisitioned by the Allies in towns and villages around the assembly centres, and others were billetted on the local inhabitants.

The variety in the origins of this vast DP population was matched by the disparities in their circumstances and health. Many of the camp inhabitants were in a poor physical condition, especially the concentration camp inmates but also many of the forced and slave labourers from the East. 'Those who had been deployed in the countryside were generally in far better shape on liberation than those found in the factories and cities. On average, the situation of Western workers was better than that of those from the East, and the condition of the liberated concentration camp prisoners was generally far worse than that of the civilian workers and deployed POWs' (Herbert 1997, p 377). The position of the workers from the East at the end of the war is vividly described in this passage from Hulme's book:

> There were some seven million of these compass-point citizens in Nazi Germany, working as slave labourers in the plane and ball-bearing factories, in the textile mills and mines, in the sugar beet and cabbage fields, and all the registered slaves carried these peculiar passports naming OST as their place of origin. ...

As she continues:

> When this vast population of slaves was uncovered by the Allied Armies in 1945, they had been OST people for nearly six years, ever since the first Nazi blitz into Poland and later thrusts onward and eastward through the Ukraine and up as far as the little Balt republics of Estonia, which stood then like outposts of democracy only some three hundred miles from Leningrad and facing out toward Sweden across the Baltic Sea. Since the majority of them had been brought into Germany as war plunder and obviously must have come from somewhere more specific than a direction in space, the Allies invented a new name for the OST people, indicating their state of being rather than a generalised point of origin. They were named Displaced Persons. (pp 5–6)

The term was inadequate and stretched to cover a wide range of people with different experiences – the survivors of the holocaust, the German expellees from the East, those who had left by choice – but regardless of the definition, the 'scale of human tragedy was enormous' (Eksteins 2000, p 113). According to Eksteins, a German deputy in lower Saxony, Heinreich Albertz, believed that the whole issue of how to respond to these displaced people was 'the greatest social problem facing the west'. The 25 women whom I interviewed found themselves classified among this group, part of what Hulme termed a 'new kind of debris of modern war' (Hulme 1954, p 6). Plate 4.1 shows an UNRRA (United Nations Relief and Rehabilitation Administration: this organisation took over the running of the camps at the end of the war) official recording the national origins of the population in a camp near Klagenfurt in Austria. The table shows that there were 35 Latvian inmates in 1946.

As the 25 Latvian women in this book had been involuntary workers for only a few short months, their physical condition was relatively favourable compared with longer-term labourers and concentration camp inmates. Nevertheless, their health was poor, affected by food shortages and epidemics. The spring of 1945 had been exceptionally mild after the severe winter and proved a fertile breeding ground for infections, exacerbated by poor and cramped living conditions. Tuberculosis was widespread among the DPs, and would later disqualify some young women from the Baltic Cygnet scheme. Typhus, the most feared illness of

Plate 4.1 Europe's exiled millions: the nationality of occupants in a displaced persons camp near Klagenfurt

Source: Photo by Haywood Magee/Getty Images (originally in *Europe's Exiled Millions* UNO 1946)

war, diphtheria and influenza epidemics swept through the camps. Relief teams from UNRRA were sent in to improve the general condition conditions, including the health of the camp occupants, through the provision of a better diet and housing. Their brief was also to organise employment for the DPs, both within and outside the camps and eventually elsewhere in Europe, the USA and Canada and in Australasia. For a second time, then, the story is one about the regulation of the bodies, health and labour power of a vast population of homeless people, raising the same sorts of questions about how to establish control and introduce the necessary mechanisms to ensure the establishment of biopower and surveillance for the Allies as the Third Reich had faced, despite the undoubted difference in their motives as they impounded, regulated, controlled and eventually shipped out Europe's displaced persons. The women at the heart of this book became, sometimes through intense effort and sometimes as much by chance as by design, residents in the British zone, inmates of camps as well as billeted on the local populace, where their reception and treatment varied. They lived 'in the strange half world of the DP camps, where two million of Europe's uprooted lived bracketed between two liberations – the first from the Nazis in 1945, and the second from the camps themselves, anywhere from 1947 to 1952, when the final families accepted for emigration elsewhere were safely salvaged at last' (Hulme 1954, p 7). These women were amongst the first to leave Germany, leaving the camps between 1946 and 1949 to start a new life in Great Britain. In the interim, they had to re-establish the norms and practices of daily life in this half-world.

In discussing this life – employment, everyday rituals, the re-establishment of communal identity and eventual recruitment as labourers for the Allies – I want to emphasise the particular experiences of young women, to assess the tensions between their burgeoning desire for a greater degree of independence and the unsurprising desire felt by many, especially perhaps the older refugees, to re-establish close familial and community ties in the face of the huge uncertainties of life for displaced people at the end of the war. In this discussion the female body plays a particularly significant part. Camp life was communal, privacy was difficult to attain as young women's bodily activities – their health, their labour and their social life – were regulated not only by adult relations and friends but also by the camp administrators, guards and employers and, finally, before leaving for England, by British officials and camp doctors, anxious to establish the health and purity of the women whom they recruited as future British workers and, perhaps, as potential mothers of future Britons. Furthermore, as the narratives reveal, hunger and poor diet were constant themes. As Mara noted: 'there really wasn't enough to eat for young women who were growing and developing'. The rhetorical construction of these young women as pure, clean, strong, as good stock, by British officials, as I explore below, was countered by their own conception of themselves as unfeminine. Hungry, dirty, with loose teeth, lice, scabies, TB, boils and scabs, and often not menstruating as the food was insufficient, it was hard for these young women to imagine themselves as settled domestic subjects, desirable marriage partners and potential mothers in a country about which they knew next to nothing.

Figure 4.1 Divided Germany in 1945: the occupation zones

Achieving refugee

The first task for the Latvians in Germany at the end of the war was to gain access to a camp or some other form of accommodation under Allied control, preferably in the British occupation zone (see Figure 4.1).

This was not always an easy task as the three long narratives and two shorter comments on the next pages illustrate. The level of detail in these descriptions of flight may seem surprising given that almost 60 years have elapsed since the events recounted. However, there seems little doubt that the intensity of the experiences engraved every aspect of the escape into these women's memories. In addition, these stories have been told and retold over the years to the future children of the women as well as exchanged within the community of escapees and exiles in the camps and many times since then: as Connerton (1989) noted, memory is an embodied performance. Subterfuge and disguise is a common theme in the narratives; Latvians pretended to be German, for example, or told Russian soldiers they were planning to return home. The testimonies are also full of a sense of desolation, as well as the fears felt by many women as they found themselves separated from friends and relatives in the confusion of the first days and weeks of peace.

The first voice is that of Diana. She left Latvia in 1944 with her parents and her sisters and had worked in German agricultural employment at the tail end of 1944 and into 1945. Diana's account – and several others – reflects the anxiety of not really knowing which zone she was in, as well as the desperate desire of both Latvians and many Poles to avoid repatriation to what had become Soviet territory:

> I ended up in a little village in Mecklenburg in the middle of Germany. We stayed there when the war was ending and then we were under Russians again. It was 1945 when we escaped from the train. We were in the Russian zone. That used to be a German city and now it was Polish and there were so many empty houses with furniture, exactly the same as we had left and so we went in an empty house and stayed. We didn't have anything else to do. If we stayed in the train we would be taken to Siberia. And so we took a house, everything was there but food was very scarce but we found we were near a nursery and we went myself and my sister and we just, a vegetable farm or something like that and so we worked there for a year. And there again the Poles, I don't know if you knew how the Germans treated the Poles, it was very bad. And now it was the other way round, now the Poles treated the Germans very bad. And there was of course the Russians there as well and so we lived in the house and we never knew if one day the Poles and Russians come and bang the door and you have to open and let them in. That was nearly a year and then we heard rumours. Because Poland was full of different nationalities who didn't want to go back to Russia. And the Polish Government, that of course was communist, they have agreed that all the Russian citizens, because of course we were then Russian citizens, they are going to collect and send back, to 'home', that's what they said. And we knew if they found us what will happen. Then the Poles sent, not by force but they did everything possible so that the Germans would leave the towns because a big part of Germany now belongs to Poland. And they wanted them to send all back and they did everything possible, they didn't give them work, they weren't brutal but they did everything possible.
>
> And really we were, did not know what to do and there was a special office where Germans had to go to leave Poland and one day, my, both sisters, we were very desperate, we went in when there was only one person and we said we want to emigrate. We speak German and they said where is your papers and I forgot to tell you earlier when they took us to Russian camps they took away all our passports, everything. We had nothing, no papers, so you are nothing so when we went to the Polish office, they said where are your papers and we said we have no papers. And in that split second we had to decide whether to lie or to tell the truth and we told the truth, that we are Latvians and the gentleman that was there, there was nobody else there, he said yes that is true. They are going to send you all back. And you know what he did? He said you come the next day and I'll give you a big pile of papers and chose one which you want. And my sisters, we went back and he said you are too many people together, you are five people, and my eldest sister and her

> little boy, he was three, we go together and my mother and father would go with my younger sister so we had different identity papers, and so we went to the German camp. You don't know how we felt, but that was all what people do.
>
> And they had again a train was there and we were all packed in and we went over the border, that was the Russian border. We went through the English zone and you don't know how I felt when we were through the Russian zone. And then from there we were taken to the American zone and then we found from there, we knew friends and we let them now we are over there and then they took us there. But my sister and mother and father were not taken to American or English zone. They were taken back to the Russian zone where the Russians are. I can't explain that. Perhaps it was illegal, there were friends who found a way to give a note to the German office to say they are so and so and so they could come across the border to the American zone. And there was, it was so complicated, at the last minute they just jumped into a train and came over.

The second story is Elvira's, who was also in the Russian-occupied territory when hostilities ceased. She, too, wanted to reach the American or British zone:

> There were quite a few families together and my cousin said, 'let's see if we can find a way to the west'. We knew there were those zones – English and American – and we thought we must see if we can find any way to get to the English zone or at least out of the Russian zone. And one of the people who stopped was from the forestry commission and he went to Berlin by himself to see if there was any way of getting out of the Russian zone and he had a radio and he heard that there is a chance. He came back and said 'yes we will go. It will take a few days to get to Berlin so we will go on Monday and then you come on Thursday'. We told the Russians we were going back to Latvia not just to Berlin so we got things together, just what we could carry and we went on the train to Berlin. And for some reason the train was absolutely packed because there was some sort of rule that all the people who had lived in Berlin up to 1939 had to go back to register, which was not really true but all the people were there and the train was absolutely packed, it was awful. We just sat there for nearly three days.
>
> We got to Berlin about 1 o'clock on Saturday and the offices were closed where we were supposed to register. And there is a station in Berlin, just before the main station, Spandau, and the train for some reason stopped there. It should have gone right through to the other station. And the friend who went on Monday with his family was waiting for us at the main station. So we had to wait all through Saturday and Sunday. On Monday morning the station was bombed, just ruins only where the tickets were collected was left and we thought 'we'll just put our things together and stay somewhere', and the ticket collector said 'don't do that because you will be robbed and murdered if you go from here'. And so we all huddled together. And one night it rained, it was really awful. This friend he was very good. He organised a van, a baker's van, for the children and the luggage. And working on the farm I had had my legs scratched and they were infected. It was awful and we didn't have any bandages either. I couldn't really walk so I was in the van with the luggage. And he took us to a British camp and we were taken in as refugees. And that was where it started.

The third long narrative is Lina's which she told me as a single, almost stream of consciousness, story, beginning with leaving Latvia in the autumn of 1944 when she was just 13 years old. Here, like Elvira, she tells of the impact that the journey on her health, and of the poor living conditions. The panic and horror of her isolation as she was left behind by the people with whom she had been travelling is clearly evident in latter part of her story and the whole narrative is suffused with vivid descriptions of the hardships she suffered, captured in bodily sensations. The soothing touch of the ointment applied by an elderly nun, the pervasive smell of cooking root vegetables, the oily floors, as well as the self-induced fears from ghost stories told by candle light, bring an immediacy to her story that draws the reader into it:

> When we arrived in Germany, at that time it belonged to Germany but it is now in Poland and I can't remember its name. In German it is Gotenhafen [now Gydnia in Poland], next to Gdańsk, very near to that and when we got there we were sent on further into Germany to an old mansion house with no electricity and no water and it was December. It was packed with people, some Lithuanians and Latvians. You had double bunks and perhaps a small table in the room and a coal stove in a corner or something like that and bunks all around. It was very, very overcrowded. I think the worst part for me, those four refugee years I had lots of illnesses and that didn't help. It started before we left Latvia, I still don't know what I had, some sort of eczema perhaps, like biggish watery blisters on my body, no it can't have been eczema. They were painful, on my buttocks and tummy and somewhere else and it was painful. When we were in the mansion house an old German nun came and she used to put ointment on them and they did heal but very, very slowly because what healed during the day I would scratch off at night. It took about three months to clear and then I got typhoid. It was very common. There was like a typhoid epidemic and I was one of the last people who got it and then they sent me to hospital. I was there for about four weeks, it was about 30 kilometres from the house. I was taken there in a horse and cart and it was an isolation hospital, no visitors were allowed and those four weeks I didn't see anybody at all. ... I could speak some German. I had learnt it at school for two years and then in the months in the mansion house there was no school but I had a German book teach yourself and I was working on that because simply out of boredom, because there was nothing to do at all, no school nothing. I just did anything to occupy my mind really.
>
> We were there [in the mansion house] for about six months. We did have a meagre Christmas party but otherwise there was nothing really and there was no electricity; there was no light at night nobody had candles or torches so people had to go to bed when it was dark. People told all kinds of stories then. Ghost stories or whatever, just to amuse themselves, for fun, for relaxation, I suppose, because things were rather grim. The food was very inadequate really. We had a kind of vegetable soup with you know carrots and swedes and another vegetable. I don't know the English name. Another root I think, white vegetable, not a turnip. We had this soup day in and day out and for ten years after that I could not stand the smell of swede because it brought back those memories. And we had some bread but very little, a small ration. But we stayed alive somehow. But that was only six months and then all the confusion started because the Russians moved in there in that area.
>
> When I was hospital all I knew was that the war had ended. There were no papers in the hospital so all I knew was that 5th May the war had ended or was it 8th May? I 'm not sure. Anyway the war had ended that was all I knew. And as I had had no visitors I didn't know what had happened [at the house]. And as it happened the

Russians had moved in there and they [occupants of the house] had told the Russians that as they were liberated they'd be going back home. You know, telling them lies. So the Russians had got horses and carts for the village people. 'Pile up your belongings and off you go'. So they did. But they didn't go home – they went in the opposite direction and somehow got out of the Russian zone and into the British zone. But at that time I didn't know that so when I had to leave the hospital they said I had to go to the local police and ask for permission to travel there and, erm, I didn't think much so off I went to the police, to the police station. And when I got there they said they couldn't give me the permission. I would have to wait some days and I was a bit worried and I said 'well where can I go? I can't go back to the hospital' and they said 'oh there is a Latvian camp in the town' and somewhere in the town there was a young man who said 'oh yes I know where it is, I'll show you'. So off we went but we only went a couple of streets with me and he left me, he said go there and left and right and there, and he left me.

I had only one German mark that a woman in the hospital had given me. I hadn't even wanted to accept it but she'd said 'well, you never know it might come in useful'. So I had this one German mark and a face towel and my clothes and that's all I had. No possessions, no papers because I'd gone into hospital you see, no belongings nothing. I couldn't find the camp. I wandered all day and I didn't feel very strong as it was, just out of hospital and all day without food or anything so I wandered around and it was already getting dark and I was a bit panicky and I thought I'd have to spend the night out in the open. And there was a queue with German women standing in it, at a shop for food and I asked one of the women and I think she saw that I was a bit down and she said she would come along and look for this camp with me and eventually we found it. And we found the place but the man in charge said he couldn't take me in. He said there was no place and I was totally at a loss. I think I started to cry and the German lady she gave the man a good telling. She said she had found this child on the street and what was she to do with this child and in the end he took me in. And anyway, there was plenty of room, the reason why he didn't want to take me, I suppose, he just didn't want the responsibility because I was on my own without parents and so on. So at least I had a place and a roof over my head and so on and people gave me a cup of tea and maybe a piece of bread and I think again the next morning, I can't remember. And then I had to go to the local town hall and get a ration book to buy some food. I got the ration book and I had this one mark and so off I went to look for food in the shops, and there was nothing in the shops. They were all empty. So what I got I was, I think I got some sugar and a pound of dried peas and so I lived on those for three days. Those days you were lucky to get that. I wasn't starving and I got tea on top of that.

I was in a shared room with other Latvian people. That town had been taken by the Americans, I didn't know that, and it was later on given over to the Russians as they divided Germany and so we were moved out of there to another camp and that was quite funny in a way because we were put in a disused factory and all the machinery was still there – all oily and black and the floor was oily and black between the machinery and people used to run around and find boards or grass and anything to put down on the floor so as not to, you know, sit or walk over that oily floor. And I didn't have anything, no blankets, no sheets, nothing so I went outside and got some grass together to cover the floor and fortunately I still had my winter coat so that was my blanket sort of thing. At that stage it was all confusion, nobody noticed me.

> [Later] I got back with my foster parents. It is amazing; I can't believe it. They were in another camp. They'd just travelled on and on until they got to the British zone. I think I was only there a couple of nights and then we moved again to a large camp which was near the River Elbe, near Hamburg and that was very large, about 2,000 people. We used to live in wooden huts but by then things were a bit more settled.

Jelena had also spent several months as a young girl with her parents in Russian-occupied territory. They left as rumours about repatriation for Latvians were rife:

> About five kilometres (from where we lived) there was a sort of centre, between a town and a village and there was another Latvian lady there. She was friendly with the Russians – she was very good looking – and she discovered we were all going to be deported so we had to go again. We went to Pilsen by train. There was a camp there for Germans from the Russian zone who wanted to go out to the western zone, who had relations there or who had lived there we were integrated with them, we had to pretend to be German. We weren't allowed to speak Latvian. I was a girl again by then (this is the girl whose father dressed her as a boy) although my hair was short. Then we were loaded on another train. It took a long time, stopping and starting, not much to eat and my teeth all got loose. Then we went to a dispersed (sic) persons' camp. They were all right. We went to one near Hanover: it was called Murbeck.

Natalija also travelled by train to the British zone:

> When war ended, the DP camps were set up and we went to a camp. There was trains and we went by train; we didn't know where we were going and we just arrived there. It was in an American zone. It was more like a transit thing – you just stayed for a little while and after that we went to a sort of real camp and that was in the English zone: Blomberg.

Three main types of refugee housing were common. The first type was what were known as casern camps (Ruta, for example used this term when talking about her time as a DP), which were former German or Italian military centres with permanent buildings. Secondly, there were barracks camps, often former forced labour camps, and largely consisting of wooden huts. Thirdly, camps based on the requisition of whole villages or parts of a town were not unusual. Vieda, for example, remembered that 'I was put in a small town where all the Germans had been evacuated and it was filled with foreigners'. While this way of housing the DPs was most resented by the defeated German population, the 'foreigners' were, in general, regarded with extreme distaste. Eksteins (2000), who himself was a camp occupant as a small boy, draws on reports in local newspapers and later research (see Benton 1984, for example) to construct a stereotypical image of the DPs:

> They swarmed like locusts over all available housing; they snatched like rats anything resembling food; and given half a chance they would carry away anything that was not nailed down. They stole money and rations coupons from the elderly; they beat up innocent citizens for fun; they slaughtered farm animals in the dark of night; they engaged in firefights with the police; they lived like monstrous beasts, filthy and licentious . . . Such was the popular image of the DPs. (Eksteins 2000, p 119)

While there was a thread of truth in these exaggerations – several women, for example, told me about stealing from fields in the night, and as I show later, there was an active black market in the camps – these images ignored the valiant attempts made in the camps, by both officials and occupants, to reconstruct some semblance of a 'normal' life. Official responsibility for running the camps was handed to UNRRA at the beginning of October 1945, taking responsibility out of military hands and providing a greater emphasis on rehabilitation. Although UNRRA had initially assumed that there would be a relatively quick resolution of the 'refugee problem', estimating that about six months would see the camps emptied, this turned out to be far too optimistic. Although over five million people were quickly repatriated from the western zones in Germany in the first months after the end of the war, almost two million people were still there at the end of 1945. And as Eksteins (2000) noted, 'many of these proved to be difficult cases. It was the Soviet citizens and Eastern Europeans, especially the Poles, Ukrainians and Balts, who presented the greatest problems. Many of these people did not wish to return home' (p 140). In mid-1947 there were still 416 camps in the US zone of Germany, 272 in the British zone and 45 in the French zone, as well as eight camps in Italy and 21 in Austria (Wyman 1998, p 47). The 25 women in this book were by that time either in a camp in the British zone or on their way to the UK, in part benefiting from the good reputation of the Balts, especially the Estonians and Latvians, in comparison with the 'lawless' Poles. First, however, before explaining how these women left, life in the camps must be described.

Becoming a woman: health, bodies and femininity

On arrival, bodily hygiene immediately became a focus for all camp entrants who were sprayed with DDT powder against typhus, as well as lice. 'We had some food, and a bath and were deliced (sic),' said Elvira. Despite recognising their less than pristine physical condition, many women found this ritual cleansing and spraying humiliating, as others did on their behalf. One young refugee, for example, recalled with indignation that 'I saw some official put a duster gun, a flea powder dispenser, up my 15 year old sister's skirt and down her blouse' (Bruce 1982, p 38). Ilona who, with three other young women, had been billeted with a German family in the British zone recalled that:

> It was a punishment for the Germans to take in these foreigners and they had to give up a room. And we were three girls in a room but we were registered with the Red Cross and we had to go to have health checks because we had lice in our hair and we had some scabies as well. We didn't have soap. We weren't in very good condition then. It was a bit of a rough time but it wasn't pleasant to be inspected.

It is clear that the journey across Europe had had a severe impact on the health of many of the women to whom I talked and that, as well as illness, food shortages, lack of sleep and fear of capture affected normal levels of physical development, delaying or inhibiting menstruation, for example, as well as affecting their skin and teeth. In the earlier quotes, Elvira mentioned her infected legs and Ilona her teeth. Pauline also recalled the problems that she had had with her teeth, in her case trouble that had become evident when she was in a German labour camp just before the end of the war: 'We had such bad food, we used to go to Germans and say look our teeth are already getting loose and they used to give us carrots and so on.' In addition, rickets, dysentery, intestinal and chest infections, TB, diphtheria, typhus, scabies and other skin infections were common ailments among camp inmates. Natalija, Ilona, Lina and Pauline, for example, all spent part of their time as DPs in hospital with, respectively, an unspecified lung disease, diphtheria, typhoid and pneumonia.

As improved diets remedied some of their health problems, the lack of privacy became a pressing issue for young women then in adolescence and early adulthood. After reaching the British zone, Elvira explains the overcrowded conditions that she experienced which gave her no space to call her own:

> We were taken to the English zone where we stayed in one camp. Oh it was so cramped. I can't remember the name now. So we tried to get somewhere else and in the end we ended up in a really posh house. The owner of it owned a brickyard and he was in hospital and the brickyard wasn't working anymore and the lady of the house she lived in a bungalow and with the refugees we were in the main house, it was really very nice but we only had one room. I was put in with a mother and her teenagers. I hated sharing with them but I suppose I was fortunate.

Even in these difficult conditions, class differences between the occupants were recognised and respected and middle class standards of living adhered to as far as possible. As Elvira commented: 'We kept the house really nice. They were all Latvian people, some with a bit more education than others. There was a professor of medicine and his wife who had been a soloist in the opera at Riga.' Clinging to older standards was one of the few ways that were easily available to combat the chaos and uncertainty of camp-life, attempting to re-establish something of the hierarchical certainties of pre-war life in Latvia.

For Natalija, rehoused in a British camp, the accommodation 'was a school, about four storeys with fairly large classrooms. We were 45 in that room; there were no beds, nothing, we had some straw, and you were very lucky if you had a blanket. After they gave us some blankets, army grey. Later on we got beds, two sort of layers, my parents below, and if I stretched out a hand I could shake a young man's'.

In these overcrowded conditions, blankets were used as space dividers in an attempt to create a sense of privacy for family groups, as Hulme (1954, p 81) describes:

> These were the rooms that always caught at one's heart, for they were partitioned off into family cubicles with the narrow wardrobes and stacked luggage built together to make one dividing wall, and Army blankets hung from ropes to close in the remaining footage authorised to each.

It was clear that she was appalled by the treatment of the camps occupants:

> You stared at these khaki labyrinths, the last ramparts of privacy to which the DPs clung, preferring to shiver with one less blanket on their straw-filled sacks rather than to dress, comb their hair, feed the baby or make a new one with ten to twenty pairs of stranger eyes watching every move. You knew then that no matter what had happened to these people in the merciless herdings of them from homeland to enemy land, there was this one thing that could be never taken from them – the sense of privacy, the essence of human dignity.

Natalija remembers being transferred to a different camp further north in Germany, which, like Wildflicken where Hulme worked, was 'a huge camp, more than 3,000 people all together – Latvians, Lithuanians, Poles, all together'. But here, her living conditions improved somewhat: 'There, we had a room for our family, a fairly largish room. We had three beds and a table.'

These living conditions, while undoubtedly irksome for all occupants, were perhaps especially problematic for young women who found it humiliating to live in close confinement with people of all ages or to have to share a single room with their family members. Nevertheless, as conditions improved and some semblance of a more normal life was introduced into the camps, young women began to find the space and independence to establish themselves as individuals with lives and interests separate from those of their families. Largely through huge efforts made by inmates, education, social and cultural activities were organised, as well as improvements to the physical surroundings in which they were forced to live. Thus, huts were kept clean, washing hung outside and flowers and vegetables planted, to recreate an image of home and the restitution of a former stable and content domestic order in the chaos and uncertainty of camp life. Many women, including Agnese, told me of the wonderful flower gardens tended by their mothers in the pre-war years. 'Well, we always had a garden and a vegetable garden, even if we lived in the army estates, or whatever. The Latvians are known for it, every farm had a flower garden and an orchard. However poor there were always flowers.' In the camps these gardens were also planted with vegetables to supplement the inadequate rations and to exchange for other items. '[Women] saved and traded seeds from radishes, carrots and cucumbers, they transplanted wild strawberries form the surrounding fields, they dug up tiny pink and white English daisies and coarse purple asters ... Sweetpeas flowered under the windows of the crowded barracks and were brought in to scent the rooms' (Nesaule 1995, p 112).

The significance of these gardens for Latvians and other Baltic peoples was also noticed by Hulme as she compared Wildflicken, housing Poles in the main and a camp where repatriation was the key policy, at least initially, with the more permanent camps where the Balts lived:

> In camps of people like the Balts and Ukrainians, whose homeland had been absorbed into the USSR even before the war's end and who had never experienced the upheaval of mass repatriation, the gardens had perennials like gooseberry and raspberry bushes, and two harvests of leaves had already been plucked from their flourishing tobacco plants and cured on strings stretched in the sun across the face of the caserns in which the inhabitants had lived more or less continuously since the 1945 liberation. Here there were landscaping effects and the crests of lost lands like Latvia, Lithuania and Estonia grew out of the earth in floral designs with marigolds, pansies and begonias spelling out the national colours. These were the 'hardcore' camps, where life had had a continuity never imagined in the tidelike turbulence of a repatriating Polish camp. (Hulme 1954, p 142)

In the camps in which the 25 women lived, choirs, clubs, schools and other youth activities were organised, not only by the camp occupants but also by the allied controllers who were anxious not only to bring some temporary respite from the hardships of everyday life to the DPs but also to the troops and other young people in the allied administrative networks. Thus, dances were often held on army bases, which despite some misgivings among parents, were not only a welcome opportunity for young people to socialise and explore their sexuality in ways that were more difficult under the watchful eyes of their relatives but also, as the extracts below show, provided real material opportunities to improve their standard of living.

Helena, who was 18 in 1945, explained that:

> There was dancing in the night, in the evenings, in a huge big camp where there was Italians and French, and all sorts of foreigners, before they went back, and we had a lovely time. I was young and carefree then. And the Americans, they were forbidden to go with German girls and so they came and took a truckload of us to a dance, all of us.

At this time the anti-fraternization movement prohibited contacts between US troops and German women (Biddiscombe 2001). As well as having fun flirting and giggling at dances, Helena went on to explain that for hungry DPs, they had another attraction, and not just for single women:

> And one woman who was married went to the dances because she wanted to take some cigarettes back to her husband. There was cigarettes all over the place. But we [Erna and her friends] wanted to go where there was good food. There was crackers and peanut butter. The food in the camp was terrible. We went to have a good time, to dance and to eat and we were given wine. Not strong drinks you know but German wine. It was a nice time.

She added:

> I grew up there (in the camp). Although my mother was there, we were treated as persons, individuals, with our own parcels from the Red Cross, and she didn't have to look after me.

While dancing with foreign men introduced an element of sexual danger into these girls' lives, the social life of the camps tended to revolve around activities that were regarded as more wholesome and in tune with the need to maintain Latvian customs and rituals. Thus, folk dancing and signing groups were formed, as well as theatre groups. A production of *Twelfth Night* has become a part of the communal memory of those years and was mentioned by several women.

Here is Jelena's recollection:

> We went to one (a displaced persons' camp) near Hanover; it was called Merbeck. It was good. By that time I was more or less coming up for 15 and it was a big camp – there were Latvians, Estonians and Lithuanians there. It was a village, it was a German village, the Germans had been turfed out as they had killed some English airman. There was about 3,000 Latvians there. There was schools and dancing and girl guides. The whole of the Latvian theatre troupe was there and they did a wonderful performance of *Twelfth Night*. It was good there. We were a proper community.

Jelena also emphasised, like Helena, that camp life could have a positive side:

> We lived there for three years. I was a teenager and there was a lot going on there. I enjoyed it.

Communal activities included, as well as leisure activities ranging from the arts and cultural activities to a numerous sports, the establishment of Lutheran churches in camps occupied by Latvians, a wide variety of forms of informal employment from tailoring to producing newspapers, participation in various forms of elected camp committees and in political discussion and organisation. As camp life became established, one of the preoccupations of young women became easier to resolve – the lack of clothes other than cast-offs arriving in the parcels from the Red Cross and other organisations. Several women told me that their mothers or other relatives recut and reshaped old clothes for them and that, as the camp tailors opened for business, other options were possible – even a special dress for a dance or a theatre performance.

In recalling these more enjoyable activities, the ways in which memories are continuously reconstructed on the basis of life-time experience became clear. Many women commented that their then youthful optimism seemed to them in retrospect rather selfish, lacking an understanding of what they had lost. Eva, like Helena and Jelena and many of the others, remembered life in the camps as being more than bearable for young women like her. Indeed, more than half of the 25, with Laura, used the term adventure to describe their life in the DP camps. For the adult occupants, however, as other studies of life in the displaced persons' camps has revealed, life was marked by tedium and waiting. Wyman (1998), for example, has argued that adults' recollections of the camp life are filled with bitterness, with memories of endless talk and, above all, the uncertainty of waiting. Children and younger adults were perhaps protected from a full understanding of their futures, whereas camp life was hardest for middle aged people, especially those with family responsibilities. As Eva noted, she only came to understand later when she settled in England that their youth had protected them from the full realisation of what had been lost:

> We had our social life there in the camps. So it wasn't bad and when you are young too that is different. It is just an adventure. But when I think about my parents, they had to leave everything behind, all their life, what they have saved and all they had, they had to leave behind. We only took a few silver spoons to exchange later on in Germany for food. They lost everything. I can imagine now what they felt and that's maybe why some people felt they could not leave.

But life for many young women was not only about leisure and education as, like their mothers and male displaced persons, compulsory participation in a range of types of work was unavoidable and once again many women found themselves forced to undertake forms of manual labour. In the camps, however, there were also opportunities for some of the older women among the 25 to capitalise on earlier work experiences they had gained before they left Latvia, so escaping the most monotonous and unrewarding forms of manual work. Before exploring the types of work undertaken in the DP camps, I want briefly to return to the question of femininity and sexuality; areas of tense struggle, resistance and negotiation for young women. Their desire to achieve some form of independence –whether social, sexual or economic – challenged the desire among many camp inmates to re-establish, under conditions of great uncertainty, older forms of familial and patriarchal control. Thus, the young women who had escaped with their families, or under the protection of male family friends, found it particularly hard to assert their right to growing independence. It was also clear that these women were vulnerable to predatory men, from harassment by other DPs and by officials, as well as being subject to surveillance under systems to regulate their sexual health.

Sexuality seemed to be a particular area of concern to the authorities, no doubt anxious to control not only sexually-transmitted infections but also the rising number of children conceived and born in the limbo between the end of the war and repatriation or migration as a worker or an asylum seeker to a third country. As well as the demeaning health checks on entry, camp occupants were also subject to periodic checks such as chest x-rays and, for women, vaginal examinations. Hulme (1954, p 50) described the tragi-comedy of a demeaning event at Wildflicken when a VD examination was ordered for all women in the camp. As she explains, the camp doctors ordered 2,000 pairs of rubber gloves for the examination but received only six from the medical supply dump and 'somehow with those six glove-fingers, our doctors managed to examine our 5,000 women over the age of 16'. The humiliation, let alone the potential health hazards of this procedure, is hard to exaggerate. Similar practices were not uncommon in British-run camps, as some of the women to whom I talked reported. It also became clear, as I explore later, that intrusive and demeaning physical examinations were part of the price these women had to pay to be admitted to Britain.

As well as officially sanctioned forms of invasive treatment, some of the women were the victims of a range of forms of unwanted sexual attention in the camps, although in most cases they reported these as a nuisance rather than serious harassment. Furthermore, it is clear that trading sexual favours for chocolate, cigarettes or food occurred. Rape, although it seemed to be a rare occurrence, was also a risk. Here, Helena explains how she narrowly escaped such an ordeal. Like Elvira's recollection of her own earlier escape, Helena's memory is also filtered through the lens of a significant material object, in her case a piece of furniture rather than a bright blouse. But Helena's recollection is far less suffused with guilt than Elvira's. Instead, she emphasises her own lucky escape:

> Well it was a cupboard, I think it's called a tallboy that saved us. We were staying in a sort of hostel and the first American soldiers must have found out there were some girls there. There were Dutch girls and a few Latvian girls, there were about 10 or 12 of us in this hostel. They came in the night; it was summer time. They didn't really treat us too bad but they wanted sex. And so we hid standing up in this tall cupboard. It was very narrow. There was one in all the rooms. Nothing happened to us, thank God. Others weren't so lucky though. They weren't, they didn't force you too much but some of the girls were raped in the garden.

While the extent of rape by allied soldiers remains uncertain, French and US soldiers, especially in April and May 1945 were accused of rape, in the main of German women (Biddiscombe, 2001; Grossman 1997; Hillel 1983; Peterson 1990). There were certainly a small number of convictions of US service men in Germany in the late 1940s in which racial discrimination played an unsavoury part as the convicted men were predominantly black Americans, in an occupation force that still segregated black from white soldiers (Smith 1987).

Involuntary labour? Work in the camps

Despite the change of overseers, hard work once again became the lot of most young Latvian women in the camps. They were directed by the DP camp administrators into a range of jobs, most of them typically feminised types of work, rather than the hard manual labouring that some of them had undertaken under the Nazis. For many young women, however, the work remained physically demanding and menial and a minority even found themselves undertaking the same work in the same location. In table 4.1 the types of work undertaken before and after arriving in the camps are shown. Lizina, for example, who was 17 in 1945, had worked in the kitchens in a camp in Schwerin when it was run by the Germans. Teenagers and women had been recruited for the lighter work and male Italian prisoners of war undertook the heaviest tasks. At the end of the war, the camp was transferred into Allied control and became a hospital but Lizina stayed in the same kitchens, doing the same heavy work. Vieda was also initially allocated manual labour. Here she describes her first job in a DP camp:

> I stayed somehow in the middle in Westphalia in Germany. There was for a while some camp or big building or something, some big barracks to go to a German hospital. I was by then 16 already and I was sent to work in a laundry which was dreadful, with the cold water and so on, though at the weekends I was allowed to sweep ... I lived in part of the nurses' room, two to three in a room. We had food and a clean bed and were paid a little, a few deutschmarks a month. I remember we had to walk across to this, part of a *landratshaus*, a town hall to get the money but you couldn't really buy anything.

But her life improved as she was befriended by another young woman who was employed in the administration: 'Then after a while I got a job in her office and by then I was fluent in German and so on and I got promotion. By then I was 17 and a half.'

Other women also found that typical 'female skills' such as secretarial or language skills that they had acquired earlier in Latvia became more valuable as they were transformed into DPs. Dagnija, for example, was from a middle class multilingual family and she had briefly worked in a bank in Riga before leaving Latvia:

> And I was lucky enough, I don't know why ... my parents both spoke English. So, well, somehow or other, the English language I was familiar with it, you know, so I got into the UNRRA (United Nations Relief and Rehabilitation Administration) office in the camp ... So I worked there, just a semi-secretary. From there I was sent to a big headquarters in Lemgo, the HQ of the British zone, in the office again.

Elvira, who had begun teacher training in Latvia, initially worked as support teacher in a camp but she was then able to attend the university set up in Germany for DPs to finish her interrupted training:

> A family friend went to the university in Hamburg when it started and he said 'Elvira, why not come here?'. Well I had been trying to teach the children there but they were young and I liked teenagers but when the chance came to go to Hamburg I took it. Four of us went together as students. I took English and History. I wasn't really set to finish, I must admit but to be in that company and society and my own

Table 4.1: Latvian women's work in the Third Reich and in displaced persons' camps, 1944–47

Name	Born	Jobs undertaken in Germany	Jobs undertaken in the camps
Agata	1927	domestic work	at school
Agnese	1926	munitions factory	school and then office work
Anya	1930	cigarette factory	school
Anyuta	1929	no information	school
Beate	1927	domestic work	school
Brigita	1930	farm work	kitchen work, then ward orderly
Dagnija	1919	office work in factory	office work
Diana	1920	factory work	camp kitchens
Elvira	1920	paper mill	teaching, then attended university
Eva	1928	munitions factory	camp kitchens
Grieta	1918	n/s	n/s
Helena	1927	domestic service, munitions	kitchen work
Ida	1914	office work (in uncle's Brewery in Germany)	kitchen work
Ilona	1926	agricultural work	kitchen work
Jelena	1931	with parents on shooting lodge	school
Lina	1931	casual domestic work	school, plus informal work (ironing etc)
Lize	1928	agricultural work	school, then clerical work
Lizina	1928	kitchen work	kitchen work
Mara	1916	n/s	kitchen work
Monika	1930	farm work	laundry, then office work
Natalija	1926	farm work	school
Pauline	1924	street cleaning	patient in hospital
Valda	1919	helper in children's home	office work
Velta	1926	surface coal sorting	kitchens, bar work, glove making
Vieda	1930	hospital laundry	office work

> age group and there were things happening, concerts and so on. First of all we were in Hamburg, that was in the museum where they gave us space for the university, and later on we were transferred to Pinneberg on the other side of Hamburg to army buildings where there was more space and room for us to live. I was there a year and a half.

The university to which Elvira refers was established by scholars from all three Baltic countries with some support from the British authorities. It opened in March 1946, initially housed in the Deutscher Ring insurance headquarters (which was also home to over 1,000 refugees) and was then moved to the Museum for Hamburg History, as Zenta recalls. This latter building had been badly bombed and so in early 1947 the university was rehoused again, this time in a former Luftwaffe School in Pinneberg. The status of the university was problematic as it struggled for recognition by British military and UNRRA officials and it was eventually officially recognised as the 'DP University Study Centre', where students studied mainly preparatory courses to aid their transfer to the established universities in Germany. For Elvira, more than a decade later, struggling to have her qualifications as a teacher recognised by a British local authority, the status of the university centre once again became important. Wyman (1998, pp 126–27) in his discussion of this institution, mentions that the students were often hungry as the diet was even more inadequate than in the camps and the Red Cross found TB was not uncommon among them, in part because of the poor nutrition. But as Elvira's narrative reveals, the sense of freedom outweighed these physical hardships. As well as the university centre that Elvira attended, the occupation authorities also required German universities to reserve 10% of their places for displaced persons and apparently these quotas were filled (Wyman 1998). Anya, for example, completed her pre-university qualifications in a camp and had been offered a university place under this scheme. In the event, her plans were stymied as she came to Britain as an EVW before she had the opportunity to take up her place.

For other women in the DP camps, unable to capitalise on their backgrounds either to claim more salubrious work or the escape from confinement entirely like Elvira, reliance on more traditional female domestic 'skills' became a way to make some sort of living. Lina and her mother, for example, established themselves as informal domestic workers, providing a service for those who would not or could not look after themselves in the camps:

> My mother, she really worked hard, poor soul and she wasn't so young any more. There were quite a few single men in the camps and she used to take in their washing and I had to do the ironing – that was my part in it. I used to feel sorry for her because in the winters it was quite cold and you had to dry the washing outside and it got frozen and cold and you had to bring it in and try to dry it. And we also used to live in wooden huts and there were great big long corridors, long wooden corridors and they had to be scrubbed every week, so we did those for other people who didn't want to do it themselves, you know for small money. The black market was really flourishing in those days and so what little money we had we spent on the black market. Sometimes I think even the German police turned a blind eye because it was just so bad anything you could buy was just a boost.

Other women remembered knitting and sewing: 'We used to knit, knit, knit for soldiers, for people in the camps, for anyone who needed something. Sometimes we sold things but not often, mostly it was for nothing' (Jelena):

> UNRRA came later on. They gave us wool and then they gave us, you know, those signals like threads and we used to pull the threads out and make little serviettes and dolls, and UNRRA used to buy them. And they gave us wool, not real wool, acrylic like you have now and we used to knit jumpers first for the men who were working outside and we just used to sit and knit and knit and knit, outside. That's how we survived (Pauline).

As well as officially regulated forms of work, usually remunerated as Vieda explained, unofficial forms of a black economy thrived, as Lina commented. In all forms of confinement beyond the bounds of 'normal' society – whether prisons, plantations or labour camps – complex systems of barter, black-marketeering and petty illegal activities, outside the market, tend to develop. The labour camps of the Third Reich, and their metamorphosis into the DP camps run by the allies, were no exception. Although the communal and educational activities that were quickly established by Latvians in the camps might be seen as mechanisms of solidarity and mutual support, the informal exchange mechanisms that were developed are better portrayed as a mirror of conventional market systems. The exchange and use value of commodities, the significance of national and ethnic hierarchies, class and patriarchal relations and force all structured the informal systems of exchange that sprang up in the camps, operating in similar ways as in the 'free' market, recreating social and economic hierarchies and inequalities. At the same, however, these activities were often vital, if not to the survival of the occupants at least to some semblance of a more than an extremely basic living standard.

Pauline, in a camp in Lübeck, remembers that looting took place in the initial weeks she was there: 'They had all the warehouses full of goods, cheeses and it started looting.' Other forms of informal exchange were common within and outside the camps. Illona, for example told me that: 'We got a ration of ground coffee and cigarettes and I didn't smoke so I sold them to the boys.' As Eksteins (1999, p 168) noted: 'Cigarettes had become the accepted currency in trading. No-one trusted the mark.' In summer 1946 'when the average factory worker in Germany earned 50 marks a week, one Chesterfield cigarette was worth six marks, a pound of butter 200 to 250 marks ... and a pound of coffee beans 400' (p 168). Black market trading was widespread, on the streets, in the countryside, in workplaces and especially in the camps.

While there is little doubt that daily life was a struggle for the 25 women they also recalled with pride the ways in which they negotiated their lives after May 1945. Their commitment to working as hard as possible in the tasks to which they were allocated, their participation in a wide range of communal activities and their careful negotiations of the conflicts between a growing desire for independence and the need to maintain close ties with family friends and the Latvian community more generally are the key themes informing their memories of these months at the end of the war. These themes and the negotiation of the contradictions between them remain central to these women's post-war lives. In their escape from the constricted life in the limbo of the camps, however, hard work and independence were to prove central. Pride in hard work is, as Skultans (1998) has argued, a distinguishing feature of Latvian identity. Becoming 'good workers' was for these young women both a way of achieving and maintaining their self-esteem and identity, as well as perhaps a way of ensuring that they were left alone as far as possible in the regulated society of the camps. Indeed, it was through their participation as workers, above all, that these Latvian women contributed to post-war society, whether the temporary society of the camps or in their more permanent residence in Britain. In the next chapter, I continue to explore the theme of labouring bodies – how they were constructed, regulated and controlled – and the establishment of a hierarchy of desirability between the different categories of workers, as they were selected to leave the camps as economic migrants and during their initial employment in Great Britain.

CHAPTER 5

BECOMING EVWS: FROM DISPLACED PERSONS TO ECONOMIC MIGRANTS

Leaving the camps

As the weeks stretched into months after the end of the war, the Allies were forced to consider how to cope with the still large numbers of stateless and homeless displaced persons who refused to return to their country of origin. It had been agreed at the Yalta conference that all Soviet citizens were to be repatriated, a decision that was to be enforced without exception and, by the end of 1945, the vast majority of displaced people who found themselves as Soviets citizens had been sent back, in many cases against their will. It is clear, however, that the Allies differentiated between those who were 'eligible' for return and it seems that people from the Baltic tended to receive more preferable treatment than other national groups. Overall, they were seen as more 'civilised' and unproblematic than, for example, the Poles, who had been living in Germany for years as forced labourers. Herbert (1997, p 380), for example, in a brief discussion of the problems facing the Allies in 1945, commented on the way in which American officers spoke of Poles as a problem and of their surprise at the level of organisation they found on liberation. He suggested that 'before the end of the war, the foreign forced workers in Germany had apparently been reduced in Allied thinking to the function of defenceless victims. They had not anticipated phenomena such as the thirst for vengeance, or the half-crazed euphoria of liberation'.

It seems that the Allies also were surprised at the extent of crime amongst the displaced persons (DPs) whose behaviour was constructed as 'malicious ingratitude' rather than a response to appalling circumstances, a view which perhaps in part explains the haste to repatriate tens of thousands of by then Soviet citizens. But more than 'ingratitude' distinguished different camp occupants, raising complex ethical questions for the Allies. It was clear, for example, that for camp occupants who had been Nazi collaborators – the Cossacks who had fought on the side of Germany – or who were suspected, whether correctly or not, of collaboration, including Estonians, Latvians and to a lesser extent Ukrainians, repatriation was greatly, and correctly, to be feared. The Soviet Union regarded anyone who had ended up in the West as guilty of collaboration by association. It was argued that soldiers should have fought to their last breath and never surrendered and that those who had worked for the enemy, or fled their country, were traitors. On 9 May 1945, Soviet VE Day, Beria proposed to Stalin that the returnees should be punished on their arrival in the Soviet Union. Almost two million people – Ukrainians, Poles, Rumanians, Yugoslavs and Balts were forcibly repatriated by the Allies between 1944 and 1947 and there is little doubt that many of them faced imprisonment, forced labour or were executed (Elliott 1982; Tolstoy 1979).

In the confusion of the first post-war months and years, it was difficult to ascertain and verify the status, motives and actions of the people who refused to return 'home', of whom at the end of 1946 there were still more than a million living in the camps. In a study published in 1958, largely based on British official records, Tannahill summaries the range and diversity of these occupants:

> There were members of the Royal Yugoslav Amy who had been prisoners of war in Germany since the 1941 campaign, Serbs who had fought as Cetniks ... some Yugoslav collaborators … various Croatian and Slovenian nationalists.
>
> There were forced labourers of many nationalities who did not chose to go home ... There were nationals of countries which had been submerged by Russia (Estonia, Latvia and Lithuania), or which had been subject to Russian rule before the war and disliked the prospect of its continuance (Byelorussia and Ukraine). The majority of these had been forced labourers or had retreated with the Germans in the face of the Russian advance of 1944 and 1945 ...
>
> There were persons displaced by boundary changes from the disputed areas of Eastern Europe, such as Macedonia, Bessarabia. Transylvania, the Bant, Galicia, East Prussia and Silesia; and there were the numerous persons of German descent (known as the Volksdeutsche) who had been removed from the countries of Eastern Europe during or after the war ...
>
> There were political refugees from various countries of Central Europe ... [and] finally, almost inevitably in the conditions of the time, there were some traitors and common criminals escaping from justice at home, a few adventurers ... and a few who preferred to gamble on the chance of economic betterment or a more peaceful life in the West. (pp 9–10)

While the distinctions between these different categories of people were often unclear, they were also to become important in determining eligibility for migration to the West: to the USA, to Western Europe and to Australasia, as schemes to recruit workers, as well as to provide homes for refugees, gathered pace from mid-1946 onwards.

These schemes, especially those instigated by the British government, are the main subject of this chapter. Seen through the lens of the lives of the 25 Latvian women, the recruitment policies of the British government are examined to reveal the assumptions about the nature of migration and the moral character of migrants that were embedded within these policies. The intention is not only to examine the particularities of this period and the categorisation and treatment of the women caught up in it, but also to illuminate debates about the origins of post-war migration policy more widely, showing how the origins of current discriminatory distinctions between economic migrants and refugees lie, in part, in the late 1940s. I want to explore the interconnections between nationality, skin colour, religion and gender in the construction of eligible and less eligible post-war migrants to the UK. The migration of white Europeans into Britain in the late 1940s both preceded and overlapped with the in-migration of Caribbean people to Britain, attracted by the expanding economic opportunities during the period of post-war reconstruction. At the same time, the long-standing migration from Ireland to the UK continued and as Kathleen Paul (1997) has argued and documented in her incisive study of British migration policy in the post-war era, a comparison between these different groups of in-migrants provides illuminating insights into conceptions of race and citizenship and the connections between them in the UK.

My aim here is to add to this debate by showing how the construction of young Latvian women as both workers and potential mothers provides a revealing insight into then current racialised conceptions of Britishness and its association with 'whiteness'. The positioning and inscription of migrants by the receiving society – both as members of the working class and yet as separate from it through their construction as 'different' – is achieved by the intersection of a wide range of official and unofficial practices, discourses and behaviours, through popular culture and the media, through political practices and in economic and academic theories, all of which combine to position migrants as deserving or undeserving, as workers or as refugees, as beneficial to the post-war reconstruction or as interlopers undercutting British wages, as victims of Soviet aggression or as fascist sympathisers, depending on the context in which they are being discussed. And in-migrants themselves also construct new versions of personhood and identity as they find ways to adapt to their lives and to attribute value and meaning to the everyday practices and communal institutions within which they are situated. Although Latvian women and the wide range of other Europeans who came to Britain in the mid to late 1940s were accepted as migrant workers, in their own view they were refugees and asylum seekers, coming not willingly but reluctantly and with little idea that they would stay for more than a few years before their homelands once again were liberated. This view, as well as their class backgrounds, ethnicity and colour, was what distinguished the EVWs from the Caribbean migrants who closely followed them. Their sense of themselves as exiles rather than economic migrants has also, to a large extent, influenced their determined efforts to reconstruct a version of Latvian identity and community in exile that resulted in the construction and maintenance of largely separate lives during the second half of the twentieth century. This is not to deny the crucial significance of these young women's value as workers. As I shall show, it was the social value ascribed to their strong, young clean bodies by Ministry of Labour officials who visited the displaced persons' camps in Germany that bought them entry to the UK and which positioned them as superior to other women workers in stereotypical female jobs at the bottom end of the labour market. This superiority stood them in good stead in their early years and for some was a mechanism of escape. Furthermore, the institutionally-ascribed superiority mapped onto a strong self-belief in their own value among these women and found its expression throughout their lives in their commitment to the values of hard work, moral restraint and self-improvement as I document in this and the succeeding chapters.

Why immigration schemes? Post-war labour shortages in the UK

In 1945, at the close of the Second World War, the British economy was in severe difficulties (Cairncross 1985; Clark 1996; Law 1994; Morgan 1990; Whiteside 1999). Weakened by the war years and short of labour, the attention of the British government turned towards in-migration as a possible solution, especially in those sectors of the economy crucial to the reconstruction programme. These included the production of raw materials such as iron, steel and coal, as well as food, and those parts of the public sector that were essential to the running of the economy and the well-being of the population. Transport, the new national health service and, somewhat anachronistically, domestic service in private homes were identified as important parts of the service sector that were short of labour. In addition, there was a huge backlog of essential maintenance and repair work that needed to be resolved and severe shortages in the construction sector. The table below from Peter Hennessy's (1993) illuminating survey of the years between 1945 and 1951 provides a useful summary of the position of the country as the war ended.

Despite the labour shortages in Britain, however, and post-war demobilisation, the total working population actually fell by 1.38 million between mid-1945 and the end of 1946. As well as the withdrawal from the labour force of large numbers of married women and elderly people who had worked beyond normal retirement age during the war, labour was also lost because of emigration. Many families decided to emigrate to parts of what were then known as the Dominions (especially Australia, New Zealand and Canada), that were themselves short of labour and anxious to encourage white settlers from the United Kingdom in an effort to maintain their old colonial links and European notions of citizenship and identity. Approximately 1.5 million British residents, for example, emigrated in the two decades after 1945, in the main to Australasia and Canada. Furthermore, the raising of the school leaving age in 1947 cut the numbers of young people who were available for work. The British government

Table 5.1: The position of Britain at the end of the Second World War

Population	46 million
Armed forces (pre-1938 0.5m)	5 million
Civil defence and munitions workers	5 million
Deaths (military and merchant navy)	380,000
Deaths (civilian)	60,000
Houses destroyed	500,000
Houses severely damaged	250,000
Gold reserves disposed of	33%
Overseas assets sold	33%
Debts incurred	£3.5 million
Direct taxation, 1939-45	+300%
Indirect taxation, 1939-45	+160%

Source: Hennessy, P (1992) *Never Again*, p 99

therefore had to look for alternative sources of potential employees and so was forced to address the prospect of in-migration to meet the labour shortages, looking to different parts of the world for prospective workers. Thus, in 1946, there began a complex process of recruitment from widely separated geographic regions, both from territories with attachments to British imperial and colonial history and from those with no connection at all, other than the accidents of war.

These post-war decisions about labour and migration initiated a complex debate, as well as a set of policy decisions, about the relative position and rights of subjects, citizens, aliens and others (Dummett and Nicol 1990) that affected the relationships between different groups of economic migrants as well as their position in Britain, as I illustrate below. In addition, that long and still-unresolved dilemma about the relative status of economic migrants and refugees and asylum seekers became an important part of post-war migration policy and remains a key issue at the beginning of the new century. Thus, the years immediately after the end of the Second World War are key to an understanding of how new and complex interconnections were established between ethnicity, cultural traditions, skin colour, class and the rights (or not) of citizenship that remain at the heart of the definitions of 'Britishness' that currently are being contested through recently-established discourses of a multi-ethnic or multicultural Britain (Runnymede Trust 2002).

State constructions of difference

In 1945, there were three main sources of potential workers that were relatively easily available to the British State and to prospective employers. The first group consisted of those refugees and displaced people, demobilised soldiers and prisoners of war, homeless and often stateless as a consequence of the upheavals in Europe between 1939 and 1945. During the war itself, for example, over 300,000 German and Italian prisoners of war had been employed in Britain in essential areas such as agriculture. While most of these prisoners were returned to their own countries, as I have explained, there were large numbers of people in camps in Germany who were anxious not to return to their homelands which in the main had been transferred into Soviet hands. In addition, sizeable numbers of Polish servicemen whom had fought with the Allies chose to be demobilised in the UK. The majority of this first group of potential employees – camp inmates and former soldiers from Central and Eastern Europe – had few if any connections with Britain nor any rights of citizenship. Although they were mainly white Europeans, they were aliens by virtue not only of their legal status but their language, religion and cultural background. They were recruited by the British State as 'European Volunteer Workers' (EVWs) – this term replaced that of 'displaced persons (DPs)' which was regarded as pejorative by British officials. It was argued in Cabinet discussions that the term European was preferable to that of foreign workers accepting that, at that time, the British population in general disliked and distrusted foreigners. The term European would emphasise the joint heritage of the incomers and the local population. But the switch in terminology had the effect of transforming camp residents' own sense of their identity as political refugees into the official status of economic migrants. In all, 600,000 European 'aliens' (the official designation) were recruited to work in Britain in this post-war period, although only a proportion of them were from the camps in Germany. Between October 1946 and December 1949 about 80,000 men and women from displaced persons' camps were recruited for work in Britain, more than doubling the then foreign-born population of the country.

The second group of prospective workers was from a more traditional source for Britain – Ireland – and in total numbers far outweighed the movement into Britain of displaced persons/EVWs. Although there had been a long-established tradition of migration across the Irish Sea in the pre-second world war period, at the end of the war Irish citizens were particularly encouraged to migrate to Britain and, despite being aliens, were given all the privileges of citizenship.[1] In each of the years between 1946 and 1962, approximately 50,000 to 60,000 Irish men and women entered Britain for the first time and began to search for work (Kearney 1990). The third source of prospective workers lay in the Commonwealth dominions. As the territories of what became commonly designated the Old Commonwealth (Australia, New Zealand and Canada) were recruiters rather than sources of white British workers, attention was perforce turned onto the colonial citizens of colour in the 'new' Commonwealth countries, especially, in the early post-war years, residents in the Caribbean, as a potential source of new employees. The migration of colonial citizens began slowly in the immediate post-war period. Between 1948 and 1952, for example, between 1,000 and 2,000 people entered Britain each year. This was followed by a steady and rapid rise until 1957, when 42,000 migrants from the New Commonwealth, mainly from the Caribbean entered. The numbers declined by almost a half in the two succeeding years but by 1960 had increased again to 58,000 and then in 1961 more than doubled in number, in anticipation of the 1962 Commonwealth Immigrants Act that then restricted opportunities for entry (Fryer 1984). Although this latter group of migrants consisted of British citizens, they were to find themselves regarded by the British population as foreign, as other, as 'coloured' and so as 'less eligible' Britons (Gilroy 1987). Indeed, in the official papers discussing Caribbean migration, potential recruits were labelled 'coloured colonial labour' and from 1962 onwards people from the Caribbean increasingly were restrained by the State from exercising their right to independent migration and residence.

While all three groups were valued as economic migrants because of their potential contributions to the British economy, there were clear differences in how they were recruited. The former and the latter groups – the EVWs and New Commonwealth migrants – were attracted to Britain through recruitment drives, while the Irish migrants moved on an individual and independent basis. The first group – the EVWs – were aliens and yet were regarded by the British state as fellow Europeans and as suitable candidates for assimilation, as I shall illustrate in more detail in the following section. Only the latter group – the Caribbean

---

1 In a move with no precedent, under the 1948 British Nationality Act, Irish citizens were to be regarded as neither British subjects nor aliens but instead as Irish citizens with all the legal rights of British subjecthood.

migrants – came to Britain with full legal rights as British subjects and yet they were to find themselves out of place in Britain where the population of people of colour in the pre-war years was tiny and subjected to a racialised discourse of 'difference', as well as to racial discrimination in the job and housing market (Smith 1996) that continues to this day. Irish in-migrants fell into an intermediate category – neither subjects nor aliens, neither British nor self-evidently 'foreign' but bearing all the connotations that being Irish carries in Britain: stupid, dirty, unreliable, feckless or in a less pejorative discourse, as emotional, fey and romantic (Curtis 1984; MacLaughlin 1997; Walter 2001). However, the entry of Irish migrants as well as the continental Europeans was regarded as less contentious than that of Caribbean migrants both by government officials responsible for immigration policy and by the UK public at large because 'they passed an unwritten test of racial acceptability' (Paul 1997, p xiii).

But even so, as the Irish found, often to their cost, and Latvian migrants drew on as a source of strength and solidarity, their common 'whiteness' and shared European heritage did not preclude their construction as different from the 'native' population and the 'othering' of their perceived or stereotypical ethnic characteristics. Furthermore, for Irish and continental European women, as well as Black women who were doubly discriminated against because of their colour, their construction first and foremost as workers excluded them from the then prevalent discourse of acceptable femininity that was key part of the British State's programme of post-war reconstruction with an explicit role for white British women. This discourse emphasised domesticity and maternity as the key correlates of womanhood. As early as 1943, for example, Winston Churchill had argued that 'our people must be encouraged by every means to have larger families'. Although not in as uniform and widespread a manner as many accounts suggest, nevertheless many British women responded to government pleas and retreated to the home to assist in the rapid rise in the annual number of births in the post-war years.

Women who remained in the labour market, but especially migrant women recruited explicitly as workers, were thus placed outside the boundaries of the hegemonic, albeit idealised, discourse of (middle class) domestic respectability (Lewis 1992; Riley 1983; Summerfield 1994). In fact, as Summerfield (1984) and others have argued, the government was also anxious about shortages of female labour in industries such as textiles and so in its *Economic Survey 1947* working class women in the relevant areas of Britain were identified as desirable, albeit temporary and part-time, workers. Thus, women were to be recruited to help in a crisis, 'for whatever length of time they could spare', and they were to undertake what was identified as 'women's work' under less satisfactory conditions and usually on a part-time basis in factories, services and agriculture, rather than, as in the war, doing the 'jobs usually done by men' (quoted in Summerfield 1994, p 63). This appeal to spare some time for employment was explicitly not aimed at 'women with very young children' (Cmnd 7046 1947). For younger married women, bearing children and then caring for them in their own homes, rather than labour force participation, continued to be seen as their duty. Thus, post-war official reports such as the *Royal Commission on Equal Pay* in 1946 and the government's *Social Survey on Women and Industry 1948* argued that no woman would or should want to work if her husband earned reasonable money, although the marriage bar to women's entry to teaching and to the Civil Service was dropped in 1944 and 1946 respectively, reflecting a somewhat contradictory attitude to married women's employment (Summerfield 1994). Thus, complex categorisations based on class, gender and marital status, as well as ethnicity, were established in these immediate post-war years to differentiate between different types and classes of women.

Although women migrant workers (and to an extent 'native' working class women) were, primarily, regarded as a commodity in the labour market, just like male migrant labourers, their gender raises vexed questions about the associations between nationality and ethnicity, maternity and femininity, as well as their suitability as prospective partners for British men. However, here too there were important distinctions between the women of different origins. The women recruited from the Baltic States may have been constructed by the state as ideal workers, but as I explore below it is clear from official documents that in the longer term they were also regarded as potential marriage partners for British men and so as future contributors to the British stock, whereas fears of miscegenation precluded consideration of Caribbean women's contribution here. It is clear, then, that the three main streams of migrant labour to Britain in the immediately post-war years were constructed in distinctive and differential ways by the institutions of the state (Holmes 1988). Continental European migrants may have been foreign, and aliens, but they were also constructed as 'suitable', even superior, workers, in comparison not only to other nationalities among the camp occupants but also to both the Irish and new Commonwealth in-migrants, who were regarded as less respectable, indeed inferior to both the native population and to women, and later men, from the Baltic (Joshi and Carter 1984).

Recruiting European Volunteer Workers (EVWs)

Britain's search for workers at the end of the war focused initially on the displaced persons' camps. In 1946 the recruitment schemes began to be established. It was not only Britain, however, but numerous other countries which saw the camp occupants as a valuable pool of potential workers. As Hulme (1954, p 203) noted: 'never on earth has there been such a focal point for mass emigration to almost every country on earth'. She described, for example, a recruitment centre set up in Germany in 1947 with a central hall that 'appeared at first sight as provocative as a corridor through Cook's, with neat signs angling out from the repainted doors naming the mission within – CANADA, BELGIUM, UNITED KINGDOM, FRANCE, AUSTRALIA, SOUTH AMERICA' (original capitalisation, p 175). And each country had different criteria for selection, looking for specific categories of labour to fill the particular shortages in their post-war economies:

> Australia would take family units consisting of husband, wife and unmarried children not to exceed three, all nationalities accepted. Brazil wanted mainly agricultural workers 18 to 40 years of age, no children under 2, all nationalities and religious groups accepted, with the exception of Jews and persons of Asiatic origin. Canada had half a dozen schemes both for mass and individual recruiting –

> for cooks, maids, housekeepers, workers for sugar beet farms and the hard-rock mines. France offered a farm-family scheme, family to go together with the worker and no limit on the number of children. The Grand Duchy of Luxembourg asked for single workers with no dependants, Balts preferred. The Netherlands had jobs for tailors, weavers, spinning-mill hands, unattached between 18 and 35 years, no dependants accepted. New Zealand sought 200 orphaned children for adoption in private homes and 300 single women under 40 to work in mental hospitals. Graduate nurses for Sweden, DPs of Moslem faith for Turkey, single women as domestics for the United Kingdom, farm workers for Venezuela ... (Hulme 1954, pp 201–02)

Some countries were rather quicker than others in recruiting workers. In total, approximately 120,000 Latvians accepted assisted passages to the UK and France under economic migrant schemes between 1946 and 1950, although others held out for entry to the USA and Canada who were relatively tardy in offering entry to their countries. The two main schemes under which Latvians, and other displaced persons not only from the Baltic states, were recruited as workers in Britain were the Baltic Cygnet Scheme, originally to recruit women to work in hospitals and then extended to domestic workers more generally, and the Westward Ho! scheme. It is the first of these two schemes that is referred to by Hulme at the end of her list. The main features of the two British schemes are outlined in the next section, showing how the claim made in the labour and DP camps by Latvian women that they were superior to other women refugees was also echoed in the official British view about the attributes of women of different national origins, informing the establishment of the Baltic Cygnet scheme as the very first of the all the many schemes by numerous western nations to recruit foreign bodies to labour in their agricultural and industrial sectors and to fill vacancies in their expanding service industries.

'Suitable' workers for the British labour market

In 1946 the government established a Foreign Labour Committee (FLC) to 'examine, in the light of existing manpower shortages, the possibility of making increased use of foreign labour, particularly in essential industries which are now finding special difficulty in recruiting labour' (Cabinet Papers 1946). Although this was the explicit and immediate aim of the seven man (the gendered term is accurate) committee appointed from among the Cabinet members, in fact the committee became responsible for Britain's 'resettlement scheme for refugees and other "displaced persons" and ultimately assumed responsibility for the transformation of aliens into Britons' (Paul 1997, p 67). As hospitals, sanatoriums and other institutions largely reliant on female labour, as well as private households, were particularly short of workers to undertake menial domestic tasks, the government decided to look abroad for suitable supplies of women workers. This decision was not without precedent. During the 1930s, for example, permits under the Aliens Order, the mechanism controlling immigration, were given on a reasonably generous basis, for female domestic helpers from Austria and Germany. Young Jewish women, for example, who were essentially political refugees entered Britain though this mechanism, paralleling the transformation in status later to be experienced by Baltic women in the 1940s.

The decision to recruit foreign workers in the post-war period was a politically sensitive one as it not only represented a substantial shift in immigration policy but it was also taken by a Labour government in the face of opposition from the Trade Union movement whose memory of the 1930s depression remained vivid. However, post-war labour shortages were so severe that the decision was taken to revoke the individual work permit system that had previously regulated the entry of aliens and land the European Volunteer Workers (EVWs) as a group, but on the explicit condition that they must accept and remain within the employment assigned them by the Ministry of Labour for a specified period, usually two years (Kay and Miles 1992; Tannahill 1958). Thus, their official status was transformed from that of refugee into economic migrant and the term 'displaced person' replaced by EVW. Despite the shift in nomenclature, however, the continuities in their position are perhaps more marked than the differences. Once again, as in the last months of the war in Germany and for some women in the camps, these young women found themselves constructed as unfree labour, regarded as a commodity to be assigned by others with little choice in the matter themselves and directed to manual employment in which their value depended on their fit, young bodies. Waiting in the camps, which understandably were riven by rumour, gossip and fear, to see what their fate would be as the 'free' nations of the world squabbled over the bodies of potential workers, the young women in this book anxiously scanned the camp notice boards listing all the options for escape, which as Hulme (1954, p 170) perceptively commented 'made you think of some kind of macabre stock market that dealt in bodies instead of in bonds'. The Allies, Hulme suggested 'were really in big business – the business of bodies for sale' (p 201). It was made brutally clear that the possession of a fit and healthy body was almost the sole criterion of acceptance. Plate 5.1 shows young women – in this case Polish women – leaving a displaced persons' camp for a new life in the west, probably in Canada. In the British zone, towards the end of the recruitment years, a military official suggested dividing all the DPs into three categories: potential 'resettlers' able to pass the medical tests, 'substandards' whose status was marginal and 'hard core', who would fail. Among the hard core were those requiring institutional care – people who were blind or chronically and mentally ill, for example – as well as 'persons over 50 unfit for employment' (Eksteins 2000, p 102).

The first stage in purchasing women's domestic labour for British institutions took place when Ministry of Labour officials travelled to the camps in the autumn of 1946 to assess the suitability of women from the former Baltic States of Latvia, Lithuania and Estonia as domestic workers for hospitals, other institutions and, despite the new climate of greater social equality after the war, for the private homes of the upper classes (Giles 2002; Thane 1991). Kay and Miles (1992) have suggested that, as well as meeting the severe shortages of domestic workers, women might have been seen as less controversial and less competition than men, so reducing the impact of the initial resistance by the trade union movement to imported labour. Furthermore, as accommodation was to be provided by employers, these women would not need to compete for housing with the local

Plate 5.1 Hired girls leaving for a new life, 1947

Source: Time Life Pictures/Getty Images

population. Thus, they would neither be a visible group in the community nor place further demands on an over-stretched and war-damaged housing stock. Nevertheless, it was also clear that the Home Office was concerned about the introduction of economic migrants who could not be deported in the event of problems. As Latvia had ceased to exist as an independent entity and the Allies had decided to disregard the provisions of the Yalta agreement in their case, they could not be deported if they proved problematic or surplus to labour requirements.

Despite these anxieties, under the first scheme, initiated in 1946, more than 1,000 women were recruited, under a programme rather ludicrously designated the Balt Cygnet scheme, or as one of the women I interviewed dismissively called it, 'that white swan thing'. It is interesting to contemplate the image that the recruiters assumed would be associated with this name – perhaps a vision of vulnerable yet attractive young swans, redolent of purity, sailing across the water to the UK and emerging from their drab protective colouring as cygnets into the full beauty of an adult swan under the guidance of the British state or public? While there are clear connections between this imagery and the differential construction of post-war migrants explored above – their whiteness for example – the appropriateness of the label for the underfed and anxious young women so recruited stretches the imagination. The theorisation of the significance of whiteness is a relatively recent development in critical social theory and until recently typically has been assumed to be an advantage in the labour market (Roediger 1991). As Linke (1999), among others, has argued whiteness is both unmarked and invisible and yet is a mark of domination and superiority in the construction of racialised hierarchies. Thus, she has argued:

> In the Western scholarly imaginary, white skin is designated a discursive construct. Unmarked, unseen and protected from public scrutiny, whiteness is said to be deeply implicated in the politics of domination. Viewed as a location, a space, a set of positions from which power emanates and operates, white political practice appears to be thoroughly disconnected from the body: Corporality then has been removed from the politics of whiteness … whiteness is perceived as a normalising strategy which produces racial categories. (Linke 1999, p 27)

Whiteness therefore represents purity, spirit rather than body and, as Dyer has argued white people are 'socialised to believe the fantasy that whiteness represents goodness and all that is benign and non-threatening' (Dyer 1988, p 45) in comparison to the dark skin of 'others'. Recent work by Bonnett (1997, 2000) and Dyer (1997), among others, has begun to unpack this polar dichotomy and the taken for granted associations of superiority and inferiority, constructing a new research agenda. In this agenda the question of the meaning of whiteness and its implications is being probed by research exploring the cultural and institutional conventions and practices that continue to normalize white invisibility. As Linke has noted: 'Until quite recently, the multiple ways in which whiteness has been politically manipulated, culturally mediated and historically constructed have in large part been ignored' (Linke 1999, p 28).

Whiteness is a relational concept rather than a singular unvarying category. It is constructed by the way it positions others at its borders, as excluded and inferior. It produces both a system of racialised inequality but also within the realms of Western representation a source of fantasy and repressed desires (Fanon 1952; Said 1978). For minority groups it produces images of objectified racialised otherness. However it is also clear that it is a fluid and mutable concept that both encompasses variation within it and also allows elision between categories. The boundaries that are drawn around the terrain of whiteness (and of colour), despite the assumed rigidity of these criteria of difference, must be viewed as decentred and permeable, thus permitting a challenge to the binary categorisation. 'Because such a space is strategic and not essential, there is movement into and out of these categories of identity' (Linke 1999, p 33). But, further, there are degrees of whiteness, distinctions within the category. Here, I am interested in how the British state constructed differential positionings, or perhaps more accurately multiple constructions of whiteness, when it is sometimes but not always the marker of superiority. In post-war Britain, the whiteness of Irish migrants brought few of the associated benefits that accrued to young Baltic women. Instead, in the 1940s, they were positioned between the EVWs and migrants from the Caribbean in a hierarchy of desirability.

While skin colour may have positioned EVWs with the majority population, it is also clear that language, culture and their experiences of loss differentiated them as separate and different. Interestingly, in conversations with white American women in the 1970s and 1980s, Ruth Frankenberg (1993) found that they experienced and talked about whiteness as 'nothingness' and of 'having no people'. While the white British population might also have spoken in similar terms in the 1940s, EVWs' sense of themselves as different from the white majority population in Britain became a key part of their identity and a source of solidarity in their long 'exile' explored in more detail in Chapter 8. While it is hard to re-read official policy from almost 60 years ago and to uncover unequivocally the meanings of its narratives, it is clear that the labelling of young Baltic women as 'cygnets' was not an innocent act but a key part of their representation as innocent virginal women, and so as suitable wives for white men and potential mothers of Britons. In this way, the migration of Latvians to Britain despite its challenge to earlier assumptions that lay behind immigration policies – and remember that the migration of these displaced people into Britain in 1946 and 1947 more than doubled the number of foreign born people in the country – was less of a disruption to conventional notions of Britishness than that of the almost concurrent migration from the West Indies. The EVWS used their white skins to achieve an invisibility in Britain that was inaccessible to black migrants. Black citizens found that they were hypervisible and so subject to surveillance in ways in which 'white others', including the EVWs in the 1940s were not. But skin colour, as the Irish know only too well, is mediated through class and religion, through age and through gender. It was the combination of their whiteness with their class origins, their Protestant religion and their European culture that positioned the EVWs as the acceptable face of the new policy of foreign labour recruitment. White, Protestant, young, and, at least at first, female, EVWs were represented as a benefit rather than a cost to the wider British society: strong young workers with a common European heritage, even potential mothers of young white Britons. In a memorandum from the Foreign Labour Committee after a visit to the camps in Germany, the advantages of Baltic women were spelt out in unambiguous terms:

> The women are of good appearance; are scrupulously clean in their persons and habits ... There is little doubt that the specially selected women who come to this country will be an exceptionally healthy and fit body ... and would constitute a good and desirable element in our population. (quoted in Kay and Miles 1992, p 50)

It was their appearance – their self-evident cleanness, fitness and whiteness – that was to distinguish them from Caribbean women, both as workers and as putative mothers. That they had no connections with Great Britain and few spoke English on arrival (Tannahill 1958, p 67) suggests less than 10% of all EVWs had even a rudimentary knowledge of the language) was apparently of no consideration at all. It was their bodies that qualified them for entry to Britain. It is clear that the apparent superiority of the Baltic DPs was recognised more widely than by just the British recruiters in the camps. The Canadian High Commissioner in London, Vincent Massey, in an inspection tour in April 1946 for example, also found himself favourably 'impressed by the quality of these people who appeared to be industrious, clean, resourceful and well-mannered ... I could not help feeling that of all the Europeans I have seen these Balts would make the most admirable settlers'. He was less favourably disposed towards Poles, suggesting that 'one did not want too many of them about' (Abella and Troper 1983, p 213).

Expanding the categories of worker

The initial aim of the Baltic Cygnet scheme was to recruit 1,000 women as domestic staff for TB sanatoriums. As this proved relatively acceptable to both the British public and the trade union movement, recruitment was extended in January 1947 to include up to a further 5,000 women for domestic work in general hospitals and other institutions. Strict criteria of eligibility were established: the women who were recruited were between 21 and 40, although in practice it seems that both some younger and some older women may have slipped into the scheme. In addition, recruits had to be single; officially, they had to have no dependants, whether children or other relatives, although it seems clear that this requirement was flouted. One of the women to whom I talked managed to come to England with her mother, and others had travelled with their sisters. They also had to be in good health which was established through an invasive medical examination. This was often a problem that had to be negotiated, sometimes through subterfuge, as TB was prevalent in the camps as well as other infectious diseases. As well as a general medical, women who were potential EVWs also had to endure questions about menstruation and, in most cases, a gynaecological examination. Ilga, for example, recalls a camp medical before she left for the UK: 'It was demeaning and offensive. We were just considered as fodder.' Other women who had come to Britain as cygnets, desperate young women, anxious to leave the camps, told me that they often lied directly or by omission in order to pass these medical inspections. Helena, for example, told me that:

> The doctor asked me when my last period was. Well, I knew then that I was pregnant but I didn't tell him. I just lied and said I was regular as clockwork.

The concern with the gynaecological health of single women who were potential workers was not restricted to the British recruitment of cygnets. Hulme, who by 1947 had been to transferred a camp at Aschaffenburg on the River Main that housed Ukrainian and Estonian refugees as well as Poles, found herself involved in what became known as the affair of 'The Flying Virgins'. A Member of Parliament from the Province of Quebec who was also a well known industrialist came to the camp to recruit '100 single girls of spotless moral quality for his spinning mill in a small town in Quebec' (Hulme 1954, p 148). They also had to be Roman Catholic so in this case, atypically, Polish young women were seen as ideal. The Canadian government was prepared to lift its immigration requirements as it considered this scheme a worthy cause. At the camp, Hulme expressed her doubts about both the legality and motives of the proposed scheme. She was anxious about the proposal to separate girls and young women from their families, especially as the Red Cross and other relief agencies had worked so hard in the months after the end of the war to reunite family members. She was also angry about the proposed exploitation of vulnerable young women. They would be going from 'slave labour to slave labour' (Hulme 1954, p 150) she furiously argued, suggesting that the camp officials were demeaning themselves by acting as 'brokers for coolie labour' (*ibid*). The overt sexualisation of these young women was deeply troubling to her. She reported that male officials repeatedly joked about the virgin tag, about how they wouldn't be virgins long in Canada, and pruriently speculating how it might be established who was a virgin. While this episode is perhaps more extreme than the recruitment of cygnets, the same sexualisation of young women workers is also evident in the British scheme of labour recruitment. While Ministry of Labour officials were instructed to size up the suitability of men on the basis of their 'physique and general appearance', rejecting the puny and the unkempt, single women might be classified as undesirable on the grounds of sexual immorality or 'general intractability' (Kay and Miles 1998, p 54).

Other aspects of health, as well as sexual, were part of the recruitment interview and examination process in the British-run camps and here too subterfuge and evasion had to be practised. Natalija, who had been hospitalised in Germany with TB, took the advice of her German hospital doctor in facing questions from the British officials:

> I spoke to the doctor to see if I could go [to England] and he said, 'yes, why not?' But sometimes they had a medical beforehand, asked questions about what illnesses you had had and that. And the doctor said 'but keep your mouth shut'. He said 'you don't know anything'. So I left the hospital one Saturday and I was confirmed in the camp's church on Sunday and we left for England on Monday.

Pauline also hoped to be recruited as a cygnet but she too had a problem with her health and was less fortunate than Natalija in evading detection. Although she failed to be recruited as a cygnet she came to England a year later as part of the Westward Ho! scheme:

> And then came the time when the first 1,000, girls, especially girls were asked to come to work in the hospitals. But I didn't qualify for it cos I had something wrong with my lungs and they said 'no, you can't go to work in the hospitals'. So they sent me to the hospital and then later on they inspected everything and they didn't find nothing cos I just had like a dry pneumonia. I was terribly coughing but after a time it dried up but they put me with everybody. There was soldiers come from the war and some were very ill, some weren't so ill and so on but they were coughing and all that and I said 'where did they put me? Why did they put me here?' It was in Hamburg that hospital. You don't know nothing and later on they said 'you are OK and you go back to that camp'. Then it came to the time when everyone could go to England and at first they picked out those that could work in the camps. So OK, I was again first 'I want a job and I want bread' and this time I was lucky. I got my things together, which was nothing cos everything got lost in the war and I came to England.

Health, cleanliness, virtue and status were thus key parts of the selection process. It seems that young women from the Baltic States, often from middle class family backgrounds, were the preferred recruits of the British officials not only for their health and single status but because they were generally regarded to be superior to the women from other nations who were often from less privileged rural backgrounds. Kay and Miles (1992, p 48) quote from an internal minute in the Ministry of Labour dated 21 November 1945 where it was stated that Polish recruits were mainly of 'the peasant woman type' who accordingly might fail to meet the high standards of cleanliness needed in British hospitals. After a preliminary visit to a number of camps in Germany, it was suggested in the Draft Report on the Recruitment of Baltic Displaced Persons that 'an exceedingly good type of woman is available for hospital domestic work in this country'. The report went on to acknowledge the superior appearance, knowledge of English and general educational standards among young Baltic women and, in a significant comment, the author of the draft report also noted that 'the volunteers have no desire to live in segregated groups while in this country, but wish to become part of the community here. In my opinion they would rapidly be assimilated and would constitute a good and desirable element in our population' (quoted in Kay and Miles 1992, pp 49–50). The contradiction between this claim and the proviso that participating employers must provide housing for their recruits was not mentioned. However, it seems probable that 'becoming part of the community' was a euphemism for marrying British men rather than for the establishment of independent living.

The belief, held by Ministry of Labour officials, in the superiority of Baltic women was also shared by many of the 'Cygnets' themselves, as my interviews revealed. Remember Agnese's comments, recorded in the last chapter, about her own mother's dislike (and pity) for women from predominantly Slavic backgrounds, whom she regarded as inferior. Agnese herself told me with no reticence that she was an Aryan. This distinction between Aryan and Slav, of course, has an awful history. It was a dominant discourse in Nazi-occupied Latvia, and indeed remains an issue today as the Russian population of Latvia is now often discriminated against in both official ideology and in practice (Smith 1999). In the first half of the 1940s, Poles in the German-occupied Baltic states had to wear a large P on their clothes and in the cities were not permitted to walk on the footpaths but must keep to the edge of the road. Several of the EVW women to whom I talked mentioned their superiority to their co-domestic workers in British hospitals, both socially and as workers. Thus, several of them were dismissive of the standards of cleanliness and capacity for work not only of other Eastern European women and women migrants from Ireland (who were also a significant minority among hospital domestic staff at that time) but also of local working class women. It became clear that class as well as ethnic differences were significant axes of discrimination. Agnese, for example, found that it was the class differences, especially as reflected in educational standards, between Latvian EVWs and the local young women who were also employed as domestic staff in Yorkshire hospitals that was the main barrier to social contacts. In her first job, she noted:

> There were three Latvians and I think there were three Estonian women and of course the English, they were, they lived there as well. But some were, you know, simple-minded. They were only for domestic work and all that you know and it was a bit, you couldn't hold conversations with many of them. We had nothing in

> common. I mean I am not a snob but they really knew nothing.

And as Eva told me these preconceptions were reinforced by the hospital hierarchy of jobs which were carefully graded. Eva explains this in the extract below in which both the uncertainly of those first days but also some of the gratitude many of these young women felt as they first started work shines through in her comments:

> When I came to England in 1947, I will never forget that day because it was Princess Elizabeth's birthday. That is 21 April. We were coming by boat lots of girls together. So we were in London, erm, I don't know whether it was in a hostel or something. I can't remember that any more but we slept the night and there came the welfare officer, you know, ladies who would offer us jobs now. 'What part of England do you want to go, and what hospital?' but what do we know?
>
> They needed four girls for this mental hospital and we were four and they said it's in the Midlands. So we thought 'oh well, in the middle that would be good, that would be best, not far away from anything'. You don't know anything, you see. But now we registered in this hospital outside Warwick but we had no idea. And then we are talking among ourselves and said 'I wonder what mental means', you know.[2] We didn't know what mental means. It was all in English and it was not so much at that time. So my friend had this what do you call it, like a little book to look in, and she looked and she said 'aagh' and we said 'oh god, we don't want to go to a mental hospital1'. And so we go to these ladies and we say 'we don't want to go to a mental hospital' and they say, 'no, don't worry, you not going to see anybody, you are not going to work with patients' and they explained to us a bit more. They are old people and we said 'all right. We will go'. Oh, it was the best thing we could do. It was a lovely hospital and me and my friend, you know who came from the same camp, we worked in the ward where you know, you have a little nervous breakdowns, you know where they bring people in. And we were naturally polishing floors and serving meals and making beds and you know, we were ward orderlies, we were not domestic help. One up it seemed.
>
> And we thought we were in paradise. We each had a room, a nice little room. We had a basement where we were just the four of us and a bathroom and a sink in your room, hot and cold water, all the time and then we had a separate like a sitting room for us, the four of us. And the surroundings, it was April you see and that year it was a very nice summer and all the fruit trees were in flower and it was lovely. When we worked in the ward, we could see all the fruit trees in blossom. It was a really nice place.

Thus, working as ward orderlies, 'one up' from the domestics, distinguished Eva and her friends from the women doing the rougher work. And, as she added, 'the matron, the sisters, they all told us that we are not really the lower class people. I am sorry to say that, but we couldn't fit in so we kept to ourselves mostly'.

This belief in the superiority of Baltic women was widely endorsed by hospital matrons who, according to the popular press of the time, found their new

---

2 Tannahill (1958, p 53) reported that there was an agreement that no young woman would be directed to a mental hospital against her will, but it is clear that this agreement was broken. In addition it is clear that many young woman did not understand the terms of their employment, in part because the interview and documents were in English.

domestics to be 'first class workers', 'keen and enthusiastic' (*Evening Standard* 5 October 1946; Kay and Miles 1992, p 51). A more material recognition of these women's qualities and standard of education lay in encouragement to train as nurses once the agreement of the National Advisory Council on Nurses and Midwives had been secured.

Westward Ho!

In 1947, the recruitment programme begun with the Balt Cygnet scheme was extended to include men as well as women, and renamed Westward Ho!: another fanciful name endeavouring to capture an optimistic spirit of adventure and so encourage applicants. It seems unlikely, however, that many of the camps' occupants would have read Charles Kingsley's historical romance of the same name: a children's book about the Elizabethan adventures of men who sailed with Sir Francis Drake. Even if they had, the analogy seems rather far-fetched. Substantial numbers of workers were to be recruited under the Westward Ho! scheme and held in dispersal camps in the UK, before being distributed to vacancies in low-wage jobs that British workers regarded as undesirable in essential industries including textiles, the iron and steel industry, coal mining and agriculture as they arose. Recruitment for Westward Ho! began in March 1947 and the first recruits entered the UK a month later. Table 5.2 shows the total number of people who entered Britain under these schemes and the jobs to which they were initially allocated, showing the clear gender division of labour embodied in the schemes.

Table 5.2: Total arrivals in the UK under the Balt Cygnet, Westward Ho! and Ukrainian POW schemes

	Men	Women
Ukrainian (Westward Ho)	16,210	4,720
Ukrainian (ex-POWs: men only)	8,320	
Polish	9,351	4,667
Latvian	9,706	2,126
Yugoslav	9,220	972
Lithuanian	4,763	969
Estonian	2,891	1,223
Hungarian	2,152	322
Czechoslovak	1,144	192
Rumanian	652	148
Bulgarian	86	
Sudeten*	–	1,319
Total	65,409	17,422

Source: British Immigration Statistics, from Tannahill, JA (1958) *European Volunteer Workers in Britain*, Manchester University Press, Manchester, Table 1, p 139.
*Only women were included in these early labour schemes.

Table 5.3: First occupational placing of EVWs

Industry	**Men (Westward Ho!)**	**Women (Balt Cygnets and W Ho!)**	**Ukrainian prisoners of war**
Agriculture	29,554	65	6,257
Army and Air force depots	1,603	–	1,347
Boot and shoe manufacture	11	63	–
Brick and allied industries	2,729	2	–
Cement	262	–	–
Clay pits	57		
Clothing wholesale	4	57	
Coal mining	10,968		
Cotton	1,083	**7,564**	
Domestic service: Hospitals	109	**3,782**	
Domestic service: National Service Hostels Corp	1,458	919	
Domestic service: others	3,589	2,058	
Flax processing/spinning/weaving	57	13	
Gas industry	60		
Gypsum mining	49		
Hosiery	24	265	
Hydro-electric scheme	250		
Iron and steel industry	1,355	1	
Jute	18	175	
Laundries	2	389	
Narrow fabrics (Leek)	18		
Nursing	169	425	
Pottery	137	31	
Quarrying	708		
Rayon	554	**1,000**	
Refractories	98		
Textile finishing	17	8	
Timber production	107		
Wool	1,113	**3,173**	
Miscellaneous	885	58	
Total	57,030	20,066	8,114

Source: Tannahill, JA (1958) *European Volunteer Workers in Britain*, Manchester University Press, Manchester, Appendix H, p 133

It proved more difficult than expected to recruit women under the expanded scheme, in part because by 1948 other countries had started recruitment and so potential applicants had a greater choice of potential destinations: the Cook's option described by Hulme.

Diana recalls this time. She came to Britain under the Westward Ho! scheme in mid-1947 and she was held in a transit camp in Market Harborough before being allocated to domestic work:

> They started to, people started to emigrate because Great Britain as the first to let refugees come here and my sister and I decided. There was nothing to do in Germany and we have to live somehow and so we came in 1947, end of July, to England. There was a camp near Market Harborough, army barracks and I wasn't very long there and then I had a job but we decided we wanted to stay together. And I was told I had a job in hospital at Hitchin and I knew how to cook. My sister was artist, she was learning in Academy of Art. She was a painter and she knew she wouldn't get any jobs like that. She was a cleaner in a sisters' home, the same hospital. ... My sister had to work to clean in a big kitchen. When I went and had a look round there were ever such unusual people, some were sitting and smiling, some were talking and later on I found it was an old people's hospital. They were all different, some were very simple and some were a little bit strange. But the first year I was frightened. We had to start working at 7 am and at 8 am we went for breakfast and I met together with my sister 'Do you know where we are? It's a mental home'. But, no. I came to England to work and I can't be choosy.

Lizina, who spent a short period in the same camp near Market Harborough after landing in England, recalls that there just three options for women: 'There were interpreters who asked you questions. The women could only do three jobs: a mill, a hospital or like a house, domestic work'. She also remembered that the humiliating medical examinations common in Germany were repeated in these British reception camps:

> And we had a health check there. I was red and embarrassed. They were matter of fact but I mean, oh my God. You had to be healthy and without any defects.

Fodder indeed, as Velta commented earlier, or the good muscular flesh identified as valuable by Hulme, which, if female, had to be unsullied as well. It is clear that despite their relative youth, and their gratitude for a job and accommodation ('It was a clean room, a big room with a clean bed and you don't know how I felt. Because in the camp there was terrible conditions and the first night when I had a bath and slept in a clean bed, you don't know how I felt'). Diana, (talking about her room in the hospital where she worked initially), the Latvian women who came as Cygnets and Westward 'hoers', were clear-sighted about their use value as a commodity, even though this clear-sightedness may have developed with hindsight, as Vieda explains:

> While I was working there (in the administrative office of a DP camp) it wasn't a very posh job but reception you know and I had to register people and nearby there was a big English army, no, RAF place or something but they had to come and check the X rays or do the health checks or something. And one day arrived this wing commander or group captain and his wife and they x-rayed and when I was doing the papers we start talking ... and they said 'well, do you want to stay in Germany?' I am only staying there because it is not so far [from Latvia] and I hope

> to go back. And they said 'we are going back to England. Would you like to come with us and work for us for a year?' ... would I be the nursemaid to the nanny? They had two children, little Fiona and little Mark.

I could still hear the condescension in their tones as they referred to their children. When I asked Vieda why she thought that they took a liking to her, she replied:

> Well, I thought well, I am quite friendly and probably I am cheap labour too. In those days you did not think like that but when I look back probably. Or perhaps they genuinely liked me, I don't know.

As well as the sort of institutional domestic work that Diana and her sister were allocated to, and the private domestic service Vieda entered, the other major area of recruitment for women under the Westward Ho! scheme was into the textile industry: wool in Yorkshire, cotton in Lancashire and artificial fibres in the Midlands. If the pure cleanliness of Baltic women captured in the image of a young swan was seen as an ideal qualification for what was in fact tough and dirty work in hospitals, then Baltic women's purported stamina and ability to withstand the harsh British climate were regarded as advantages by the textile manufacturers. Here, Baltic women were constructed in official discourse as superior workers, but this time not in comparison to Slavic women but to the women from the Caribbean who were just beginning to be recruited by British employers, by both private factory owners and by the public sector, typically, once again, to meet shortages in hospitals. Addressing the post-war recruitment by Lancashire mill owners, Webster (1998, p 35), for example, quotes from a government working party which had been established in 1948 to examine the possibility of extending foreign recruitment into the cotton textile industry beyond EVW women to workers from the Caribbean. The working party report suggested that it was 'unlikely that West Indian women could stand up to the Lancashire climate for any length of time'. Furthermore, in comparison with the relatively high educational standards of many EVW women 'it was understood that most of the women available [from the Caribbean] were illiterate and thus unlikely to make suitable textile operatives'.[3] In the same year, by coincidence, the United Nations General Assembly criticised the British government for admitting too few European immigrants into the UK and in a discussion of whether to increase their numbers or those from the Caribbean, the former route was chosen. A Ministry of Labour official rather frankly admitted that 'it is one thing to maintain the traditional policy under which British subjects are free to enter Great Britain without restriction, but it is quite another to organise migration from one part of the Empire to another', even though organising a mass move from Germany to Britain seemed not to raise similar difficulties. However, as he

---

3 Interestingly, Kay and Miles (1992) suggest that EVW men were compared favourably not only with Irish but also British men transferred from areas of high unemployment to work in coal mines or brick works in the 1940s. They quote the manager of a hostel for miners suggesting that 'of the British residents who are arriving, 80% are the scum of the earth, are filthy, have a police record, are either wanted by the Police or are awaiting trial on counts ranging from indecent exposure to robbery with violence. This, compared with the 'superiority of the foreign residents, to their sobriety, to their cleanliness and to the little trouble they give' (quotes from Ministry of Labour records, 1949: see Miles and Kay 1992, p 210).

continued, 'the 500 men from the Empire Windrush have caused considerable political embarrassment by their mass arrival' (quoted in Hennessy 1993, pp 441–42, original source PRO, LAB 13/259).

These attitudes about the lesser eligibility of Caribbean migrants, despite their Commonwealth origins, have permeated the discursive construction of Caribbean women throughout the post-war decades, especially in the early years. Thus the 1953 Report of the Working Party on Coloured People Seeking Employment in the United Kingdom alleged that African Caribbean in-migrants found work difficult to obtain because of their 'low output ... high rate of turnover ... irresponsibility, quarrelsomeness and lack of discipline'. Black women were seen in official eyes and in official documents as less suitable, although than who was not entirely clear. As Paul argues, in this report '"Coloured" women were described as "slow mentally" and "coloured" men as "more volatile in temperament than white workers ... more easily provoked to violence ... lacking in stamina" and generally "not up to the standards required by British employers"' (Paul 1997, p 134).

Narratives of identity: British or alien? Workers or mothers?

It is clear then that there was significant discrimination between women (and men) of different origins. White European migrants were constructed as superior to Irish and, especially, to Caribbean workers. The aim of the post-war British government was to transform these European migrants into good Britons, despite their legal status as aliens when the other groups were either *de facto* (Irish) or *de jure* (Caribbean migrants) citizens. Right from the start of the policy to admit displaced persons from German camps, ministers took active steps to achieve the policy of 'insertion' or assimilation, initially identified as a possibility in the first draft report on the recruitment of displaced persons from the Baltic, as I noted above. Deals were struck with British trades unions, for example, to ensure that the newcomers were fully accepted in the workplace, rather than treated as temporary workers. However, although integration was a key aim, it was also recognised that potential competition should be nullified. Arrangements were made so that the in-migrants were initially placed only in sectors of the economy where there were significant labour shortages and they were unable to compete in the open job market during their first two or so years in the UK. For women recruited to hospital work, employment by general hospitals rather than TB sanatoriums and mental hospitals had to await union agreement and, similarly, their eventual promotion to nursing from domestic service in hospitals also depended on careful negotiation between the employers and the unions. Through these regulatory mechanisms, it was clear that however 'superior' the Baltic migrants were to other economic migrants, they were categorised as second class workers in comparison with British workers, especially the male manual labour aristocracy whose privileged position was protected in the Fordist years from the end of the war until about 1972 (Harvey 1989).

In the first months of their entry to Britain, action was taken to help EVWs 'to settle down'. English lessons were arranged in camps and in workplaces, for example, as well as instruction about the British way of life. Although some of the women had learnt some English in school, for the majority German had been the second language during their secondary schooling. Although the commonalities of a joint European heritage were stressed in official discourse and in the orientation programmes (indeed, as I have already noted, the very term 'European' volunteer worker was officially adopted to avoid the term 'foreign' as the Ministry of Labour believed the indigenous British population despised foreigners (Kay and Miles 1992, p 130)), the key aim was to encourage assimilation, for the EVWs to feel British, rather than to encourage both migrants and the local population to explore their joint European heritage. As Paul (1997, p 65) has argued, 'the intention ... was to transform aliens into subjects by clothing them in a discourse of potential Britishness'. As potential Britons, the marriageability of these young European in-migrants was discussed in terms that strayed dangerously close to eugenicist arguments. Thus, the Baltic immigrants were referred to in a parliamentary debate as 'the spirit and stuff of which we can make Britons' and 'first class people' who would be 'of great benefit to our stock'. As a Ministry of Labour official suggested in a letter to a senior civil servant in 1948, the EVWs 'are coming definitely for permanent settlement here with a view to their intermarrying and complete absorption into our own working population' (quoted in Paul 1992, p 464). While this may have been the aim of the British government, the reality proved somewhat different.

While marriage may have been a goal for the EVWs, perhaps especially for the male in-migrants who entered under the Westward Ho! scheme and who outnumbered their female compatriots, (the women interviewees, for example, mentioned their initial relish of their independence as single workers and their hope of avoiding too premature a 'settling down') intermarriage with the local population and the production and parenting of little Britons was not the aim of either sex. Stripped of their citizenship rights and mourning their vanished homelands, the reconstruction of a national identity in exile was the central aim rather than assimilation into an unknown and, in many senses, unchosen nation. For the young women who entered Britain in the post-war period, circumstances were complicated. That difficult contradiction between the British ideals of post-war femininity and the dire shortages of labour in many previously female-dominated sectors of employment had to be negotiated both by women as individuals and by the state in its attitudes to female EVWs. It is important to stress that these women were recruited first and foremost as employees rather than to expand the British stock. It is clear that in the early post-war years, the qualification for mothers of future Britons was itself British nationality. As William Beveridge (1942) noted in his report on the future of national insurance, the future role for British women was as wives and mothers, financially dependent on male breadwinners. These pronatalist assumptions were echoed in housing policy where Beveridge argued that 'those who design homes of today should realise that they must be the birthplaces of the Britons of the future – of more Britons than are being born today. If the British race is to continue there must be many more families of four and five children' (Beveridge 1943, p 172).

This view was reconfirmed in the post-war Royal Commission on Population. Its 1949 report on the connections between population change and labour market shortages continued to represent British women as potential or actual mothers rather than full-time workers. While British women might be encouraged to combine motherhood with part-time work as the concept of 'dual roles' was popularised (Lewis 1992; Myrdal and Klein 1956), for post-war economic migrants, whether from Europe or the Caribbean, full-time paid work was the norm. Thus, whatever the advantages of their 'stock', EVW women were employed on a full-time basis and were expected at the very least to fulfil their initial period of directed 'volunteer' (albeit financially remunerated) labour. As one Yorkshire mill owner, a Mr Cartwright noted forthrightly in the *Yorkshire Post* in 1948, one of the main advantages of women EVWs as employees was their single status:

> These women ... have no husbands to cook for in the evening, no children to wash and put to bed, and as they live in a hostel their shopping, cooking and cleaning is done for them.

Their single status did not last long, however. Outnumbered three to one by male EVWs from Latvia, the women whom I interviewed found themselves eagerly courted as potential marriage partners. Within four years of landing in the UK as single women, 17 women were married and by 1954 all except one of them, who was to remain single throughout her working life, were married – 20 of the 24 to Latvian men. Of the other four, only one married an Englishman. Thus, the state's ideal of intermarriage was thwarted from an early date. Contacts within a developing Latvian community, based around, in the main, cultural activities such as choirs and dance groups, but also in these early years, through the Lutheran Church, were an important way of cementing national ties as well as a way of meeting potential partners. The significance of women's work, not only their continuing employment as paid workers but also their roles in the family and the community, in constructing a version of deterritorialised Latvian identity in Britain is the focus of the next chapter where the post-war lives lived by Latvian exiles in different parts of Great Britain are explored. Returning to the concept of the total social organisation of labour introduced in Chapter 2, I want to look at the ways in which Latvian women, their husbands, family and friends organised their daily lives in 1950s Britain at a time when the differences and separation between men's and women's lives were perhaps greater than at any other time in the twentieth century. First, however, in the rest of this chapter I want to look in more detail at the types of work Latvian women undertook during their period of 'volunteer' labour, exploring the conditions under which they laboured, the divisions of labour involved, their relations with their co-workers and the parts of the country in which these women worked. To a large extent, their initial allocation both to a specific job and to a particular place determined their future prospects for social and geographical mobility, or, more commonly, stability.

Working as 'volunteers' in 'women's' work in 1940s Britain

In this final section of this chapter the types of work to which Latvian women were allocated on their arrival in Britain from October 1946 onwards are explored. The aim is to show how the organisation of the task undertaken, the social and gender divisions within the labour force and the geographical location of work combined to influence the types of social relationships that these young women were able to establish on arrival, as well as the ways in which their initial circumstances set the parameters for their future lives in Britain. The three main types of work to which these women were allocated were, as Lizina noted earlier, domestic work in hospitals, domestic work elsewhere and work in the textile industry. While the first of these three types of work proved to be the most agreeable, in terms of offering opportunities for social and geographical mobility, in all three locations Latvian women found that not only was the work hard, menial and physically demanding but they were also often lonely, either finding it difficult to, or choosing not to, develop contacts and friendships either with co-workers and or within the local community where they found themselves living.

Domestic work in hospitals

The women who came to Britain to work in hospitals were sent wherever recruitment of British workers was difficult. Six of the 25 women whose narratives I collected were recruited as 'cygnets', and a further five women were also allocated to domestic work in hospitals under the Westward Ho! scheme. They were sent to hospitals across the country; these women found themselves working in Dartford in Kent, in a small town near Edinburgh, Scotland and in a range of places in between. While there was no explicit policy of keeping women of specific nationalities together, whether or not these women were part of a group of EVWs that included other Latvian women, and later Latvian men as well, the hospital's location within the United Kingdom had a significant impact on their future lives. Life in isolated TB hospitals could often be lonely, especially when there were no other Latvians in the locality. As Valda, sent to a small hospital in a rural part of Scotland, noted: 'It was awful there. I was completely on my own and I was so lonely.' She also disliked the work, even though she recognised that she had been treated relatively well, emphasising, like Agnese, the status distinctions between different categories of support staff:

> In Scotland I was a ward orderly, partly nursing really. We were called ward orderlies but we helped with the patients. It wasn't cleaning or that. We had to wear uniforms. It was much better than now with all these mangers. Every one liked Matron. We lived in. I wouldn't say it was hard work. The first month though I worked in laundry there, and that was hard. We had to accept, you know, what we were given at first. Later on the matron just gave us different jobs and so on. I enjoyed it really. I had never been very keen really on hospital work but I had to do it and I did it.

But, she added emphatically, 'I wouldn't do it again if I can help'. Beate was perhaps luckier, at least in her geographical location. She travelled to the UK from Germany early in 1947, accompanied by her mother and sister. They had each applied to enter Britain as single women but they had managed to stay together and were all sent to work in a mental hospital in Kent. There Beate was initially allocated work as a ward orderly. There were 18 Latvian women in total at this hospital in Kent when Beate worked there and so they were able to create a sense of workplace-based community, establishing both a choir and a dance group which performed for patients and the medical staff and eventually toured other hospitals in Britain with EVW staff.

Conditions of work in these hospitals in the late 1940s were not easy. Hospitals then were extremely hierarchical institutions in which domestic workers and ward orderlies barely featured at all and certainly were not consulted about anything. These women told me about the rules that enforced the hierarchy in which matron was next to God, outranked perhaps only by the head doctor. EVW domestic workers were not permitted to speak without being first spoken to, they had separate entrances to the hospital and to their accommodation, as well as uniforms that differentiated them from the nursing staff whose status far outranked their own. As Beate noted: 'We shared the nurses' home but we really had not much to do with the nurses. The domestic staff kept to themselves and we had separate dining rooms.' Agnese describes her conditions of work as a hospital domestic, also commenting on the status differentials that were so important in hospitals in the late 1940s as follows:

> We landed in Hull, on 29 May 1947, on the Westward Ho! scheme and we were taken to Pocklington which was near York, to a transit camp and there we waited for jobs. It was about three weeks we were in the camp and then my mother, myself and a school friend of mine went to Leeds General Infirmary. We worked as maids, you know domestic staff. And it was difficult. It was an old hospital and we lived in domestic quarters and the nurses lived in another, you know, camp, another wing and we weren't quite allowed to go there. They were a bit higher and it was, well, erm, like a caste system: matron, and the hierarchy and sisters and nurses. It wasn't said but it was understood that you hadn't to get any contact with nurses and everything. And it was difficult to go on your knees on these stone floors scrubbing, and crowds of students coming. And one stepped in the bucket once and upset all the water. And it was, you know … I don't mind working, but it was … You felt repressed and in hospitals you had to work Saturdays and Sundays and later on when the people in the factories, they had Saturday and Sunday off and the Latvians developed a social, there was a choir and a dance group and a theatre group and you couldn't join in because you were always working.

Ilona also remembers the hard unremitting work, and how she escaped from it before the end of her indentured period:

> I had come on my own with a group of volunteers and I was put in the Fountain Hospital, a mental hospital and I had to scrub the floors and wash the dishes and polish the wooden floors, light the coal fires. You go into a place and light the fires to keep the place warm. It was in Tooting. There were four of us, two elderly ladies and a friend of mine. We kept together. But her sister came over and was sent to Bradford and she wanted to join her. So she left me alone and I developed the housemaid's knee because of scrubbing and all that work and I lost a lot of weight and was crying a lot. I didn't like it all. And there was an old German doctor and he kept talking to me and he saw that I had all the education. I showed him my papers and so on and he said that he would try to help me that I could do nurses' training. So I, before my time, before a year was out I was already a student nurse.

For the young women sent to hospitals, while their geographical isolation, as well as the long and anti-social hours mentioned by Agnese, often made community participation difficult, their occupational position proved to be an advantage.

Several of them, including Ilona, trained as nurses and so found a route to both social and spatial mobility. The potential for hard work by these young Latvian women that had been identified by the initial recruiters, soon made itself evident among the women who started as hospital domestics. Resigned to menial work, they determined to do it well. 'Work is work and whatever we had to do, we done it with greatest pleasures as long as everyone was pleased with our work' (Ida). Matrons, sisters and other nurses found the Latvian EVWs to be willing workers and several of them were given additional responsibilities, a form of preferential treatment that was not always welcomed by their English and Irish domestic co-workers. 'There was some jealousy in the hospital. We were good workers and some of the English girls were jealous. They thought the overseer was giving me preferential treatment' (Eva). Thus, as I noted earlier, class and ethnic differences between the foreign workers were sometimes a source of conflict. At times, this reinforced the differences between local and foreign workers and strengthened feelings of isolation, especially among the women whose language skills were poor and who found themselves in small or isolated hospitals without the company of other Latvian workers.

Domestic work outside hospitals

If domestic work in hospitals could be lonely, for women who were allocated to domestic service in private homes, isolation was often the defining characteristic of the job, except in very large establishments. For the six women initially allocated to domestic positions other than in hospitals, the common experience was one of exploitation and loneliness. Lina, for example, after spending six months in the kitchens in a camp for male EVW agricultural labourers, was sent to a private household where first of all she was the kitchen maid and then, in a step up, promoted to be a parlour maid. Her experiences in this house typified the exploitation that had been common in domestic service in the pre-war era: the main reason why British-born working class young women preferred other types of work after the war. As Lina explains she felt powerless. She was a young girl, only 17 years old, alone in a large house in the Warwickshire countryside:

> I didn't know anything. I didn't know the laws, I didn't know my rights, I didn't know anything and also in domestic service in those days there were no trade unions. People could ask you to work any hours they liked and they did. And in this house I worked from seven basically until ten o'clock, well not exactly, let's say nine when the washing up was done. I had my meal breaks, you know, coffee at 11 and then lunch and teatime, but you are tied to the place. You can't say I am going to my room for 15 minutes, you couldn't do that; it wasn't done. People never complained. If you didn't like it you left and tried to find a better place. But you couldn't say I am not going to do it, because you are there and that's it. You are in service you see. So when I finished there, I thought never again because basically you really do have no life of your own really.

Vieda's experiences working for the son-in-law and daughter of a titled family in Kent may have been better, but she too regarded the job as exploitative and wanted to leave as soon as legally possible: 'I wanted to get on and do something with my life.' For Vieda too, nursing proved to be the route to advancement, even though she did not begin her working life in Britain in a hospital.

Like Eva, for several other women their first employment was as domestic workers in the transit camps set up by the British government to process incoming EVWs and at least there loneliness was not an inevitable problem. Pauline's early work history, for example, included two jobs where she worked in kitchens and in canteens in reception centres. On entering Britain in April 1947, she was allocated to a transit camp in Hull where she worked in the kitchens until the August of that year. When the camp closed, she was moved to East London to undertake similar work in a hostel for Polish ex-servicemen. The work in Hull was relentless; in London she found it less pressurised and her living conditions were better:

> Sometimes 500 people from Germany would stay for just one night [in the camp in Hull]. We had to feed them and send them off the next day with sandwiches. After the camp closed they distributed the people all over because it was Ministry arrangements. We could not go and look for jobs ourselves because the five years weren't up. You had to stay here and that is that, and be more or less controlled. After the camp closed they sent four of us – two Latvian girls and two Estonian – to London and here was one camp, it was in Canning Town and we were working there ... I was in the canteen serving food, collecting dishes up and that ... We lived in a barracks but the barracks was nice and clean and we didn't need to clean it ourselves as we were doing the shift work.

Natalija also started work in Britain in an institutional setting and, like Lina and Pauline, she found herself in a male-dominated environment:

> I had to be in the dining room to serve the people with a meal and to clean afterwards. It was an agricultural college for the ex-servicemen: there were sailors and pilots and soldiers after the war who wanted to go into farming or didn't know what else to do – a very mixed company. Well, there was fun, not understanding English I had my dictionary under one arm. They joked but not cruelly. They were nice. I was still only 17, it was very funny sometimes. Generally they were not nasty, I can say. The only nasty person there was the housekeeper ... we started to work at six in the morning and very often we didn't finish 'til 10 at night. There was not much time off in between, half an hour after lunch in the dining room, that sort of thing. I remember it was about six weeks that I stuck it.

She was able to leave after an enquiry into the conditions of employment and was then allocated a position in private domestic service:

> ... but that was again, that was a house where they expected you to work from early hours until late at night. They both were business people ... Very rich people, but slave drivers.

The young women who were initially allocated to private domestic service were the ones among the 25 women to whom I talked were the most dissatisfied with their employment. All of them left as soon as they were able to, in more than one case breaking the terms of their agreement. Through contacts with other Latvian EVWs they moved into factory work, in the main in the textile industry or in hospitals, first as domestics, and then as nurses or, in one case, as a dental nurse. None of these women moved into other forms of employment in the wider economy as I shall explore in more detail in the next chapter. Their occupational choices were mirrored by their locational decisions; they moved mainly to towns in the Midlands, the North West or Yorkshire where other Latvian EVWs had first been sent. It is hardly surprising, however, that in the early years of residence in Britain, that personal networks dominated employment decisions. For the textile workers, the third main category of employment to which Latvian women were allocated, while the work was demanding, their co-workers proved to be more friendly, untrammelled by the status and class distinctions that characterised hospitals and their geographical location in towns with other industries and employment for male EVWs led to the growth of wider social networks. However, ironically, it was these women who were to experience little mobility and perhaps the hardest lives in the post-war decades.

Textile work

It was this form of work which was to prove most unfamiliar to the Latvian women. From predominantly middle class urban backgrounds or from smaller towns and villages, they had no previous experience of industrial work. Many of them spoke vividly of the shock of the harsh and noisy environment of the mills and factories, of the noise and dust, as well as the speed and dexterity required to complete the tasks they were allocated. It is interesting that these women spoke at length about the nature of their tasks in the mills, often describing in great detail to me exactly what they had to do, compared with the women who became domestics and who hardly mentioned the characteristics of their work. In part this was a reflection of its newness to them (and perhaps too my own interest in industrial processes). However, the women allocated to textile jobs also recalled the real kindnesses of their co-workers, their landladies and other townsfolk, as well as the rugged beauty of the northern mill towns, although they too found the work physically demanding.

Here Elvira, who came as part of Westward Ho! to work in a textile mill in Yorkshire, even though she had completed her teacher training in Germany, captures some of the ambiguity and complexity of these women's early working lives in England, their reception by and reaction to locals and to their co-workers. She also describes the division of labour in the firm, both between men and women and the task that she was set to do, as well as reflecting on the now-familiar rhetoric about the inferior qualities of Polish EVWs:

> Then the chance came to come to England. Someone came from England to the camp to recruit. It was just for single people. I came in 1947. Before I came people were taken only to work in hospitals. I was still hesitating then when those people came. I was offered work, weaving in Bradford. I had seen weaving with frames on the farm but that was different. It was a laugh at first but not easy. They [her co-workers] were laughing at us. They put two girls together; we put cotton wool in the ears because all machinery working, not like weaving by hand, the noise. But the people were marvellous. First of all we were in Bradford. Well, we lived at Bradford, the work was in Oxenholme, Keighley, Howarth; beautiful place. Real Yorkshire. More or less all the people who worked at the factory lived in houses belonging to the factory but it was lovely. That was my first place of work. The people were marvellous. We were the first people there, not just the two of us but

> others. Then later on some Polish girls came and they were dirty and awful. We felt quite ashamed. I don't know why. In the toilets they wouldn't sit if I may say so. Anyway, there were nice people. We lived with a couple who didn't have any children. They were so helpful. She was Irish, Mrs O'Donnell. I can still picture her and she had a piano and I could play there. The man was just demobbed from the army and they had some money and that'd bought the piano.
>
> In the mill there were just the two of us [Latvian women] there in Oxenholme. But there were more with the firm in Bradford. At first we had lived there in Bradford and went on the bus there. It seemed unreal to me but we thought its not for ever, it is just for now. I think we had agreed to work for a year in a hospital or factory, we could chose. Or domestic help in posh houses.
>
> It was women in the mill, except there were some foreman I think, and men who set what we had to weave, all the yarn. It was fun. First of all because the spools they shoot through a wooden handle with a bit of leather, through the cloth and when the spool gets nearly empty you have to catch it. The number of times it landed in the middle. First of all we got odd pieces of cloth to weave, to get the rhythm. To catch it you had to stop the machine, the whole thing and it comes out at each end on a little sort of platform or box and you had to catch it there and rethread it. You stopped it by hand with a lever.

Velta also started work in a woollen mill near Bradford:

> The first job was in a woollen mill. I was a weaver. I were deaf for a fortnight – all that noise. I couldn't speak English a word. I'd never seen anything like it, all those looms and shuttles. I had six looms and if the yarn was broken you had to stop them by hand. It wasn't automatic then. I was so lonely. I sat and cried and cried and I didn't know what I was going to do.

Across the Pennines, other young Latvian women found that the conditions in the cotton industry were similarly unfamiliar and equally demanding. Monika was sent to Marple in Cheshire:

> … to work in the cotton mill. It was a spinning mill. We worked in the cardroom … I had never been in a mill before. It was quite horrendous at first you know. Noisy, dusty … There were about 20 or 25 women in there. There were all these spindles going round and you had to go round putting new ones on and join them together again and when the bobbins get full you had to take them off and put them on again. It wasn't hard, not very very hard but it was dusty and you not being used to it. I didn't like it, to tell you the truth. I wasn't happy at the work.

Agata was also unhappy. 'Oh, that mill … I started first in spinning and erm, it was noisy and pretty filthy. When I first started doing I thought I will never do it, came home in tears, thought I'll never do it … But you get used to it.' This stoical acceptance characterised these women's attitudes.

The final description of working in the cotton industry is from Lizina's life story where she describes a more complicated gender division of labour than that remarked on by Elvira in the woollen mills. Here gender and age in combination produced a segmented division of labour:

> It was machining, making bobbins for passing on to weaving. It was a cotton mill. When the cotton comes it's in big bales. There's a machine where it first goes and it's still thick when it comes out. And the next machine, it's smaller and then it goes,

> until it comes to the binding. It goes three or four machines and then it makes the yarn, and then it goes to weaving. They were all women on the machine, with a male overseer and then there was the bobbin boys who wheeled your full bobbins away and brought the empty ones. It was all done standing up. And we made the cones. It was 25, you had to service 25 of those, all whizzing round. And then you had the knotters; when it was broken you put one end through from the top and one from the bottom and it knotted and you let go. The faster you worked, the more money you made.

It seemed clear from Lizina's description that this was hard work, demanding concentration and dexterity. She went on to explain:

> The first day at the mill I wanted to kill myself. I'd never been in a mill before. All the noise and the dust and the people – oh Lordy. After the first day, I got back to the room and I screamed and cried. My mother said 'you wanted to come to England, so here we are and I don't want to hear another word'.

And Lizina, who was only 18, like a good daughter, buckled down to work and was to remain a mill worker until 1953, working evening shifts after she became a mother in 1951, and later returning to the mill after a short spell on an industrial assembly line.

As well as jobs in Yorkshire and the North West, a few women were sent to make artificial fibres at the Courtaulds factory near Coventry, where the labour process was almost identical. Here is Lina, who escaped from domestic service by agreeing to this job, describing her work in very similar terms to Lizina:

> I did shift work there. I did two shifts: 6 till 2 one week and 2 till 10 another week. And you have a half day free so you have got your own life, you see. The first job I don't even know how to describe it. It was a rayon machine and there was a great big rack with spools of silk on it and you had to watch when the spools ran out. You know put another spool on it and join up the threads you know and make sure that everything goes through the machine and the silk sort of winds round, a bit sort of like a huge bobbin and then that goes to the knitting department where they used to knit. And then after the first job I got a second job in another department when the material is already knitted and it's checked for faults and then it goes to the dyeing department where it is dyed various colours. I think there all these sort of materials were rolled and weighed and marked because the dyes are used according to the weight of the material so that was quite interesting in its own way, you know, but the shift work that was the main thing; that was really good.
>
> The work was mainly with other women. There were one or two men but mostly women. The spinning department was all men and that was three shift work with nights as well. The other women were all kinds of nationalities, Latvian, Lithuanian, Polish, German as well, there were quite a few Germans girls as well, and English as well. People were friendly but I didn't go out with them as I was already engaged.

Other women also commented on the friendliness of their co-workers. They told me that both local women and Irish in-migrants were generous to them, helping them initially, showing them the tricks needed to cope with several machines at once and often sharing food at breaks. But, like the domestic workers discussed above, EVW textile workers also tended to have limited social contacts with their co-workers. 'Most of our friends were Latvian. It was all right. There were lots of our ladies [at work]. And the English ladies – well, they let us be' (Agata). And, less positively, Anyuta noted that: 'Nobody asked us to their home. It didn't seem to be an English custom.' But as Elvira explained in these first months in England: 'our social life at first was with the men in the camps nearby, not with the English.' As she later explained: 'then we got married and life was either work or at home, we didn't have time for socialising with the English workers.' She paused and then added thoughtfully: 'in general most of us had, and still have, rather separate lives from British women.' But the author of a report carried out for the United Nations (Vernant 1953, p 2) on the settlement of refugees in the immediate post-war period also noted that England was 'probably the most difficult of all countries in which to be a refugee'. Whether English reticence or different social customs are the explanation it was not usual in the 1940s and 1950s to invite strangers into the home.

The separate lives of Latvian women in Britain are the subject of the next chapter. In this chapter, I have attempted to reclaim the largely forgotten early history of these remarkable women, as they left the relative security of life as a displaced person in the camps in Germany and came to England, in the main as single and independent young women, although as the narratives revealed several of them managed to maintain family contacts in their initial placements as EVWs. I have shown how the social construction of Baltic women as superior to other women ran though both the official discourse of the Ministry of Labour at the time and the narratives of individual EVW women who were from Latvia. Despite this rhetoric, all these women were allocated to manual and menial tasks. Their value was predominantly as healthy labouring bodies, despite a secondary motive that lay behind the recruitment schemes – the renewal of the British stock. In fact, this motive was never fleshed out in the bodies of small Britons. Whether these women were seen as potential wives for other EVWs, for the demobilised Polish forces in the UK or as suitable brides for Englishmen remained unclear, despite the evident desire that these women, and later men, would be assimilated into the then dominant and hegemonic version of a white, middle class Englishness. But, strangers in a strange land, housed in the main in specialist employment-related accommodation, often speaking little English and anxious about their families left in Germany, as well as relatives still in Latvia, it is not surprising that these young women looked to their compatriots for solace and social contact. They had little desire to assimilate, fervently hoping that their sojourn in Britain would be temporary and that they might soon return to Latvia, once it was freed from Soviet control.

At the end of the 1940s then, EVWs tried to keep out of trouble, to get on with the work to which they had been allocated and pray for return. In the main, the British public permitted this. As long as EVWs were not seen as taking valuable jobs and other resources from deserving Britons, especially ex-servicemen, their presence was tolerated. As the 25 women at the centre of this book were employed in 'female' jobs and largely housed by their employers they seldom experienced lack of sympathy for their plight or outright harassment. One of the few complaints about EVWs concerned a protest by a number of northern MPs in 1947 and repeated in 1949 that foreign hostel dwellers received a larger meat ration than their constituents (Hansard, vol 443, col 497 and vol 463, col 816). Otherwise, there was little officially documented protest. But tensions were common, nevertheless. There was widespread anti-German feeling in Britain after the war and some DPs/EVWs were suspected of having fascist sympathies or backgrounds. Some of the national newspapers carried unsympathetic editorial comment in the initial years of recruitment. *The Daily Mirror,* for example, published an editorial on 20 July 1948 headed 'Let them be displaced', suggesting that Britain had recruited 'most of the scum' from the camps rather than the cream that other nations had taken and suggesting the EVWs were responsible for swelling the crime wave by engaging in black market rackets. Six months later a perhaps surprisingly negative editorial appeared in the *New Statesman and Nation* (8 January 1949) which, while appreciative of the efforts of some EVWs, suggested that 'the illiterate, the mentally deficient, the sick, the aged, the politically suspect and the behaviourally disruptive' should be excluded. It is significant that these editorials postdated the Baltic Cygnet scheme.

Male migrants were seen as far more threatening than women, both in general and as competition to British workers. Thus, some foreign workers were resented by the trade unions as well as by their fellow workers in, for example, the coal mining industry, where British workers wanted to reserve the highest paying, coal face jobs for themselves. And Tannahill (1958, p 70) suggests that it was unions representing the most highly skilled workers who were most unsympathetic to EVW recruitment. But here too, it seems that the Balts received a less hostile reception than, for example, the Poles and the Volkdeutsche or ethnic German women who were recruited under the North Sea Scheme for domestic work as the number of women DPs 'volunteering' for this type of work failed to meet demands. While local newspapers sometimes carried articles about the EVWs, especially in the northern textile towns where the numbers of workers were greatest, coverage was generally, although not always, sympathetic. *The Bradford Telegraph and Argus* in 1951 for example, carried three articles – on 17, 26 and 30 July – explaining the efforts of EVWs to fit into local 'ways' and two decades later, as I mentioned in an earlier chapter, the Sound Archive housed in Bradford library recorded a series of interviews with a range of post-war economic migrants including a small number of EVWs. During the late 1940s and into the 1950s, numerous voluntary and religious organisations were mobilised to provide material and spiritual assistance and to facilitate the hoped-for assimilation. However, as in the labour market, the EVW population was to demonstrate a commitment to self-reliance and to separatist organisations that came to mark both their working lives and retirement and old age in Britain in the decades since their recruitment.

Finally, it should be emphasised that the original reason for establishing the Baltic Cygnet and Westward Ho! schemes was utilitarian. Their aim was to find workers for parts of the economy suffering severe shortages. They were not a humanitarian response to the huge problem of people displaced by the Second World War. From the start, the aim was to recruit people who were portrayed as 'free' foreign labour, while being anxious to avoid Soviet accusations of exploiting 'slave labour' (Paul 1997, p 83). Suitability of recruits was uppermost among the criteria of selection and the Home Secretary at the time, James Chuter Ede, hoped that 'the intake could be limited to entrants from the Western countries, whose traditions and social backgrounds were more nearly equal to our own' (Cabinet meeting, 3 April 1946, quoted in Paul 1997, p 85). Labour restrictions, although often difficult to enforce, were imposed on the movement of EVWs until 1950, and it was also hard for workers to gain permission to bring family members to Britain. It is clear that the authorities involved failed to consider or, at least, make clear to the general population that the EVW schemes were, in fact, resettlement schemes. Indeed, Ede initially had recommended in March 1946 that only individuals whom it would be possible to deport and repatriate should be recruited, warning the Cabinet against conceding rights to permanent settlement. Thus, the initial undertaking which all recruits were asked to sign included a statement that 'the period of permitted stay (an initial 12 months for most participants, although it was clear from the interviews that many women were unclear about their terms, mentioning periods between one and five years) will be extended further if the individual complies with the employment condition set out immediately above and behaves as a worthy member of the British community'. However, there was little the government could do if this condition was broken. To return Latvian EVWs to the camps in Germany was not feasible and to return them to Latvia was impossible.

In his early assessment of the schemes Tannahill (1958) argued that the British government should have lifted labour restrictions earlier and, furthermore, that right from the start it should have been open about the permanent nature of the migration. As he notes, it was only in an afterthought to an answer to a question in the House of Commons on 11 November 1948 that the Minister of Labour actually admitted that: 'this is settlement of a permanent character. These people came here, working their passage to British citizenship.' In fact, as I show later, British citizenship was not what Latvians themselves wanted. Rather, they desperately wanted to go home, if only the British government would support them in their struggles to re-establish independence in their own country. At least in the early years, the Latvian EVWs had no plans for permanent residence in Britain and little interest in assimilation.

CHAPTER 6

SURVIVAL STRATEGIES: WOMEN'S DUAL ROLES IN POST-WAR BRITAIN

No longer 'slave workers'

As the EVW population settled down in Britain, and the first months of unfamiliarity with the work to which they had been allocated stretched into boredom and hardship, dissatisfaction with their conditions of employment began to manifest itself. As I have argued earlier, many of the Balts who left their countries in 1944 were from middle class families, often well-educated, many with professional qualifications and with previous experience of non-manual forms of employment. And yet all these people were allocated to manual employment, separated from their partners and other family members and forced to remain in the positions to which they were allocated for a period of up to two years. Over time, a degree of liberalisation was introduced by, even forced on, the Government because of evident dissatisfaction among groups of workers. As the rates of marriage within the European Voluntary Worker (EVW) population in the UK increased, for example, women petitioned to move to be closer to their husbands, other women left their employment without permission (Marta was in this group).

In 1949, the Ministry of Labour decided that it would be as well to face the fact that EVWs 'are not 'slave workers' and must be allowed a reasonable degree of freedom to change from one employment to another' (Ministry of Labour and National Service 1949, quoted in Kay and Miles 1997, p 107). There was a sting in the tail of this memo, however, as it continued: 'so long as they are willing to take a job in one of the undermanned industries for which EVWs as a class were recruited.' Thus Lina, who fled an unsatisfactory position in domestic service was allocated a new job at Courtaulds. Elvira, still to her shame as is clear in her recollection, also left her first job before completing the required period, using the greater willingness to unite partners as her excuse:

> I knew that there was a relative of mine in Leicester. I'd met him in Germany and he had married a Latvian girl there. And he wrote to me and said 'come and see how you like Leicester' so I went and I liked it very much. There was quite a gathering of Latvians, quite a few and we went to a concert. And I said 'I would love to come up here but how can I?' And my relative said 'oh just say you have a boyfriend or a fiancé', so that is what I told my boss in Oxenholme. And they were too nice to say you are lying and they let me go. I felt awful really, I should have stayed at least a year because I think I started in September and, or a bit later probably. I came in August, and they let me go and I came to Leicester just before the annual holiday so there was a week to wait. I got a job at a hosiery factory and I had a week to wait and I almost died really, from shame. I thought they will find out what I said is my fiancé, he is married and I'll be put in prison. But no-one said anything and I started work.

Plate 6.1 A young machinist working in Leicester's textile industry in 1948

Source: Picture Post/Getty Images

Plate 6.1 shows a young woman working in a job similar to the one Elvira found in Leicester in 1948.

Thus, as the 1940s drew to a close, there began a period of some movement, both between occupations and between different parts of the country, as Latvian men and women moved to locations where they were likely to find a significant number of their fellow country folk as well as, for some, the prospect of more congenial employment.

A decade of change?

In this and the next chapter I explore the lives of the 25 women as they moved between jobs, found marriage partners and began to establish roots in Britain in the 1950s – that decade of growth, expansion and improved living conditions. This was the decade that has come to symbolise the dominance of a particular version of domesticity and an extreme gender division of labour, as marriage and birth rates remained high and so it is seen by many commentators as a decade of social stability. This apparent stability is, however, more accurately represented as a decade of change as what might seem like the re-establishment of older ways of living in fact was the beginning of a new post-war era of rapidly rising consumption, in part based on women's rising participation in paid work, albeit largely on a part-time basis, and new ways of living. Even the baby boom turned out to be more of a 'blip' in the twentieth century decline in birth rates. It might be argued then, as Royle (1994, p 8) has suggested:

> In several important respects the decisive break with what we think of as the nineteenth century, or the late-Victorian world, does not come with the death of Victoria a few days into the twentieth century, nor even with the First World War, but in the period after 1945. The major trend in this latter age of transition, has been an accelerating discontinuity with the past.

Thus, the late 1940s and 1950s might be better represented as a significant watershed in British society rather than a period of continuity. The years in which Latvian EVWs escaped the bonds of their 'unfree' or indentured labour for the British state and established independent working lives and households were, as Royle suggests, a period of deep-seated changes in British society in a range of areas including the family and household structures, the rise of consumerism and its associated technologies, the position of women, and in class, race, religion and education than years of stability. I want to describe these changes and position the Latvian women within them, assessing the extent to which their deep desire to (re-)establish a version of Latvian community and identity in exile ran counter to or paralleled the changing climate, the renegotiation of men's and women's roles and the new opportunities for women opening up in 1950s Britain.

All narratives of social change include ambiguity and complexity, however, and the interpretation of social changes depends on perspective. Men and women in different class positions would have experienced the changes taking place in the 1950s in different and often contradictory ways. Although these years were undoubtedly ones in which a particular version of familialism was dominant – the age of marriage, for example, continued to fall and more couples were able to establish independent households as the post-war house building programme expanded – they were also years of change in ways of living as families. 'The older pattern', as Royle (1994, p 11) noted, 'prolonged by depression, war and housing shortages, was for the relatively late formation of households –occurring even after marriage and thus acting as a brake on the birth rates'. But by the early 1950s and certainly as the decade progressed, young people were more easily able to establish themselves as householders and become parents at an earlier age than in previous decades. In 1951, for example, the number of women who were already married by the age of 24 was no less than 84% greater than in 1931. This was accompanied by a rise in birth rates (which rose after the end of the war to peak in 1964, after which they started to fall until 1977). However, the late 1940s and the 1950s were also the years when the links between age and birth rate and marriage and birth began to be broken by the introduction of more reliable and accessible forms of contraception, by changing social norms and rising rates of illegitimacy and by the development of greater opportunities for young people to live independently, perhaps in shared households, before marriage. This latter trend, however, was not to become really significant, particularly for women, until the expansion of the higher education system in the mid-1960s. Thus, the establishment of both a particular form of domestic privacy and nuclear-family living and the seeds of its decline can be traced back to the 1950s.

The new consumerism

The great shift in consumption patterns that occurred in the second half of the twentieth century also has its origins in the 1950s as new opportunities that were radically different from those of pre-war society began to expand across the social spectrum. Although the immediate post-war years were undoubtedly 'a time of continuing drabness and shortages' (Morgan 1990, p 32), traditional sites of pleasure such as football matches, dance halls and cinemas were quickly re-established. Indeed, Addison (1985) has suggested that spending on leisure was almost the only outlet for pent-up spending power in the early post-war years as rationing was still in force and most shops were short of goods to sell. In the mid and late 1940s 'the leisure industry [was] a licence to print money' (Addison 1985, p 114). 1946, for example, saw record attendance at cinemas: a staggering number of 1,635 million seats were purchased and about 30 million people in a population of 46 million were regular cinema-goers. As Morgan (1990, pp 32–33) noted, for example, 'teenage girls ... would go to their local Gaumont, Odeon, Ritz or Regal three or four times a week'. Erna told me that the cinema also played an important part in the lives of young Latvian women in their first year in the Britain – 'I went to the cinema several times a week, by myself as well as with the other girls at work. It was warm, good for learning English and I enjoyed it'. Hollywood films dominated the output and, as well as offering escapism, showed a world with no food rationing or shortages and a less hierarchical society in which 'automobiles and refrigerators were as much a common culture as smoking cigarettes' (Clarke 1996, p 249). This image of hedonistic pleasure, or at least domestic comfort, was countered by British films such as David Lean's *Brief Encounter* (1945) in which social constraint and marital responsibility win out over an adulterous passion. In addition, the British film industry had to be encouraged as the US distributors were siphoning off millions of dollars from a dollar-starved Britain. In 1948 Harold Wilson set up the National Film Production Council and imposed a requirement that 45% of the films shown in future should be made in Britain (Hennessy 1992, p 326).

Later more sustained forms of leisure than cinema attendance became important. The Holidays with Pay Act, for example, which had been passed in 1938, was widely implemented in 1950s. By the early 1950s, 25 million British people were spending a few days away from home each year, both in the UK and, in increasing numbers, outside. In 1951, for example, two million people had been on holiday abroad. The population was also on the move internally and both geographical and occupational mobility began to alter traditional attitudes and ways of living and their association with specific geographic localities. The managerial and professional classes expanded from 1951, new grades and skill differentiations fractured the ranks of the workers and the gradual drift south meant old industrial communities were losing population. Instead, new suburbs round London, Birmingham and smaller southern towns began to grow and a type of family-based, less collective way of living was established, especially in the south of the country.

The 1950s also saw the beginnings of a new type of consumer society. As Morgan (1990, p 96) has noted, in the 1950s the 'official cult of sexual and cultural puritanism conflicted with the emergent consumer culture, or plain boredom of young people with a drab welfarised society, conflicted with the emergent consumer culture, and an urge to create a land fit for consumers to shop in'. Thus, Obelkevich (1994, p 141) suggests that: 'the 1950s were the starting point. They saw the early stages of a long consumer boom that brought the biggest improvement in the material standard of living in Britain since the Middle Ages. What previously had been luxuries for the rich – cars, refrigerators, televisions, overseas holidays – now were enjoyed by the majority of the population. In the long haul from poverty to affluence, this was the great leap forward'. Thus, the 1950s heralded the start of a significantly different era from the depression years of the 1930s, wartime shortages and post-war austerity. Peter Lewis (1978, p 9) dates the start of this new era as 1953. 'The first two years of the Fifties were a continuation of wartime in civilian clothing. Rationing, which still applied to meat, butter, cheese, tea, sugar and sweets, actually became more austere than it had been in 1945' as the aesthetic, vegetarian Chancellor Sir Stafford Cripps urged continuing sacrifice on the British population. Queues, shortages and high income tax restricting disposable incomes were common. But when all controls on consumption were finally lifted in the mid-1950s, (food rationing, for example, came to an end in 1953) there was a great explosion of consumer spending and in the Festival of Britain, designed to give the long suffering population a 'pat on the back', an official recognition that 'fun, fantasy and colour' might be part of the new Britain (Lewis, p 11).

Urged on by the example of the USA, people began to buy new forms of consumer goods, rock and roll music and the exaggerated suits of the Teddy boys. Class privilege came under attack by 'angry young men' including the playwright John Osborne and the novelist John Braine and 'ordinary people' began to fill their homes with new consumer durables. The ownership of television sets is a good example. In 1946, the first year that licences were issued, only 15,000 households had a set. By the mid-1950s this had risen to an astonishing 4.5 million. Elated by this consumption boom, fuelled by an average rise in real disposable incomes of almost 30% in the 1950s, Harold Macmillan announced in 1957 that 'most of our people have never had it so good' and two years later the Conservative government won an unprecedented third term as the working class, seduced by 'soft living' in the view of some commentators who were nostalgic for a gritttier way of life (Hoggart 1957; Jackson 1968; Seabrook 1982), deserted traditional patterns of voting in large numbers. As Caroline Steedman (1986) documented in her memoir of her mother's life, the stereotypical working class version of 'our mam' in the back kitchen (Hoggart 1957) failed to match women's own longings for the 'new look'[1] and many working class women voted Conservative for the first time in the 1950s and 1960s. As the reality began to change, the stereotypical image of northern communal solidarity took on a new lease of life as a virtual image in Coronation Street, which was first screened in 1962 providing a 'sepia-tinted portrayal of a traditional Lancashire working class community as a

1 Dior's new look, first unveiled in 1947 required yards and yards of material in the skirt, whereas the slim bodice demanded new corsets, still classified at the time as 'luxury garments' by the Board of Trade (see Hopkins 1963, p 95) and yet many women managed to buy or make a 'new look' dress.

vicarious substitute for the real thing' (Clarke 1996, p 254). And yet, as Clarke argued, it is important not to exaggerate the scale and speed of these changes in ways of living. 'The remaking of the English working class was a long and continuing historical process, one hardly confined to the sudden advent of consumerism in the 1950s' (p 254). However, this decade was a significant one in the establishment of a more privatised form of domestic living. Whether Latvian households, many of them living in northern working class towns, shared in this new form of affluence is the subject of the next chapter.

While general housing standards improved and overall living conditions were made easier by technological improvements – the proportion of households with electricity and decent indoor bathrooms continued to rise though the decade for example – a more detailed look at women's lives perhaps tempers the conclusion that there was a radical shift in social relations in the 1950s. Clarke may be correct to err on the side of caution in his evaluation of the first post-war decade and a half. While the significance of the introduction of the post-war welfare state is hard to exaggerate in its impact on overall health and living standards, the Beveridge Report (1942) which set the basis for its development, uncritically accepted the continuation of the pre-war notion that 'the crown of a woman's life is to be a wife and mother' (Spring Rice 1939, p 95). A woman's role in the brave new world was to be a housewife, albeit in the new guise of a manager of the new domestic technology that she might expect in her kitchen. Beveridge did, however, emphasise the value of a more companiable form of marriage and suggested that women should be released from the former drudgery of domestic labour, both by the introduction of domestic improvements including piped water, electricity and modern kitchens and the help from the welfare state such as subsidised food and housing, family allowances and, of course, the introduction of the National Health Service. It is also important to remember, however, that perhaps surprisingly Beveridge also advocated the expansion of collective provision for tasks such as washing, cooking and childcare that took so much of women's time. He suggested that 'the housewife's job with a large family is frankly impossible and will remain so, unless some of what is now done separately in every home – washing all clothes, cooking every meal, being in charge of every child every moment when it is not in school – can be done communally outside the home' (Beveridge 1942, p 264). His plea was echoed by Lord Reith's suggestion that communal nurseries might be an appropriate part of British New Town Policy then being devised to improve housing conditions (Reith Committee Report 1946, p 42; McDowell 1983) but these radical proposals were never introduced. Indeed, the expansion of laundrettes as well as the growing individual ownership of domestic washing machines had replaced communal laundries almost completely by the 1960s. The subsidised British restaurants introduced in the war were closed down (Roberts 1991) and, most significantly for women's future pattern of labour market participation, nursery provision was drastically reduced after the Second World War. Ministry of Health subsidies were removed from wartime nurseries and local authorities failed to expand their provision, except in areas of great labour shortage (Summerfield 1989). Thus, by 1956, there was nursery care for only 10% of 3–4 year olds, back down to the same level of provision as in 1938. Mothers were expected to look after their own children, a view firmly endorsed in the publication in 1953 of John

Bowlby's authoritarian but best-selling book *Child Care and the Growth of Love*. It was this work that warned of the consequences of maternal deprivation, sternly insisting that 'the mother of young children is not free, or at least should not be free, to earn'. Without a great deal of evidence, Bowlby argued that during the first five years of a child's life, a mother's almost continuous presence was essential. Even a week's holiday without the child was too much in his view (Lewis 1978, p 44). Clearly, the patrician Lord Reith had rather different views in his proposals for night nurseries in New Towns.

But behind Reith's recommendations lay a recognition of the 'servant problem' for middle class women (McDowell 1983), rather than an acceptance of the economic need for two earners in working class families, especially it they were to share in the post-war affluence and possession of a growing range of consumer durables. Middle class women, used to help in the home, found it increasingly hard to secure in the post-war years. There was a marked decline in domestic service in the 1950s, or rather a failure to re-establish it after the end of the war: the two million domestic workers employed in 1931 had shrunk to 750,000 by 1951 and to only 200,000 by 1961 which meant that, for middle class women who had been the main beneficiaries of domestic service, it was actually harder to combine a career and a family in 1950s than it had been in the pre-war years (Mitchison 1979). As I suggested in the previous chapter, the EVW schemes to recruit women for domestic service to address the post-war shortage had little impact on this decline and, indeed, was doomed to failure in the more egalitarian climate of 1945. Most women, therefore, had to become the main provider of domestic services to their households, a shift that may be represented as a growing proletarianisation of women (Wilson 1977), as a closer coincidence in women's conditions of living became apparent than in earlier decades. As the class differences that had divided women became relatively less important and women began to recognise their common interests based on their gender, perhaps the seeds were sown that saw the establishment of the second wave women's movement from the mid-1960s (Phillips 1987). Although the conditions of household labour might have improved during the 1950s, more women were doing this work on their own account. Further, the total amount of work and the time spent on it barely fell and indeed may have increased, especially for mothers at home who were encouraged to reach ever higher standards of cleanliness and comfort. So, for example, as the emphasis on austerity and thrifty housekeeping that had dominated women's magazines and advice columns in the early post-war years began to be superseded by an emphasis on the affluent consumer, women readers were encouraged not only to purchase more household goods and a wider range of food items that then needed time spent on them to produce a meal but also to spend growing amounts of time keeping themselves healthy and attractive, aided in the main through rising spending on clothes and cosmetics (White 1980; Winship 1987).

It has been suggested that women lost a degree of power as household managers during the 1950s (Bourke 1994), although the rise of home-based activities among both men and women (the rise of home improvement, for example) and more companiable marriage may have reduced power differentials based on gender (Brooke 2001; Hart 1989) the evidence is complicated and contradictory. After the war, however, it became more common for women to voice their resentment if husbands did no domestic work at all and increasingly it was assumed that men should participate in at least some of the tasks of domestic labour. Women's magazines, for example, began to advise women to encourage men early in marriage to play their part at home, especially as more women entered the labour market on a part-time basis as the 1950s drew to a close. But even a decade earlier, in 1948, when Mass Observation[2] asked its panel of volunteers about housework, many women said that their husbands had begun to help so that they might have more leisure time together as a couple. This survey provided clear evidence that there had been gradual but significant change over time. None of the respondents, for example, could remember their fathers helping with any degree of regularity except for tasks such as cleaning the family's shoes. Women married in the inter-war period also reported that their own husbands did little to help. However, Roberts (1995) urges caution in assessing the meaning of these changes, noting that men's contributions to domestic tasks typically were framed, and continue to be even in the new millennium, in terms of help and not responsibility. Thus, Langhamer (2001, p 151) concluded that 'the sexual division of labour often allocated specific, time-limited chores to the husband and the less defined, more time-consuming ones to the wife, with the attendant consequences for the distribution of spare time within the marital relationship. Masculine housework consisted of a series of "jobs" rather than an omnipresent "duty"'. The types of jobs that men did in the 1950s and 1960s included gardening, decorating, bringing in coal, window cleaning, mending and fixing, chopping firewood, washing up and table setting. While Bourke (1994) argued that the advent of new housing, particularly in the post-war era, combined with a reduction in working hours and rising real incomes, effected an expansion of 'manly housework' in the period, as did the expansion of DIY in the 1950s (pp 81–94), Roberts (1995) suggested that there was some reluctance on the part of women to let husbands perform more than a limited range of tasks based on women's sense of fairness or equity in the distribution of those tasks that comprise the total social organisation of labour (TSOL) (Glucksmann 2000). Many of the women who responded to the Mass Observation survey in 1948, for example, had a keen notion of housework as a skilled occupation as well as a desire to maintain control within the household. It is clear that the reasons that lie behind the particular division of household labour in the 1950s, and each individual household's negotiations about who did what, are complex and not always open to easy interpretation.

Divisions of labour and women's paid work

There is no doubt, however, that changes in the gender division of labour were evident throughout the 1950s, both within and outside the home. In large part it seems that the change was encouraged by women's greater participation in employment, even though this was typically on a part-time basis, and in routine

2 Mass Observation was a documentary project started in 1936 by three young men, Charles Madge, Tom Harrison and Humphrey Jennings, who recruited ordinary people to keep diaries. Volunteers were recruited through newspaper advertisements from the mid-1930s onwards. Garfield's (2004) recent book draws on these diaries to explore the everyday lives of the British civilian population after the war.

and inadequately paid jobs. As I suggested earlier, the widespread acceptance at then end of the war that domesticity and maternity were to be women's primary purpose in life had formalised women's position as second class workers. The rise in consumer spending through the 1950s, reflected in a more comfortable home-life was, in part, both a cause and a consequence of women's growing participation in the labour market, as well as a reflection of high employment among men and rising wages, at least for the labour aristocracy and the expansion of professional and white collar occupations for middle class men. In her splendid study of the reordering of everyday life in France in the decade preceding 1968, Kristen Ross (1994) documents the impact that the large-scale mass consumption of goods in French homes over this decade had on ideas of femininity, masculinity and good housekeeping. As she argues, a discourse about hygiene and cleanliness, in part purveyed through women's magazines, became a significant part of the idealisation of a version of domesticity for white women and part of the racist exclusion of in-migrants. Webster (1998), as I noted earlier, also documented the same coincidence of whiteness, cleanliness and domesticity in the UK that constructed minority women, but especially those from the Caribbean, as 'less eligible' mothers and so more appropriate as full-time workers than white women. While Latvian women, because of their class and skin colour, were largely excluded from this assumption that minority women make bad mothers, many of them did continue in full-time paid work through the 1950s and 1960s. Even so, they were not in the vanguard of the new consumerism. Ownership of the new consumer durables that made domestic life more comfortable came late to their households As I show later, for these women, employment paid for necessities and their purchase of cars and refrigerators – in Ross's book (*Fast Cars, Clean Bodies*) the key iconic possessions of modernity – had to wait. Indeed, in their commitment to re-establishing forms of communal activities, it may be that the home as a space for leisure and entertaining was less important for the Latvian population than for the increasing affluent British middle and lower working classes, although as I noted above, the Latvian women also recorded their initial surprise that their British co-workers never invited EVWs to their homes. For Latvians, the home was a space for communal activities and entertaining friends rather than a display case for the iconic symbols of the new consumerism.

While many of the Latvian women remained in the types of manual employment to which they had been allocated in the late 1940s, British women in general moved into white collar, or what were sometimes called 'pink blouse', jobs (Westergaard and Resler 1976) in the post-war decades. At the start of the 1950s, women still accounted for just under a third of all paid workers (31% in 1951) which was almost exactly the same proportion as in 1931 (30%). But the decade was to witness a slow but steady rise in women's participation and, significantly, increasing participation rates among married women and women with children (see Tables 6.1 and 6.2). This reflected the lower age of marriage and its growing popularity, as I noted earlier, as well as the tendency for women to have fewer children closer together in age in the early years of the marriage (Elliott 1991). It also began to weaken the idea that marriage and maternity were the crowning achievements of all women's lives which had been so firmly established in 1945. Slater and Woodside (1951, p 82) might have argued that most

Table 6:1: Percentage of women in different age groups in employment, 1931–61

Year	Total no. (millions)	% of women in each age group in labour force under 35	35-50	60+
1931	5.6	69	26	5
1951	6.3	52	43	5
1961	7.0	45	49	6

Source: National Census

Table 6.2: Percentage of women's employment participation by marital status, 1931–61

Year	single*	married	widowed
1931	77	16	7
1951	52	40	8
1961	40	52	8

Source: National Census

*The decline in single women in the labour market was partly a consequence of growing educational participation by young women as well as a reflection of rising marriage rates.

women are uninterested [in work] regarding their jobs as a short-term expediency until marriage but increased participation rates began to challenge their claim.

The overall shift in participation rates throughout the post-war years, however, disguises important differences between women. Women in full-time employment were largely unmarried or childless and there was little significant increase in the proportion of women working on a full-time basis until three decades later. It was not to be until the 1980s that women's participation on more equal terms with men, at least in terms of time, was to occur. In both 1951 and 1981, for example, only 30% of all adult women worked full-time and they were mainly women without children or women whose children had grown up (Joshi 1989). Even so, wages for women did begin to creep up. Single women working full-time after the war saw a considerable rise in their wages compared with the pre-war years. Fowler (1995) suggests that young women starting work in the 1950s were the beneficiaries of a post-war increase of as much as 400% in young workers' wages from the inter-war period. But this increase seldom brought with it a concomitant independence for these young women, who continued to hand over their wages, after an allowance for 'pocket money', to their mothers (Jephcott 1954). In the rare cases of girls who lived separately from their families, they were still expected to send money home (Kerr 1958).

Throughout the earlier post-war decades, however, most women were employed on a part-time basis, especially after marriage. As I have already noted, married women, especially mothers, were still encouraged to see their domestic labour as their primary aim and role in life, with paid employment constructed as secondary, undertaken for 'pin-money'. Once the war had ended, women were recruited into appropriately feminised forms of work, resulting in significant gender-based segregation in the labour market. As Harvey (1994) commented in her book on American women in the 1950s, after the war 'Rosie the Riveter didn't necessarily leave the workforce: she just moved – or was moved – over into clerical and sales jobs, or the "helping professions" of teaching, nursing or social work' (p xix). *Life* magazine (24 December 1956) justified women's predominance in these fields in stereotypical terms: 'Household skills take her into the garment trades; neat and personable, she becomes office worker and saleslady; patient and dextrous, she does well on repetitive, detailed factory work; compassionate, she becomes teacher and nurse' (quoted in Harvey 1994, p 129). These patterns and attitudes were mirrored in the British labour market. Indeed, the segregation of the sexes in Britain was so marked that in the 1950s 86% of all women workers were employed in jobs in which their co-workers were predominantly other women. Not unexpectedly, employers saw an opportunity to pay for this segregated, 'secondary' and insignificant work with commensurately low financial rewards. There was a yawning gap in the 1950s between men's and women's rates of pay. Throughout the decade, women earned only 51% of the average weekly earnings of male workers, a figure which by end of the 1960s had crept up to 54% and to just about two-thirds by the time of the Equal Pay Act in 1974. Further, the belief that women's work was secondary meant that women's wages were conceptualised as a supplement to the family income rather than a vital contribution, even when economic necessity dictated women's participation. Too often their income was seen 'merely' as a way of contributing to the purchase of 'family extras' – a car, holidays and perhaps a house as home ownership rates expanded in the post-war period, rather than belonging to the individual woman and subject to her control. Nevertheless, the gradual expansion of women's participation rates from this time began to make the idea that women, including wives and older women, could work outside the home acceptable. Paid work was no longer just for single women or a wartime necessity but increasingly a part of many women's lives.

In the 1950s, the 1960s and well into the 1970s, the idea that women had 'two roles' (Myrdal and Klein 1956) was central to debates about the connections between paid and domestic labour. Women's two 'jobs' were seen as complementary rather than in conflict. And while part-time employment in suitably 'feminised' occupations was to be encouraged, women's paid labour was officially portrayed in the 1950s as marginal, both to the economy and in women's own lives. The publication of John Bowlby's influential *Maternal Care and Mental Health* in 1952, for example, reinforced official views with its frightening depiction of the drastic impact that maternal deprivation would have on 'latch key' children, forced to fend for themselves as their selfish mothers went out to work. Contemporary surveys do seem to suggest that many women in the 1950s were themselves persuaded by these arguments. It was to be another decade before Betty Friedan (1963) identified the 'problem with no name' afflicting housebound wives (especially well-educated women) and the Women's Liberation movement portrayed paid employment as a key way to counter the oppression of women.

As a range of publications documented, women in the 1950s and early 1960s seemed keen to enter the labour market only when the terms and conditions were appropriate, which typically meant that the hours had to fit in with family demands. Further, their reported motives tended to be based on a desire to improve the general standard of living for the family as a whole (Hunt 1968; Jephcott *et al* 1962; Klein 1965; Smith 1961) rather than rooted in a wish for individual independence. In general, it was widely assumed by both the institutions of the state and by individual households that the main economic responsibility for the household should rest with the male breadwinner. After the war, in official documents and reports such as the *Royal Commission on Equal Pay* (1946) and the *Government Social Survey on Women and Industry* (1948) already discussed, it was assumed that no woman would or should want to work if her husband earned reasonable money. Even among the women who had been employed during the war, attitudes to continuing or expanding women's employment were ambivalent. In a survey carried out in 1947 (Thomas 1948) to assess the extent of interest in full-time work for women, for example, the results showed that two-thirds of the women surveyed disapproved of women working longer hours. These conclusions are hardly surprising responses, however, to a survey carried out in 1947 when memories of wartime hardships would have been vivid. But as Elizabeth Roberts (1984) found in her oral histories with working class women in the North West – a region where there is a long tradition of women's employment (McDowell and Massey 1984) – women who worked full-time were certainly not regarded as emancipated by their contemporaries but rather as drudges to be pitied.

These attitudes modified as the 1950s progressed and as more married women entered the labour market. However, their participation on a part-time basis barely disturbed the gender division of labour that came to dominate the post-war years of growth. As a long effort by feminist scholars addressing employment has established, one of the key elements of gender inequality in advanced industrial societies lies in the relationships enacted through the gendered division of labour in paid and domestic work (Okin 1989; Pateman 1988; Phillips 1987). As I explored in Chapter 2, this gender division of labour is based on an ideology of separate spheres for men and women, embodying widespread assumptions about the social construction of masculinity and femininity that influence the social construction of gendered identities and the moral responsibilities attached to these identities. While women's moral responsibility and role in life was to be the care of others in the private domain of the household, increasingly associated with the nuclear family, men's was the care of others through their individual efforts in the labour market. Institutionally, the entire society is organised around the assumption that childcare and care for other dependants should be provided primarily by family members – almost always a woman – without compensation. Often labelled 'traditional', this gendered division of labour almost certainly reached its apotheosis in the mid-twentieth century in Great Britain (and the USA). It was into this moral climate that Latvian women and, not much later, women from the Caribbean entered Britain as workers rather than as mothers which, as I have argued, influenced their reception in Great Britain. However, despite the significance of this extreme gender division of labour, it is important to remember that post-war Britain remained a society in which significant inequalities based on class and ethnicity divided women and men and stratified the population into identifiable groups with widely differing access to resources, incomes, wealth, standards of living and daily lives. Despite the growing similarities in many women's lives that I documented earlier as they single-handedly undertook almost all the domestic work then necessary to keep a household running, women from working class backgrounds or married to men in working class occupations were themselves more likely to be forced into the labour market where they faced a far more constrained set of opportunities for reasonable and rewarding employment than their middle class sisters. These women perhaps really were drudges to be pitied, although as we shall see some of the Latvian women, especially but not only those who became nurses, also found considerable satisfaction in their paid work.

The key sector of employment for working class young women before the war had been domestic service. In 1931, for example, an astonishing 31.1% of the female workforce aged between 14 and 20 was in 'personal service'. During the Second World War, the numbers in domestic service declined dramatically as women from all class backgrounds undertook a wider range of employment in response to the war effort. At the end of the war, employment in light industry – in the manufacture and assembly of consumer goods, for example – and especially in the service sector grew, accompanied by a noticeable shift of women workers out of manual employment and into white collar jobs. By the end of the 1950s, women had become the majority employees in clerical and sales work (see Table 6.3), whereas their share of total employment in manufacturing had fallen to a quarter. But many working class women were still employed in factories, in dead end jobs with no prospects. After the war, the types of manual work undertaken by women tended to be classified as unskilled rather than skilled. And for working class women with few educational credentials, even the

Table 6.3: Occupational distribution of employed women as a percentage of all employed persons, 1931–61

Occupation	1931	1951	1961
Employers, proprietors	20	20	20
White collar	36	42	44
clerk	46	60	65
foreman, inspector	9	13	10
higher professional	7	8	10
lower prof, technician	59	53	51
manager, administrator	13	15	15
salesman (sic), shop assistant	37	52	55
All manual	29	26	26
skilled	21	16	14
semi-skilled	43	38	39
unskilled	15	20	22
Total working population	30	31	32

Source: National Census

expanding white collar office sector brought limited prospects with few opportunities for promotion. It seems, however, that higher wages in factories were a partial compensation for the monotony, drudgery and lower status of factory employment as the differential that had opened up during the war between factory and office work persisted throughout the 1950s (Fowler 1995).

Class differentials in women's employment participation were exacerbated by differences in ethnic origin and nationality and by in-migration as the post-war period advanced. The growing numbers of migrant women workers from the 1950s found themselves in the most disadvantaged positions in the labour market, recruited for the types of work that British-born women were least prepared to undertake. As Rex and Tomlinson (1979, p 107) argued: 'whereas the white woman typically becomes a secretary or a shop worker, the immigrant woman works in a factory, or in a hospital, or rather less frequently in service industries.' And as Morokovasic (1991) has noted, in an analysis of more recent flows of women migrants into 'Fortress' Europe, immigrant and refugee women are amongst the most exploited in the labour market. Even if migrants do not enter the country as units of labour, as economic migrants, as the Latvian EVW women did, but as asylum seekers or as trailing family members, they usually enter the labour market soon after their arrival to counter the economic hardships most migrants experience. These migrant women workers find themselves firmly positioned on the bottom rungs of 'the wage, social security and social-status ladder' (Morokovasic 1991, p 75), often in informal work situations, unable to gain access to more secure employment with better prospects. Latvian women, as they moved from their controlled and allocated occupations, or in many cases remained in similar work, also found themselves disadvantaged and in the main competing with other migrants for the types of jobs that were of no interest to British women. But even here, at the bottom end of the labour market, they had some advantages, based on their white skins, their middle class origins (of some) and their deserved reputation for hard work.

In the next chapter I explore how the 25 women who came to Britain as EVWs combined employment with the reconstruction of a type of family life that they themselves had experienced, usually as children, in Latvia. Although Latvian women were not to fulfil the hope of the British government that they would marry British men, most of them did marry and have children, many of whom became British citizens. Indeed, just as the government had hoped, these women became mothers of future Britons, even if their fathers were Latvians rather than British men. But in most cases these women themselves were reluctant to apply for British citizenship. Their loyalties continued to lie with Latvia and much of their energy was invested in reconstructing an idealised version of Latvian community over these years. This was an unexpected outcome, not the hoped for assimilation. The Ministry of Labour officials who recruited these women in Germany probably would have been surprised at how little these women's loyalties and nationalist ambitions changed over the years in the UK, had they ever been interested enough to ask them again in the decades after Tannahill's (1958) study in the mid-1950s.

CHAPTER 7

PLACE, LOCALITY AND GENDERED LOCAL CULTURES

In this chapter, I move from the discussion of the general conditions of women's lives in post-war Britain to look at the specifics of the 25 Latvian women's lives as their stay in the UK lengthened from months into years. I look at the types of paid employment that Latvian European Voluntary Workers (EVWs) undertook after they were released from their legally-required period as involuntary or directed labourers, both in the formal and informal labour markets, in family businesses and otherwise and assess the extent to which they achieved occupational and social mobility in the post-war decades. I also explore the conflicts and contradictions of everyday life and their resolution and capture something of the pleasures and delight, as well as toil and strife, these women experienced as they combined employment with marriage and motherhood. Next, in the following chapter, the focus is extended, moving out from the home to address Latvian's women's community involvement and their stalwart efforts to establish forms of communal solidarity through political and other forms of organising in the UK. In this current chapter, however, the emphasis is not only on the types and conditions of work that Latvian women undertook in the labour market in 1950s Britain, on their home lives and they ways in which they combined the two sets of responsibilities but also on the places in which they lived in their initial years. Their geographical location in particular parts of the country played a significant part in structuring the opportunities and disadvantages they faced in their lives in Britain.

As feminist historians and geographers have documented, there is considerable evidence that persistent and long-standing differences between places affects people's lives. Analysts have shown that there are evident differences at a range of spatial scales from the national to the local in what have been variously termed gender contracts (Fosberg *et al* 1998) or gender bargains (Kandiyoti 1988). The ways in which men and women negotiate the gender division of paid and caring work that makes up the total social organisation of labour (TSOL) vary between and within nation states. At the level of the locality, for example, differences in the structure of local and regional labour markets both affect and reflect the ways in which men and women combine paid work and domestic labour and an expanding number of feminist geographers have begun to document empirically the ways in which 'geography matters' (Massey 1984) in structuring and differentiating gender divisions of labour across the space-economy. As I outlined in Chapter 2, regional variations in gender divisions of labour that developed with industrialisation in Great Britain continued to be reflected in and affected local geographies of work and caring in the twentieth century. During the first part of the last century, before the Second World War, a marked spatial division of labour was evident in which regional economies not only tended to specialise in particular economic activities but also exhibited a distinctive gender division of labour. In regions dominated by heavy male-employing industries, such as coal mining and iron and steel manufacturing, employment opportunities for women were more limited than in, for example, regions where the textile industry was significant (notwithstanding high female unemployment in the textile industry in the 1930s and even during the war when output increased, textiles, especially cotton textiles continued to shed labour (Hennessy 1993)) or in the expanding local labour markets of the more affluent southern regions where the service sector as well as light manufacturing created opportunities for women's participation even before the end of the war. It was into this regional pattern of specialisation and gender divisions of labour that Latvian women were inserted between 1946 and 1949, at the very time that it began to change.

Structuring the TSOL (or deciding who does what at home and at work)

Men's and women's decisions about how to divide all those tasks that have to be done to maintain a household – the multiple responsibilities for earning a wage in the labour market, looking after children and other dependants (often elderly relatives for Latvian migrants), doing the housework, decorating, maintaining the growing number of consumer durables that became accessible even to working class households during the 1950s and 1960s – are taken within a nexus of relational ties that both differentiate and bind social groups, whether based on class, gender, ethnicity or co-location. Further, a set of social assumptions and values about femininity, motherhood and child rearing that take a particular national form at any one time but which are also subject to regional variation influence the decisions that households make. These decisions therefore are social ones, not just individual decisions based on negotiations between two (or more) individuals within the privacy of their home. Thus these ties – of kith, kin, ethnicity and value positions – structure decisions both about labour market participation and about men's and women's respective roles and their claims on resources. People of different nationalities, from different classes, particular backgrounds or different generations, have particular ideas about who should do what for whom that are based both on individual and societal vales.

In research based on cross-national comparisons Daly and Lewis (2000) have documented the differences that are found between nation states in the value attributed to women's caring responsibilities. As they show, these different value systems find a reflection in diverse forms and rates of state support for mothering and parenting in different countries. Pfau-Effinger (2000) has argued that it is possible to distinguish between a small number of different models of welfare provision in Western nation states, contrasting countries that continue to depend on what might be termed a modified breadwinner model, that is one in which the responsibility for earning a wage is still assumed to be a primarily male responsibility whereas women's role is as a home-based wife and mother (the dominant model of 1950s Britain), from those that are turning towards a dual-earner pattern of employment participation and family resourcing where responsibilities are shared and gender divisions are not so marked. But as a consequence in this latter type, the value placed on mothering may be lower. Some of the Scandinavian nations fall into the first category, whereas the USA and the UK currently seem to be moving towards the latter model.

Within these broad social frameworks which establish the national norms on which gendered social relations are based, individual men and women in different class positions, with different household arrangements and living in different localities, negotiate their respective responsibilities for caring and earning. These local resolutions, however, are equally strongly shaped by social circumstances, by class position and ethnicity, for example, which have an impact on the resources available to families, including money but also informal help from within the family. It seems likely too that migrant families will have ideas about acceptable divisions of labour and responsibilities that have been developed in a different national context from the one in which they find themselves as they search for work and start their families, producing a complex interplay of factors operating across widely different spatial scales. All these factors have an impact on what families decide and whether they choose to, or have to, rely on extra-familial resources and forms of care. It is clear too, then, that what is available in an area, the mix of provision by the market and the state, as well as voluntary forms of care, will affect choices and decisions. Thus, both the local availability of employment and childcare provision has a significant impact on women's propensity to work (England 1996; Gregson and Lowe 1994; Hanson and Pratt 1995; Holloway 1999; Pinch 1984). But Duncan (2003, p 8) argues further that 'regional and local differences in women's employment are not only influenced by geographical variations in the availability of jobs at the local labour market level or by the varying provision of welfare services supporting working women [but] are crucially influenced by local social and institutional ideas about what men and women ought to do'. As he and his colleagues (Duncan *et al* 2003; Duncan and Smith 2002; Duncan and Edwards 1999) have shown, there is a local geography not only in the provision of caring and mothering but also in the value attributed to these forms of work.

Duncan *et al* (2003) identified what they have termed 'gender cultures' that vary between different regions of the UK, in part related to the history of gendered divisions of labour in the workplace and the household in these regions, as well as to the mix of class, ethnicity and religious affiliations among the populations within particular localities. Based on statistical analyses, Duncan and Smith (2002) have shown that there are deep-seated and long-standing differences between, for example, the textile towns of Lancashire and Yorkshire, as well as between Manchester and smaller towns within the North West (see also Glucksmann 2000). There is also a more general north–south distinction between the assumptions and arrangements that are common in these former towns and cities and those that distinguish the smaller towns and suburbia in the South East of England. As I explained in the last chapter, it was in the South that forms of companionate marriage and a conjugal domestic privacy developed most quickly after the war. For Latvian women, directed to, and later choosing to move to particular areas, often in Lancashire or Yorkshire, local differences may have had an impact on how they decided to share the total burden of paid and reproductive work between household members.

In his work with Ros Edwards, Duncan (Duncan and Edwards 1999) has suggested that there are also a number of distinct types of 'gendered moral rationality' that mothers draw upon in making choices about, for example, how to combine paid work and childcare, how to divide household labour and how to choose childcare. These socially and spatially variable 'moral rationalities', they suggest, are the product of an interaction between material circumstances and beliefs about gendered rights and responsibilities. Based on research with single women, Duncan and Edwards (1997, p 71) distinguished three ideal types of what they termed gendered moral rationalities based on women's domestic and employment orientations. The first ideal type is primarily a mother who 'gives primacy to the moral benefits of physically caring for their children themselves over and above any financial benefits of undertaking paid work'. The second they labelled mother/worker integral: women who 'see financial provision through employment as part of their moral responsibilities towards their children' (Duncan and Edwards 1997, p 72) and, thirdly, primarily a worker: women who 'give primacy to paid work for themselves as separate to their identity as mothers' (*ibid*). Sarah Holloway (1998), in her work on how childcare decisions are made in different areas in Sheffield, a working class city in Yorkshire, combined these two sets arguments – about the significance of locality and morality – defining particular 'moral geographies of mothering', which, she suggests, become dominant within particular localities over time in interaction with the local social organisation of childcare provision. Thus, these 'moral geographies' consist of institutions and networks through which notions of 'good mothering' are circulated and include the sorts of decisions and contacts made at local groups as well as more general value systems. Further, as Himmelweit and Sigala (2004) have argued, women's choices about childcare and employment are not static but evolve over time, depending on their experiences and the extent to which they find particular arrangements satisfactory.

In the analysis of the Latvian women's transcripts, I utilised these ideas about moralities, localities and satisfaction. To capture the complexity of their interaction, I prefer the term 'situated understandings', rather than moral rationalities as it is a less judgmental term to capture the decisions made by parents as they combine paid work and childcare (see also Jarvis, Pratt and Cheng-Chong 2001 for a similar argument). This term or approach recognises the competing discourses of appropriate forms of mothering and care arrangements that women (and men) face, as well as the complex ways in which women modify and renegotiate their values over time in interplay with their experiences of using a particular type of childcare or of finding work. These factors interact with the web of social relationships (with partners, other family members, work colleagues, local community structures) through which women's self-identity is constituted (Griffiths 1995). Thus, commitments to care for kin apply to specific relationships in particular times and places and are established through processes of active negotiation and renegotiation over time (Finch and Mason 1993; Mason 1996). For young Latvian women moving into the open labour market at the start of the 1950s, establishing relationships within and beyond the community of other

Latvian EVWs with whom they have contact, marrying, starting families and so coming into contact not only with local women in the same positions – at work, in ante-natal groups, in hospital, and later at schools – but with the local institutions of the welfare state; a network of ideas, discourses and power relations influences the ways in which they organise their lives and divide the responsibilities with their husbands.

The choice about this organisation, however, is not an entirely 'free' one for women as they are constrained by the dominant moral beliefs about feminine identity. A commitment to care – for partners and elderly dependants as well as for children – is for women deeply implicated in the construction and maintenance of their moral identity and reputation. This commitment to care exercises a powerful hold over individual women, Mason (1996) argues, precisely because the responsibility emerges through negotiation within social and personal relationships and in this way is experienced by individuals as a consequence and reflection of their own choices and decisions, rather than being seen simply as a set of pre-given expectations about men's and women's respective roles. It seems then, to many women, that these choices about caring are personal choices, rather than societal ones. Nevertheless, notwithstanding this experience of choice, such negotiations are intimately shaped by the social and cultural contexts in which they occur, including the ideologies of motherhood and child rearing dominant at any one time and the often unequal social positioning of the parties to the negotiation. In the 1950s, as I documented in the previous chapter, women's wage-earning capacity in the labour market was lower than men's which, in combination with the widespread social commitment to the establishment of a particular domestic version of family life, made it seem a 'rational' choice for men to take the breadwinner role and women to shoulder the bulk of caring commitments. At the end of the war, too, women and men were deeply affected by wartime dislocations and hardships. For the native British population and, in particular, for EVWs, where both men and women had experienced the loss of home, family and, in the case of people from the Baltic States, their very country, the desire to rebuild a secure home and family life was extremely strong.

Whilst different social groups may display different situated understandings, both the social groupings and the understandings expressed are fluid and changeable. The processes of decision-making for individuals will always be shaped by the webs of relationships in which they are enmeshed. Thus, for Latvian women, their notions of 'good mothering' in the 1950s were based on a combination of their own experiences as children, advice passed on and tales told by their mothers if they too were in Britain, ideas from talk in the workplace, in the factories and hospitals where many of these women continued to work after being released for their labour contracts, as well as on the deeply gendered national policy framework at the time in which notions of childcare and rearing based on an idealised middle class concept of the family were dominant. Thus, the national ideology about women's place, the belief in the 1950s that mothers should be at home, is filtered through geographical differentiation at the local level. Within this nexus of relationships and at a time in which the former EVW population was attempting to establish a version of 'normal' family life at a time of severe economic constraints, these women negotiated a gendered division of domestic and paid labour within what were often multigenerational households.

Although Latvian EVWs deviated from the hegemonic ideological construction of femininity, initially through their involuntary labour and later, seeking employment through economic necessity, their employment and domestic arrangements histories were affected by their location as well as by their personal circumstances. Thus, through a complex interplay of local labour market opportunities, local attitudes to women's work and mothering, the types of employment to which Latvian women (and their future husbands) were allocated, as well as their 'in between' or hybrid positioning in Britain, differences as well as commonalities in their lives in contemporary Britain were constructed. In different places, Latvian men and women began to remake their lives. As I explore below, Latvian EVWs, as Elvia presciently remarked, constructed for themselves lives that continued to be largely and remarkably separate from those of the rest of the British population as the post-war years passed. The British government's hope for assimilation never materialised as these women clung tenaciously to a sense of themselves as Latvian nationals, despite the loss of independence of their homeland.

Latvian women's lives in the 1950s and 1960s: combining employment and motherhood

One of the most noticeable features of these women's lives is how hard they worked, both for love in the home where many of them supported and looked after their parents as well as children, and for money in the labour market. In an era when domesticity was the ideal and idealised option for married women with small children, these women were exceptional in their continuous participation in paid work. Table 7.1 provides a summary of their lives between 1946/49 and 1960.

The particular ways in which they combined their 'dual roles', however, were, in part, affected by the social and material circumstances in which they found themselves in different localities that structured the opportunities and constraints on their paid work and so on their domestic lives. As well as the availability of different forms of work, locally and regionally-specific beliefs about whether women should take up paid work or primarily be home-makers influenced the ways in which Latvian women were seen to conform to or transgress local cultural expectations. Further, the extent to which they might draw on networks of support from kin and countrymen was also partly dependent on the type and location of their first jobs. Those women who had been allocated to private domestic service, or to domestic work in isolated hospitals, for example, were less likely to be surrounded by fellow country folk than the women who were sent to the cotton or woollen textiles industries; as the previous chapter showed, they were more likely to be working with other Latvian women. Furthermore, living in an industrial town also meant that these women were more likely to find themselves closer to male Latvian EVWs, to the men who had been directed to work in the iron and steel industries or into coal mining in adjacent labour markets under the Westward Ho! scheme. In addition, the textile districts,

Table 7.1: EVWs' jobs, family status and childcare arrangements, late 1940s to 1960

Name	Born	1st EVW job	D of marr	No of children	Childcare	Work when children small
Agate	1927	textiles	1950	2	none	school dinner lady
Agnese	1926	hospital domestic	1952	2	mother	nurse on nights
Anya	1930	textiles	1952	4	husband's mother	part-time nursing
Anyuta	1929	domestic	1950	2	none	piece work at home
Beate	1927	hospital domestic	n/a			
Brigita	1930	textiles	1949	1	neighbour	textiles f/t + lodgers
Dagnija*	1919	clerk in camps	1948	1	none	housewife
Diana	1920	hospital domestic	1951	2	none	housewife
Elvira	1920	textiles	1950	3	neighbour	textiles + lodgers
Eva	1928	hospital domestic	1949	5	mother	ran guest house
Grieta	1918	domestic	1943	2	father-in-law	dental nurse
Helena	1927	textiles	1946	2	nursery	factory work
Ida	1914	hospital domestic	1948	2	husband	cleaning
Ilona*	1926	hospital domestic	1950	2	none	housewife
Jelena	1931	textiles	1950	1	mother	farm and mill
Lina	1931	maid in private h/h	1950	2	Latvian friend	mill and shop
Lize	1928	hospital domestic	1950	2	mother	factory work
Lizina	1928	textiles	1950	1	mother/self	shift work in mill
Mara	1916	domestic	1942	1	friends	cleaning
Monika	1930	hospital domestic	1953	1	mother/self and nursery	nursing p/t
Natalija	1926	domestic	1954	1	mother	hospitaldomestic
Pauline	1924	domestic	1953	1^	n/a	
Valda	1919	hospital domestic	1953	2	neighbour	postal assistant + lodgers
Velta	1926	hospital domestic	1949	2	mother	nurse, then shop buyer
Vieda*	1930	maid in h/hold	1949	2	au pair	housewife

* Married to Englishmen. Although the numbers are small, all three women married to non-EVW men were not employed when their children were under 11, whereas all but one Latvian woman continued to work.

^ Died under three months old.

especially in Lancashire, but also in Yorkshire, have a tradition of women's full-time work (Glucksmann 2000). In these areas, women have long been seen as workers as well as home-makers and mothers and, at the time when Latvian women first entered Britain, had not yet begun to experience the rapid rates of de-industrialisation and unemployment of more recent decades, although even then the textile industry was losing workers. Women in more isolated communities without the support of local traditions of women's paid work or community-based support from their compatriots may have felt a stronger pressure to conform to idealised views of domestic femininity.

Gender bargains and local gender cultures

In the rest of this chapter then, the variations in the ways in which women combined their paid work with domestic responsibilities are investigated, in an attempt to assess the relative significance of 'local gender cultures' or what I have termed situated understandings of appropriate gender roles. Did Latvian women find that local ideas affected their decisions about how to live in 1950s Britain? To what extent did they conform to one or other of Duncan and Edwards's idealised categories? Did they exhibit one of the three gendered moral rationalities Duncan and Edwards defined or are perhaps these distinctions less relevant to the circumstances of married women, with husbands who might be able and willing to share caring responsibilities? Or perhaps, their common origins and the experiences of loss and migration shared by Latvian women united them in efforts to recreate an idealised Latvian family that had more in common with the domestic hegemony that at the time dominated British culture than with either local working class patterns and beliefs or with the new negotiations beginning to emerge among middle class couples from the 1950s onwards? Re-establishing a stable family life was an important part of countering the sense of loss and dislocation among the EVW population and, as bell hooks (1991) insists, it is important not to neglect the home as a source of strength and a site of resistance for minority women. For Latvians in Britain, their homes were perhaps important as a place of resistance to the forces of history and the relations of power that positioned EVWs as supplicants and as highly regulated alien workers in 1940s Britain. It was in the home, and as I shall show later in the organisation of cultural events, that Latvian EVWs were most easily able to re-establish a version of 'normal' life based on the traditions and customs that they had learnt as children and teenagers growing up in Latvia.

Both Latvian men and women were quick to enter matrimony on arriving in Britain and most of the marriages have lasted. It is interesting that in a discussion about the failure of mixed marriages (between Latvian men and British women) Tannahill (1958, p 90) quotes a Latvian man who placed the blame on the British side. British women, he argued, were too independent to accept the husband as master of the house and, furthermore, as the type of partner EVW men were likely to meet were sometimes 'girls of a rather poor upbringing' they had little sympathy, he suggested, with the different customs and beliefs of these European migrants. A Lithuanian respondent was perhaps more honest when he also suggested that many EVW men tended to excessive drinking! It seems clear, however, that the establishment of a traditional form of patriarchal marriage in which men continued to be dominant in decision-making, even though most women were in employment during all or the majority of their married lives was most common amongst these couples.

As the initial geographical location, combined with the type of work, as well as nationally specific views about the nature of marriage and appropriate gendered responsibilities and behaviours, had a clear impact on what is now termed work/life balance decisions, the lives of the textile workers are discussed first and then compared with those of the women initially allocated to domestic work, whether in hospitals or elsewhere.

Gender cultures and communal support in textile towns

The women who had 'volunteered' to became textile workers quickly settled into a 'dual role' in Britain, combining continued paid work with domestic work and with childcare. Before marriage, and indeed afterwards, despite the hard work described in the last chapter and poor living conditions in these mill towns, young Latvian women were able to benefit from the establishment of locally-based Latvian communal activities, which were organised right from 1946. Choirs and dance groups were set up, language classes organised, Lutheran churches founded and the women textile workers also quickly established shared households based on ethnicity and family ties. Through communal savings schemes, terraced houses in towns such as Bradford and Bolton were bought, as property was relative inexpensive in these northern towns, and rooms were let to other Latvians. In the early years, married couples, parents and children and acquaintances all shared a house, often living a single room with shared access to a kitchen and bathroom (when there was one). As I shall illustrate later, for many women EVWs providing rooms and meals was either a significant supplement to the incomes from their paid work or an acceptable alternative way to contribute to the total household income while 'working' at home to care for their dependants.

All the young women allocated to the textile industry soon married, ending their status as single independent women that had been one of the key criteria in their recruitment. In the space of a few busy years after arriving in Britain they married, established households, typically in the locality to which they had first been directed, and most of them had children. As several women had succeeded in bringing other members of their family to Britain – usually their sisters or mothers but sometimes fathers too, these households typically included several generations or sets of interconnected relatives, rather than the small nuclear family then coming to dominate Britain. Helena, for example, married almost immediately after she arrived in 1946, and all the textile workers, except Anya who married in 1952, were married by 1950 (see Table 7.1) and quickly became mothers.

Unlike their English peers, however, most of these women continued in employment even when their children were young. Many, although not all of them, continued to work in the mills or moved into other forms of manual work.

Helena, for example, had initially been allocated work in Courtaulds 'in viscose, where you make the threads', which she left before completing the two years that had been required of her. She moved to a Goodyear factory where the wages were higher for a short time: 'I was trimming the edges from soles and heels. It was sitting down so that was good but it was hard and dirty work and dangerous. Oil dripping onto two turning blades and if you weren't careful many of a time you cut your [finger] tips off.' One of the first to marry, Helena's children were born in 1948 and 1949 and she returned to Goodyear's on a part-time basis as soon as they went to school. Other women initially allocated work in the textile industry either stayed there or returned to the industry after trying something else. Lizina, for example, worked in textiles almost all of her working life, apart from a brief nine-month period when she tried assembly-line work in a factory making TVs. Like Helena, she valued this job because 'it was sitting down work' but 'it was so boring and I didn't last long'. She saw an advertisement for morning shift work (in fact from 6.30 am until 2 pm) in a local mill and applied. 'I got it. Winding, so I were back where I'd started.'

Jelena also returned to mill work after a spell in agriculture. She worked right through the years of child-rearing with only a few weeks' break at the time of childbirth. She had been allocated work in the textile industry as an EVW, and then in 1950 she had moved into farm work with her Latvian husband so that they could be together, before returning to a mill to work. Here she explains how she met her husband, in a disarmingly frank statement about the marriage prospects of single Latvian women at the time. Her comments also include a thoughtful reflection on the difficult position of those young Latvian men who had been recruited into the Latvian Legion by the Nazis. It seems likely that her husband came to Britain as part of the Westward Ho! Scheme, although strictly he should not have been eligible:

> I met my husband in Buckinghamshire at a wedding of someone I knew. She was getting married to a Latvian from one of the agricultural camps and she invited four girls to the wedding and I met my husband there. He was already in the agricultural camps. So I went to the wedding. There was all these lads there and we could take our pick because there was a shortage of girls. They had all been in the army. They were conscripted in the army although that was against the Geneva Convention. They were called volunteers but they weren't really; they were conscripted. My husband was just 18 and he had just finished school when he was conscripted and at the end of the war they were prisoners of war in Belgium and the Belgians didn't understand their position and they were treated as Germans. They had quite a hard life there. There was a lot of young men about in England, the Latvians and so I met him in about 1950 and we got married in 1951.

When her son was born in 1952 on the farm, she told me 'I put him in a pram and took him in the fields with me'. Later when she moved back to mill work in north Cheshire she continued working, combining paid work with her family responsibilities by drawing on both the local tradition of shift work and the support of her mother. 'My mother and I were both there, doing shift work so whoever wasn't at work looked after him. We brought him to the mill at the changeover and whoever wasn't working took him home again.' Lizina, who took six months' leave from her job in a Bolton mill when her son was born in 1951, had the same arrangement: 'I was working the evening shift and my mother days. I used to go to meet her with him on me arm. She'd walk out, I'd hand him over and I'd walk in.' Other women working in the textile industry had similar arrangements, sometimes sharing the caring responsibilities with their husbands rather than their mothers. Lina, for example, who was working shifts at a Courtaulds factory in the Midlands when she became pregnant, took a short break on the birth of her first child in 1952 but returned to work within a few months. Like Jelena, the shift system in the textile industry allowed the household to manage without paying for childcare.

> The first child came along and for a period I didn't work and things were quite hard so, by that time he (her husband) was doing two shifts. So for a while we did like the opposite shifts so we could look after the child. The factory was quite close and we could change over very easily and the child would sleep at midday and so we did opposite shifts.

By the time her second child was born in 1954, she and her husband had both left the factory and had opened a grocery and continental foods shop. Again, Lina felt compelled by economic need to continue full-time work in the shop when the child was born, even though she had two young children.

> I worked in the shop and we had baby sitters, Latvian women, but later on I worked part-time and I got people working in the shop instead of me, part-time, so I could spend more time with the children. But at the beginning I had to be there myself. It was quite difficult really.

Acquiring a home

For most of these women workers, as is common among migrants, economic necessity was the key factor in their decision to remain in the labour market, even after the birth of their children. For this reason they are less likely to conform to Duncan and Edwards's ideal types of gendered moral rationality, or at least not through choice. Once they completed their initial compulsory period of work and were free to move, they had to establish themselves in the housing market and struggle to achieve a decent standard of living for themselves and their families in a country in which they had none of the advantages conferred by recognised educational qualifications or property ownership. For many, finding somewhere to live independently outside the control of their employers and of British landlords was a crucial part of their decisions about employment once released from their contracts. It was usually this desire, even if housing initially had to be shared, that lay behind most women's decision to remain in the labour market. In their early years in Britain, many EVWs began to buy residential property. Both as individuals and then later as families, EVWs started their independent housing careers in Britain in shared accommodation, almost always in furnished rooms in multiple occupation houses, sometimes let by indigenous landlords but more typically in rooms let by Latvian landlords. One of the key motivations to move, once their indentured work was over, was their shock at the generally poor housing conditions that were common in northern towns and, indeed, more widely. Several women commented on their surprise at finding how primitive

British standards of living were in the late 1940s. The lack of indoor toilets, hot water and central heating shocked them. Most homes still relied on coal fires which not only polluted the air (smog was common and the first Clean Air Act (1956) almost a decade away) and made towns look grimy (there were no high pressure hoses to clean bricks and masonry until the 1960s) (Hennessy 1993)) but also increased women's domestic work. Poor housing conditions, especially in the private rented sector were a key spur to Latvian in-migrants to aim for home ownership as soon as was financially possible. Here, Eva comments on the rented room in which she started her married life:

> First place, oh it was an awful, a little bedsitter above a bakery. My husband said 'oh, I can't get anywhere to live, a room or anything'. He was lucky; he came out of the camp and lived with an English family in Coventry – they rented out rooms – with his friend. So he found a room, he let me see it. We got married in 1949, on 30 April and I said 'oh, it is all right'. I thought it didn't matter what it is like as I would improve it. Wherever the Latvians go they always like to improve their surroundings. I said it's all right but we didn't stay very long there because the landlady was nasty. Those days you had to put 10 pence in the bath to get hot water and it was included in the rent. But we could only have the bath maybe once a week or something but I said to my husband 'but I want a bath more often. What about we put our own shilling?' And we did that and I went into the bath and the landlady had turned off the hot water. She didn't see I had put my own 10 pence in. She was simply nasty. It wasn't very nice.

Buying property then was seen as an important way to improve living conditions. As is common among many migrant groups, forms of community saving schemes were established to enable households to gain a foothold on the housing ladder. Several women before or as they married pooled resources with their parents or in-laws, and sometimes, but less commonly, with friends of the family, to get on the housing ladder. This was Agnese's route to home ownership:

> Anyway, we decided that we should marry some time and in autumn we decided to buy our own house. My mother's friends lent us £100 here, £50 there and my mother and her friend, of course, gave us some money as well and came to live with us. And they lived in one attic, my future husband in the other attic. I lived in the ground floor front room, and then we had couple with their mother who lived in two bedrooms, all in this terrace house. And so we paid it off, these hundreds of pounds and, you know, in one year. That's how many people started their lives here. Buying a house and filling it with other people until they saved enough money to buy a house and moved out.

Some of the women to whom I talked had also borrowed money through informal channels within the community: forms of self-help savings and loan schemes. One household would purchase a property and rent to the others as all the members of the scheme continued to contribute to each house purchase. Jelena and her mother not only shared childcare but also pooled their resources to buy a terraced house in Hyde in north Cheshire where the two generations lived and throughout the 1950s and also rented rooms to single Latvian men.

Home ownership was a key element in the establishment of a sense of belonging in Britain, even though at the same time, the women to whom I talked insisted that they remained optimistic about returning to Latvia during the first decade of their residence in Britain. In the comment below, Lizina explains the significance of home ownership among the Latvian refugees:

> It wasn't unusual for people like us to buy a house. I think the psychology of it, because if you have a house you have a sort of a foot, a room in the place you are not in somebody's way, you have a house. And also we had to take in lodgers to help with payments and so on so. Every room in the house was let. We only had one room to our selves. That is how everybody did and also some other women sort of cooked for the lodgers which I didn't. Well, I did for one but I don't like cooking for other people but I did for one man. He sort of insisted but some women did for a whole crowd of people, did cooking and what not but I didn't. So, yes, I mean, yes, people wanted their own place. That is how you can explain it. You don't want to be sort of underfoot or in the way of other people all the time, you want to have your own little corner sort of thing. All the lodgers were Latvian, people were looking for places and word was passed round. There were a lot of single men looking for rooms.

For Eva, renting rooms became more than a temporary resolution of housing problems. Her husband was a builder and they moved during the 1950s and early 1960s between a succession of larger and larger houses in which she rented rooms to and provided meals for both families and single men – all of them Latvian. At the same time, she raised five children. Eva never took an independent income from her work. The profits went straight back into the family business and so she would have been recorded as a housewife in official figures. As she worked extremely hard throughout her married life to increase the household income, I have included her among the women who continued in paid labour after marriage and motherhood. When her husband was still working in the pits, for example, the job to which he had been directed as an EVW which he stayed in for some years, they rented for themselves part of a large house, then virtually derelict, which had been used as a stop-over for lorry drivers. They eventually took over the whole place and set up as a business sub-letting rooms with the help of Eva's father. Here, she describes what the house was like when first lived there:

> It was a historical house. So we went there to see the lady. Oh, my God, the place was awful. It has been standing empty over the war. And there were stables further down there were gardens, there was a quite an old clock tower and a lot of land with it. We went in and oh my god she had in there lorry drivers and she never made it up the place, she was thinking maybe of doing it up bit by bit. Oh, and when we looked in the rooms! They slept on the floors, you know and downstairs she had this huge kitchen where she made breakfast for them. And lorry drivers didn't mind how they slept as long as they got their good breakfast, you know ... And she took us upstairs and oh God, the ceiling is falling down. The place is terrible. It is like a nightmare. So we looked over and she took us upstairs and she showed us three rooms in the corner of the house. My husband never having been a handy man said, 'oh we have to bring Dad', my father and we brought Dad and he said 'of course we can do it up. We can do it up'. So she let us have the place.
>
> I had a baby by then. We had a big sitting room, the kitchen was smaller and a bedroom and we done it up very nicely and there was another couple too and they did it up. We shared a bathroom. In the kitchen we didn't have a sink, just a cooker so buckets to take the water out to the toilet and the water to be brought in by hand from the bathroom, you know. It was quite difficult but compared you see, maybe

> compared to the hospital [Eva's EVW placement], it was maybe a little bit backwards going but we thought 'well, it's our home, our own little place'. We bought our furniture hire purchased.

After living there for a year, Eva and her husband took over the lease to the entire house and began to improve it:

> So we got the place, first of all for a year and then the owner said 'we will see whether we will extend the agreement'. So Mum and Dad came to live with us and Dad has a lot of work, lot of work. He done the ceilings, nice and clean and Mum cleaned the house and helped me. But it was hard, you know, we only had this one bathroom in the whole house and I had two children by then. The rooms were in such a state and we had to do it all ourselves. We did it out and we furnished the rooms too and then we let it out as bedsitters.
>
> And a lot of Latvians came to live those days. There was a big kitchen and my husband bought a lot of cookers and each one who rented a flat or a room had his own cooker so they didn't need to wait for anyone else and there was no rush. Then there was some single men, Latvian chaps who lived there and for them I was doing the meals. And oh then we had an Indian couple – for them I didn't cook and then we had an Arab family, I don't know he was maybe studying and his wife and daughter and son lived with us and I cooked for them, so I was busy in that respect. We had a kitchen upstairs and by that time I had my taps and sink in the kitchen but the bathroom! It is amazing how we managed, everybody had their day when they went in the bath. I think they had the sinks in the room too. And by that time I think I had my first washing machine, oh that was a funny machine, with a mangle. I was very happy those days.

Other married couples yearned for a house of their own, but once achieved they often found that the financial demands were high, usually necessitating dual earnings: 'We had nothing when we got the keys to the house, not even a cup and saucer. We had to buy everything. We couldn't save, so I had to work' (Natalija). Earning enough money meant that some women held multiple jobs, usually at the bottom end of the labour market and thus poorly paid, but which was the only way to make ends meet. Here, Lize outlines the jobs she and her husband undertook in the early 1950s:

> It was a difficult time. We were short of money. We had bought two derelict cottages and we were working on them ourselves. Mother was living with us then so she looked after the baby. I did all sorts of work locally – soldering batteries in a radio factory, making rubber tubes to go round car doors. Later I worked in a bakery, then I was a machinist. My husband was in a hosiery factory and for some time we even worked in the evenings too, cleaning offices. Those were hard years.

Local networks and traditions

When I asked about the knowledge of local traditions of women's work, about attitudes to mothering, and the significance of long-established networks of mutual support, these women assumed that I was referring to specifically Latvian mutual aid, as it was almost entirely within the networks established by EVWs that these women would look for support to enable them to continue in employment. In these textile towns, there were sufficient numbers of compatriots within easily accessible distances so that life could be spent almost entirely within a national enclave, in a reimagined and reconstituted Latvian community. British local cultural traditions and customs seemed in fact to have had little bearing on these women's lives and yet, as they were living in towns and localities where women's paid work was not unusual, it may be that these traditions had an indirect impact on their lives, relieving them from local disapproval or their own sense of being different. In these early years, however, their lives, especially outside the workplace, barely overlapped with those of local women. As they explained in the last chapter, when they were still EVWs, they had tended not to socialise with the women with whom they worked and this pattern continued as they moved into other jobs or were released from their obligation – and of course in the early 1950s they were extremely busy with young families. At home, those women who had married Latvian men continued to use their own language, typically bringing up their children to speak Latvian as a first language. Indeed, many of the women told me that their children had spoken not a word of English until they first started school in the mid-1950s. Elvira explained how she did not realise that this would disadvantage her eldest daughter when she started school:

> We speak Latvian all the time at home. First of all when we only had one girl she did not know any English at all when she started school at four. So I sent her to the nursery school at four before proper school at five but she was very quiet for months and never talked. And I realised then poor kid and I thought no, it's wrong in a way, so with the other two we spoke English too and they had their elder sister to talk to too. But we still speak Latvian and they answer in English although they speak Latvian too. When they were younger they went to weekend school, and all the words and the tears and they complained 'what do we want Latvian for? We will never go'. But now [post-independence] they have all been and they said 'good job we learned'.

Indeed Grieta, whose son also spoke only Latvian until he went to school, was not even aware of the official age for starting school in Britain:

> 'I didn't know that at five years they must go to school and the doctor said to me 'have you registered your son for school?' and I said 'why? He is only five years old'. Because in Latvia they start at seven.

Once children reached school age, perforce more contacts between former EVW women and other mothers of similar aged children did develop and they began to have slightly more, although still limited, exposure to local traditions and beliefs. Even so, while geographical concentration and proximity in textile towns undoubtedly had a key influence on these women's lives, longstanding local gender cultures apparently had little direct impact on the negotiations of childcare and domestic labour in the home and the combination of paid and unpaid work.

However, as becomes clear in comparisons of these women's lives with those who had been allocated to different sectors of employment, their initial location as textile workers and their marriage to men also allocated to manual industrial employment in the main in the north of England had another lasting impact. These families were socially and geographically immobile, neither moving elsewhere in Britain nor experiencing social mobility. Until retirement they remained in working class occupations in working class localities. In his work on cultures of mothering, Duncan has suggested that the construction of differences is based on the combination of the specific division of labour in a locality – a economic factor – with local gender cultures. These cultures seem close to what the great socialist critic, Raymond Williams (1980) termed 'structures of feeling': the ways in which economic and social conditions in an area are mutually constituted to produce a distinctive way of living, and as Williams noted, distinctive patterns of political allegiance. He also argued that a particularly distinctive structure of feeling was significant in the north, characterised by both a strong allegiance to left wing politics and labour voting and an extreme gender division of labour, in the workplace and in civic culture, including local political organisations and working men's clubs. But for Latvian families, economic factors – in terms of both the jobs available and the need for men and women to earn an income so that they could begin to accumulate the conventional possessions of everyday living in post-war Britain – led to a rather different way of living. As I have shown, it was not usual for Latvian men to help with childcare. Economic necessity combined with the strong and continuing commitment to building Latvian networks of mutual support thus outweighed the local cultural distinctiveness of the northern towns and the largely separate lives led by local working class men and women. Latvian former EVWs managed their lives largely within the migrant community to which they maintained allegiance and neither local attitudes nor the provision of childcare had much effect on women's decisions to remain in the labour market or the ways in which they combined this with caring for their dependants.

Domestic labourers: escape through social and geographical mobility

The lives of women whose initial allocation was to domestic employment, whether in a private or institutional setting, is now the focus. Ten of the 25 women whom I interviewed initially were allocated to domestic work in hospitals and a further seven women to domestic work either in institutions or in private households. For all of these women, a complicated set of inter-relationships between place and mobility was evident in their early lives in the UK. Unlike the women allocated to jobs in textile towns who tended to remain in the same place and often in the same type of work throughout their adult lives, the key theme for these women is their effort to escape from this type of work. The initial location of this group of women – both in a geographical and an occupational sense – then made a considerable difference to their early experiences in Britain. As I argued in the previous chapter, the women working in hospitals and other institutions were far more likely than women who became maids in private households to have co-workers, often other EVW women, but also local women and/or Irish immigrants. But for all these women it was the geographical location of their first job that made the key difference to their opportunities early on in Britain to establish social networks within the Latvian community in Britain. Whether in an institutional or household setting, it was distance to the towns where significant numbers of other

Latvian EVWs lived that seemed to determine these women's strategies. If they were able to travel to communal cultural and religious events without too much difficulty or at too great a cost, then they tended to settle in the place where they were allocated their first employment but women who found themselves in isolated rural areas or small towns moved as quickly as they were able to other areas, even in some cases breaking the legal requirement to remain in their allocated job for two years. Beate, for example, as I explained in Chapter 5, was one of 18 Latvian women sent to a mental hospital in Kent where they were able to create a sense of community locally through the establishment of a choir and a dance group. It was also possible for these women to travel into London in their free time to participate in cultural events organised by the growing Latvian community in the capital. Beata was confirmed in the Lutheran church in London soon after her arrival and she also travelled weekly to the capital for harp lessons. Silvija was also allocated to a job reasonably near London: 'once a week I used to go to London and sometimes there was a Latvian dance, so I went and met other people. It wasn't bad at all.' These women's early circumstances contrast with those of Valda, who had been allocated to a TB sanatorium in a tiny Scottish town where she felt completely isolated as she explained in the earlier chapter.

Nursing as an 'escape'

For the women originally allocated to domestic work in hospitals, in TB sanatoria or in mental hospitals, geographical and occupational location interacted in a particular way in their decisions, leading not only to geographical mobility but also social mobility for several of them. The same 'superior' qualities that had been an important factor for the British government in the initial recruitment schemes also attracted hospital matrons. These Latvian women were not only hard workers but many of them were also prepared to study to improve their social position and, in some cases, regain the middle class status they had foregone on leaving Latvia. In 1948 the National Advisory Council on Nurses and Midwives agreed to proposals that suitable candidates among the EVWs should be trained as nurses and so, in some hospitals, Latvian domestic workers were encouraged to apply to join training schemes: 'the matron was so nice to me; she was encouraging' (Vieda). In other cases, however, it was against considerable odds that individual women were able to jump the gap separating domestic workers from nurses. As Vieda elaborates here, despite the encouragement she received, a rather odd condition was imposed on her acceptance onto a nursing course:

> I met the matron and I said I wanted to do nursing. Once I have a profession I can do anything. That was 1950, I was 20 by then and before she would agree to my training, I had to stay with the matron as her maid in the hospital. To brush up or something. Maybe she wanted to see if I was a suitable sort of girl.

Agnese had less support and encouragement. Indeed, she had to face and ignore the dismissive assumptions of both the hospital dispenser and the matron:

> I asked this man (the dispenser) what are the chances to study pharmacy and he said, 'well, girl, if you have no money, you have no hope to study in England'.

> And, of course, at that time we didn't know there was a world organisation of refugees you know, to help you. Anyway I went to see the matron and asked if I could train as a nurse there. And she said, 'what, and all your friends in the domestic staff!' But she did give me a list of hospitals where you could train and so I applied.

Interestingly, the social mobility afforded by gaining nursing qualifications also brought with it the opportunity for spatial mobility, permitting these women to choose to relocate to towns with a significant EVW population, and so in many cases moving to the types of industrial towns and cities to which their compatriots in the textile industry had been sent in the late 1940s. Thus Agnese, who was originally a hospital domestic allocated to a small hospital in Nottinghamshire, moved to Bradford to complete her nursing training. Agate, who originally had been allocated work as a duffer – changing the spools in a cotton mill near Manchester – had managed after her first year there to be reallocated to domestic work in a TB sanatorium near Hexham in the North East and then later to another domestic job in Halifax General Hospital. 'I was encouraged to start nursing there,' she explained 'but it was only a thought. I'd met a boy working in a pit near Newcastle. When I came to Halifax, he came to Bradford. Nursing just went. Oh well.' Later, however, Agata did return to the health sector, becoming a technician in radiology in Bradford Royal Infirmary. Anya also had a similar early working life – domestic work in Hexham, then a move to Bradford where she too was recruited for nursing and in her case completed it, becoming an SRN in 1953. 'It was hard work and I missed out on the social life in Bradford but at least I had work that I enjoyed.'

It is clear that, once they were permitted to move, the textile towns described above and other industrial towns in the north of England became an important magnet for many Latvian women, attracted by the burgeoning local Latvian organisations. Even those who had not trained as nurses, or had the option like Agata, knew that through their contacts in the local industries they would be able to find employment in these northern towns. Anyuta, for example, who was originally allocated to domestic work in Shrewsbury near the Welsh border, also moved to Bradford and found factory work in a woollen mill, initially as a spinner and then burling and mending (working in spare threads into finished pieces) which was both quieter and better paid than spinning and which later in the 1950s, by doing piece-work at home, she was able to combine with raising her children. 'When children came you could do some pieces at home. A manager bought some pieces to the home. So I was home for him [her son] and I could earn a little bit of money.' When her children went to secondary school she started full-time as an assembly-line worker in an electrical factory. Valda, who had worked in a sanatorium in Scotland and who had herself contracted TB, moved to Chesterfield once she was released from her initial employment. Unlike some of the other women, she rejected the opportunity to train as a nurse. Although she had started a higher education course in the camps, she found that manual employment or other low status work was the only option open to her in Chesterfield:

> I said 'I don't want to go in factory and I don't want to go in hospital any more' and somebody said 'oh, there is good pay on buses'. So, of course, I started on the buses as conductor. I worked from '53 – summer time I started – and our daughter was

> born in 1955, so nearly two years, as conductor. It was hard job, and shifts. Mind you I was younger, but it was good money. Double deckers, up and down. I was very thin then. Especially winter times was very hard but you get used to it. When you need to do it, you have to do it.

Like the women initially allocated to employment in the textile industry, most of these women who started as domestic workers also married within the Latvian community and combined the early years of child rearing with paid employment. For the women who completed nursing training the opportunity to do shift work, especially night work, meant that combining caring, household and paid employment with the aid of husbands on alternative shift patterns and, especially, with mothers (or mothers in law) was possible, albeit demanding and exhausting. Anya, for example, returned to nursing on a part-time basis doing a few night shifts each week when her first child was eight months old. Agnese, whose mother lived with her during the early years of her marriage, made the same decision. Here, she explains the arrangements she set in place for childcare during the years when she worked nights as a nurse, and later as a sister. Her comment includes an interesting echo of Bowlby's thesis, showing that she was not unaware of the then widely held view about mothers in paid work:

> My mother looked after them when they were smaller and when it was holidays she came and looked after them and then went home and I always got up at four o'clock [in the afternoon]. When they got home from school I was always there. They weren't children who went with a key in the hand.

But as combining work, whether on a full- or part-time basis, and motherhood was common among Latvian women, and of course, for many working class British women, especially in the textile towns, most of these women did not seem to feel in any way that they were less legitimate mothers, although they all recognised the compromises they often had to make. One or two women expressed regrets but also argued that they had had no choice at the time. Here is Lina's reflection: 'Looking back I shouldn't have done it but that is what we did ... a child needs more attention, needs the mother more, you know.' Most women, however, did not express similar regrets and strongly rejected the notion that 'the image of the mother in the home, however unrealistic, haunted and reproached the lives of wage earning mothers' (Rich 1977, p 52).

Motherhood and childcare

As I noted above, joint household decision-making, often including the older generation, was a key part of getting all the necessary work of social reproduction done most efficiently. It was common for the parents of EVW workers to share accommodation with their children and in a number of households, the mothers of the women to whom I talked had given up work to care for their grandchildren, enabling their daughters to take a better job with longer hours. Leaving 'work' or reduced hours also often entailed new forms of income-generating activities for women, such as taking in lodgers and improving houses, as well as financially unrewarded but essential work such as caring for those, in the main elderly parents, for whom adjustment to life in the UK proved difficult.

While all the women who became mothers regarded motherhood as a key part of their lives, as Table 7.1 shows, complete withdrawal from paid employment apart from when their children were very young was atypical. Of all the women who married EVW men, 22 in total, several woman (Diana, Elvira and Vieda among them) were not employed during the early years of their children's lives but all of them, apart from Diana who did not re-enter the labour market until 1972, had returned to work by the early 1960s so that the family budget would stretch to owner occupation and the purchase of a gradually growing range of consumer durables. Valda, for example, who described her work on the buses above, worked full-time until the birth of her daughter and later her son and then returned to full-time employment, as a post office clerk, in the early 1960s, after working on a part-time basis in the intervening years. She describes below how life became a little easier for the family as her contribution to the total budget increased:

> I didn't have a washing machine till I started work again after the children. To tell you the truth we were very hard up at that time when the children were small ... Up till I started work, we were very hard off really. If we needed something you had to count your pennies but I didn't have a washing machine then. I did all the housework. Coal fires were dirty. We didn't have any fridge cos we didn't need it! We had a big cellar, a cold cellar, then.
>
> Life was bit easier when I started at the Post Office. Then we bought a car it was small and second hand but it was all right. I didn't drive. I still can't even though I have a mechanical mind.
>
> We had a holiday nearly every summer. We went in caravan or a bungalow – Wales, Scarborough, Isle of Wight and Brighton. We have been to a lot of places really. We always managed to have a good time somewhere.

Diana, as I have just noted, was the exception in her singular commitment to child-rearing. In the long extract from her narrative below, she outlines the reasons for delaying her return to the labour market, as she talks about her early working life after leaving the hospital to which she was sent as an EVW and then her eventual return to paid work when her children reached their mid-teens. Among all the women with children, Diana was the one who most clearly held to an ideology of mothering in which the moral benefits of physically caring for her children herself were overriding. For the other women who left the labour market, their absence was typically much shorter; they often returned on part-time basis when their children first went to school. For these women the cost and difficulties of arranging childcare were an important factor in their choices, although this is not to deny their commitment to mothering. But it was only Diana who was so clear about the role of a mother in children's lives. She was also clear about the material costs her decision entailed.

During her married life Diana lived in Leicester in the British Midlands where about 200 Latvians lived in the 1950s:

> And when I got married I said that although the hospital job was all right for me, but I had to work Saturdays and alternate Sundays and my husband, he was an electrician and he, he was Latvian, and this hospital was sometimes 8 til 2 and 4 to 8, and I said I didn't want it. They said 'stay. We can change the hours' but I didn't

> want it. Having shifted from place to place, now I wanted to be with somebody ... I got married in 1951. We had a song festival in 1949, or was it 1950, I can't remember now and I was in charge of supplying sandwiches and I met him there. ...
>
> After I was married I worked in different places. First I worked in a factory and then I worked in a café and then I had my daughter and I decided if I had children I want to bring them up, even if we have to struggle. I had my daughter and then a son in 1956 and I didn't work, well paid work til my boy was 14, my daughter was 16, 17. And then again I started to work: in a factory because I could have Saturday and Sunday free. Everywhere else you see, in a hospital you had to work Saturday.
>
> I found work in a shoe factory, making children's shoes. It was piece-work but you know I have been through so many things, you learn and you cope. It's a special name: it's called skiving. It's a special machine and you have to work very hard. The leather tops are cut out and you have to cut to make it thinner so if you put a sole it is not so thick, it turns round. Different things, but I learned that. I worked full time and we were buying. At the beginning my husband had a house with a job and we paid rent and he was an electrician with a brickyard and when the brickyard changed hands they wanted to get rid of the houses. And they said if you want to you can buy the house and we thought what else can we do, we have nowhere to go and that's when I decided to work and all my money went to buying the house, that's how it was. I stayed at the factory until I was 60. It suited me. There was the shops at dinner time I could do my shopping. On Saturdays I cleaned the house and everything and then on Sundays we sometimes went out.
>
> When I got my first washing machine? That was very late, very late, I think it was the 1970s or something and then it was second hand because we had to pay for the house and the children's clothes. They cost quite a lot of money. But slowly. We didn't have television for ages, the first colour television was when my husband retired in 1979. And we never had a car, we couldn't afford that but, do you know, we were very happy together, that was the main thing. And my sister lived near. Her husband was a gardener and there was a house, a bungalow and they lived there and at weekends we went there. And I had two children and she had two and they played together. Sometimes you don't need much to be happy.

Three other women – Dagnija, Ilona and Vieda, all of whom married a British resident, although only Dagnija's husband was born in the UK – withdrew from the labour market after marriage or when they had their first child. Interestingly in all three cases these women married men in middle class occupations who were able to afford to buy into the domestic ideology of the 1950s. Dagnija and Ilona agreed with Diana that motherhood was, and should have been, their key role in the 1950s, but for them it was not necessarily a financial hardship to assume this role. Of the three of them it was only Vieda who expressed some dissatisfaction with her life as a full-time housewife. She told me that she felt trapped by her husband's insistence that she must withdraw from the labour market, clearly enunciating a then common belief about how the worth of a man was reflected in the provision he made for his wife: 'it was all for show, you know, to show he was making good money and could afford a wife at home. I was so bored; I had too little to do, and we even had an au pair.' Vieda eventually returned to nursing when her younger child was a teenager, in the face of some opposition from her husband.

For most of the 25 young women, however, who came to Britain as refugees and directed labourers over half a century ago, the domestic ideology of the British state and the wider population during the 1950s barely had an impact, despite the regrets and guilt mentioned by Lina. But it was also clear that the notions of personal fulfilment through employment that were beginning to develop among middle class British women were insignificant. These Latvian women's reported behaviours were similar to those that Elisabeth Roberts (1984) found among working class women in north Lancashire in the inter-war era, and both support the earlier, then controversial, arguments of Jane Humphries (1977) about joint family decision-making for mutual benefit among working class households. For women whose daily lives involved material hardships, decisions about their own employment were often inseparable from overall household survival strategies. This is not to deny that some women were trapped in unhappy marriages nor to underestimate the sense of loss experienced by many of the individuals – women as well as men – who came to Britain as EVWs to spend most of the rest of their lives in the sort of manual employment that they had never expected to be their lot. Their commitment to hard work was not only to establish independence in Britain but also to be able to provide the sorts of opportunities for their children that they themselves had had to forgo after 1944. A significant proportion of these women's children, for example, were successful at school and nearly half went on to university. But in retrospect some women also regretted the extent to which their own, and especially their husbands', hard work kept them out of the home for long hours. Here, Eva talks rather ambivalently about her husband and the distinct division of labour that characterised her household when her five children were growing up:

> He had a hard time, his mother died when he was 14 and he had three half-brothers as well and I think he wanted to prove something in his life, to do well. Sometimes I thought, when I was young I thought 'my God, we don't see Dad much. He is always doing something, he is always working, he is always away'. I thought is it worth but now I understand more, now I have lost him. And when you get older too you understand more, for a man that is his life, his work, his ambition that is his life. You know the family is not the same. I don't agree that man are like, they are sharing too much now. My boys they like cooking and sharing, but I think sometimes it is too much. I know a woman should not complain if a man does his job and does well, you can't do everything well.

This is an interesting critique of the then prevalent ideology of domesticity, predating the now more common notion that men too might gain from greater domestic involvement, especially with their children, by several decades. Among the Latvian households in the 1950s, where leisure time was a precious commodity, the division of labour in the home tended to follow traditional and strictly gendered lines and it was women who not only carried out the majority of the domestic labour but who also assumed the responsibility for its organisation, whether they themselves were in the labour market at the time or not. As I noted earlier, Latvian men continued to hold strongly patriarchal views about marriage and family life, even though they sometimes helped with childcare when their children were babies, aiming to reconstruct the type of families in which they themselves had been brought up in the inter-war years and most of their wives concurred with these views. It was clear that the strong sense of nostalgia for the way of life that was lost in 1944 was influential. As one woman told me: 'he [her husband] grumbled a bit if I was not a home when he was. He liked to be looked after.' But this same woman also returned to work, finding a manual job in a local factory when her son went to school: 'I just told him I was starting work. He grumbled a bit but it was OK.'

In the 1950s among the population in general, a more equal or companionate version of marriage began to gain ground, albeit unevenly among women and men. In a book published in the mid-1950s, exploring what men and women expected from marriage, Gorer (1955) found that women had higher expectations of companionship, valuing understanding and thoughtfulness most highly in their husbands and selfishness, especially in domestic matters as their greatest failing. Men, on the other hand, wanted wives who were good household managers and who did not nag them, suggesting a fundamental incompatibility in expectations. Indeed, the 1956 Royal Commission on Marriage and Divorce pointed out the 'greater demands imposed by the new style of companionate marriage' (para 45). Similarly, Richards and Elliott (1991, p 47) in a study of marriage in the 1960s and 1970s concluded: 'there is abundant evidence that women, especially, are likely to seek closeness and shared understanding and that their high expectations are not always met.' In the early years of their marriage, Latvian women accepted that holding down hard manual jobs placed pressures on their husbands but many also suggested that in later decades they did develop a form of companionate marriage rooted in joint participation in Latvian communal activities. And even the women who married outside their own community found pleasure in their joint participation in Latvian events. As Ilona, who married 'out', told me: 'I dragged my husband with me into the Latvian community. We had a lot of fun together.'

Almost all of these 25 women remained in largely working class areas all their lives and seldom achieved more than an adequate standard of living. While a number of women were able to improve their own occupational position through training as nurses, very few of the others were able to achieve upward social mobility on their own account. Just two of the 25 women entered what might be termed as middle class occupations: Elvira who, after a long struggle to have her teaching credentials acquired in Latvia and in Germany recognised in Britain, eventually became a primary school teacher and Lina, who took a university degree in London and then became a university administrator, although Diana, for example, among the nurses was successful and became a sister. But, of course, the class position of married women is closely linked not only to their own employment position but to that of their husbands and to the overall standard of living of the family. Latvian men tended to find it even harder to escape manual labour. both Elvira's and Lina's husbands remained trapped in low-paying working class jobs. Here is Elvira talking about her married life:

> There was an exhibition at the YMCA in 1949, our first big one and I met my husband there. He was staying at an agricultural camp and working at a farm. He was a farmer in Latvia, he had been to an agricultural college. And so we married. I did not want to move from Leicester. On the farm it would have been very isolated and I persuaded him to come to Leicester and I think he has regretted it ever since. First of all he worked at a factory where they made those knitting needles,

> machinery I mean, because there is quite a lot of hosiery factories in Leicester. But that was not a job for him, used to being outside all the time and then someone introduced him, well told him, about a brickyard and he worked there 30 years, poor thing.

These women clearly recognised the cost of downward mobility paid by many of their husbands.

It seems probable that women adapted more readily and quickly to life in the UK than Latvian men. Several of the women to whom I talked, for example, mentioned that their husbands struggled initially to learn English. It also seems that women were less resentful of their downward social mobility and experiences of discrimination in the labour market. Women in the 1950s expected to become mothers and as they did they had a key role not only in the family but in the transmission of Latvian values and language to their children in the home and through community and cultural activities. For men, especially the older men who had had middle class positions in Latvia, the discriminatory segregation in the UK labour market, their recruitment into working class jobs initially and the difficulties they experienced in escaping this class location resulted in the loss of social status in the UK. As men's sense of themselves as men, their very masculine identity is so bound up with paid labour that it is hardly surprising that these men had difficulties adapting to life in the UK. As Franz (2003) has shown in an interesting recent study of Bosnian refugees in Vienna and New York, gender-based differences in adaptation are not unique among either Latvian or post-war migrants but continue to be significant. Furthermore, the imbalance between male and female Latvian EVWs (more than three to one), magnified these gender differences. Exacerbated by many men's fervent desire to marry within their own community, the imbalance in numbers resulted in a large proportion of Latvian men remaining single, some of whom suffered from depression or alcohol abuse in later life. Women, on the other hand, in the main married and defined themselves through their family relations and their cultural and religious traditions. For both men and women, however, their continued identification of themselves as Latvian structured their lives and social relations, as I shall show in more detail in the next chapter. Through continued nostalgic tellings and retellings of old stories and the maintenance of older traditions, their identities remained strongly attached to their place of origin. For this reason the too easy associations between a fluid and changing multicultural or hybrid identity has to be resisted in theoretical explanations of the Latvian diaspora. But so too does the too easy assumption that their working class jobs and residential location defined their lives.

Class, status, attitudes and a sense of self, as Skeggs (2004) has recently argued, is about more than occupational position. Class is made and given value through culture. For these women, as well as their desire to maintain and strengthen links within the Latvian community, a strong commitment to the value of hard work and a desire for social improvement, for their children if not themselves, dominated their sense of identity and their position in Britain. Just as they had entered Britain with a strong sense of their superiority to EVWs from other parts of Europe, so too during their long lives in Britain they maintained a sense of themselves as different from, and superior to, many of their working class neighbours, in large part because of their strong belief in education as a path to social mobility. Although many of the women lived in northern working class neighbourhoods where few of the local children went to grammar schools, almost half of the children of these women passed the 11+ examination (at a time when less than 20% of the age group did so) and went to the local grammar school rather than to secondary modern schools with the majority of their primary school cohort. Diana once again speaks for the entire group in explaining her commitment to a better life for her children:

> And education was what matters, our people believed ... if you were a worker you wanted your children to be at least a foreman, always something higher than yourself. It wasn't like here when you read, or even know, that if your grandfather and father was a miner, you have to remain a miner. That was the difference in our country.

In their belief in the opportunities for social mobility through education, these women placed themselves centrally within a particular version of working class respectability. Their beliefs perhaps had more in common with an older version of respectability emphasising the values of sobriety, discipline, morality, restraint and self-improvement than the view of working class culture that was became more common as the post-war decades passed. The new version was portrayed as one dominated by instant gratification and self indulgence, outlined with disdain in the work by members of the old Left and other contemporary social commentators (Hoggart 1957; Seabrook 1982; Williams 1961, 1980). They saw a new world, influenced by the expansion of consumer durables and new forms of culture, often dubbed disapprovingly as 'American' (Priestley 1956, 1973) and ready to sap the sturdy self-reliance, developed by the working class as a response to conditions of hardship. Herein lies the commonality of the Latvian community in 1950s Britain and (part of the) 'native' working class – their determination to get by through their own efforts despite material inequalities and limited financial resources. For the Latvian women and their families, this determination to survive and succeed through their own efforts was strengthened by their experiences of loss and dislocation and their determination not to depend on the efforts of others, be it the British State, other social institutions outside their own community, or even the support of non-Latvian friends and neighbours. In part, this determination to be self-reliant lay in their fear and dislike of any form of politics or social provision that had any relationship to their hatred and fear of Soviet communism: a set of attitudes that I shall explore in more detail in the next chapter. As Tannahill noted in 1958, the EVW community as a whole was 'known to be unitedly anti-Soviet' (Tannahill 1958, p 64). Their self-reliance also lay, of course, in the loss of their homes and belongings in 1944 and the necessity of re-establishing their lives in a foreign land. Neither the instant pleasures of conspicuous consumption that began to penetrate British leisure culture from the 1950s onwards, nor the dominant version of a middle class, moral and domestic femininity had resonance for these women, as they struggled to build their family lives and hold down paid employment in different parts of the country in 1950s Britain.

Place matters

In this chapter the connections between paid and domestic labour among EVW women have been explored. After spending the early years of their lives in Britain as directed labourers, EVWs moved into the open labour market as independent workers. At the same time most of the 25 women in this book also relinquished their single status and became wives and mothers. One of the aims here was to assess the significance of specific local gender cultures in the bargains made within households about the division of total reproductive labour, as well as to evaluate the strength of the national ideology of domesticity in the 1950s. It is clear that economic necessity was the overriding factor in the decisions made by the women to whom I talked and their households. As is common among most migrant communities, survival strategies crucially depend on maximum participation in local labour markets for women as well as men, with the exception of communities with strong, often religiously-based, beliefs that exclude women's labour market participation. For Latvians too, as Vieda Skultans (1998, p 119) has argued in her study of post-independence Latvia, 'historical stereotypes of Latvians as determined workers' are a significant part of their sense of identity and self-worth and in part lie behind most of these women's commitment to paid work. Jelena spoke for most of her contemporaries when she commented: 'We didn't mind working hard – we had a house and jobs, after losing everything.' Figure 7.2 shows two typical employment trajectories, illustrating the long labour market attachment of these women.

However, place, location, particular traditions of women's work and a sense of communal identity are also key parts in the construction of a narrative of belonging in these women's lives in which the specific geographies of 1950s Britain connect to notions of an imagined Latvian community in exile. The long traditions of women's work in Lancashire and Yorkshire textile towns meant that EVW women's lives paralleled those of locally-born working class women and, as several of my respondents noted, meant that they did not feel so very different from other women in their position who also combined employment with domestic labour. However, locality and the specificity of place had another meaning too for these migrant workers who were also, it must be remembered, refugees. Reconstructing a sense of national identity in the face of the long Russian occupation of their homeland was a crucial part of the decisions of many Latvian EVWs to move to towns where they might participate in communal and religious activities and events and, as several women told me, live lives that were largely separate from those of English people.

Creating a sense of belonging to a people in exile was and still is a key part of the everyday lives and activities of Latvian women and their families. Thus, more than geographic proximity, a common workplace or a particular gender culture in which paid employment was acceptable binds these women together. Their common experiences of fleeing their country and living in camps in Germany before being shipped to Britain to work and the community ties recreated there unite them. Consequently, the desire to live in a Latvian diasporic community resulted in a degree of geographical mobility within Britain, as well as socio-spatial separateness, that was uncommon among indigenous women in similar

Table 7.2: Typical employment trajectories of EVW women

I: From domestic to nurse

1926	'44	'45	'45/6	Mar/May '47	'47/8	'48/51	'51/3	'53/8	'58	'59/86
1	2	3	4	5	6	7	8	9	10	11

1 Born in Dagopils, Latvia
2 Left Latvia
3 Directed labour in a Nazi munitions factory
4 School in displaced persons camp
5 Secretarial work for UNRRA
6 EVW domestic worker Leeds General Infirmary
7 Training as a nurse at Bradford Royal Infirmary
8 Staff nurse, full-time
9 Daughters born, at home mother
10 Back to nursing part-time
11 Full-time employment as a night sister until retirement

II: (Almost) a working life in textiles

1928	'44	'45	'47/48	'48/50	'51	'51/3	'53/65	'65/70	'70/1	'71/88
1	2	3	4	5	6	7	8	9	10	11

1 Born in Riga, Latvia
2 Left Latvia, and directed labour in army camp kitchen
3 Work in camp hospital kitchen
4 EVW in textile mill
5 Moved to a different mill in Bolton
6 Son born, six months off work
7 Evening shift in same mill in Bolton
8 Sewing work for Burton tailors
9 Moved to Bradford: similar sewing work in a different clothing factory (making skirts for M&S).
10 Assembly line work in TV manufacturers
11 Morning shift (seven and a half hours full-time) in Bradford mill

class locations in the 1950s. Thus, the combination of the specificities of local labour market circumstances and the cultures connected to them, as well as the chance allocation to an original occupational position in Britain, in conditions of economic hardship, resulted in a particular gender division of labour among Latvian households that challenged the dominant construction of women in 1950s Britain primarily as mothers. For these women, paid work was also a key part of their identity and the idealised division of labour dependent on a gendered moral rationality that distinguished men's and women's responsibilities and position in post-war Britain was largely irrelevant and anyway financially inaccessible. As most of the women whom they knew were also in paid employment, they did not seem subject to the guilt that many working class women felt because of dominant notions of 'good mothering' (Rich 1977; Skeggs 1997).

It is clear that the connections between place and identity are constructed through a complex set of interconnections that work across a range of spatial scales. International migration flows, national economic circumstances and local labour markets, as well as, *inter alia*, ethnic origins, local place-based cultures and personal decisions about, for example, marriage, combine to construct a particular set of connections between place and identity, as well as revealing their complexity. As Massey has argued, a sense of place is composed of a set of networks of social relationships rather than a bounded conception of the local. Similarly, local notions about appropriate gender cultures are always intercut by social differences between women, whether based on class, ethnicity or other characteristics. So complex are these interconnections, that the very notion of 'place-rooted cultures of mothering' (Holloway 1999, p 438) may be challenged by the diversity of strategies that exist in a locality in order to combine productive and reproductive labour. For Latvian EVWs the desire to build a strong imagined community in a country that they continued to see as their place of exile meant that they lived most of their lives within a separate sphere from their British neighbours and co-workers. Their self-reliance and the networks of mutual support that these women built in their early years in Britain also meant that they tended not to depend on local provision of goods and services such as, for example, pre-school groups or nurseries. Thus, here too, spatial differences between localities was a less significant factor in their decisions of how to combine paid and domestic work than for many other women.

In the next chapter, I change the focus to look at wider community networks and the ways in which these women reconstructed an imagined Latvian community in exile. I want to look at these women's political identities and challenge some of the ideas about diasporic identities that are currently dominant in studies of transnational migrants. For these women, the long dominance of Latvia by the Soviet Union during most of the second half of the twentieth century was the dominant focus of their politics, their sense of themselves as Latvian and their desire to create an imagined community in Britain. The re-recognition of Latvian independence in 1991 may have seemed the fulfilment of their dreams and yet, as I shall show, it created feelings of guilt and ambivalence and unsettled these women's sense of themselves as Latvian – the very belief that had supported and comforted them during their long years elsewhere.

CHAPTER 8

YEARNING FOR 'HOME': NARRATIVES OF BELONGING AND IMAGINED COMMUNITY

In this final substantive chapter, I want to look out from the home and the workplace to explore the ways in which, through participation in communal activities in the locality and neighbourhood and in the institutions of the nation state, these Latvian women constructed a sense of their communal identity and belonging – to an imagined Latvian community as well as to, or instead of, to an idealised version of Britishness. Latvians, and the many other European Voluntary Workers (EVWs), came to the United Kingdom as strangers, connected neither by geographical proximity nor colonial heritage, separated by language and to a large extent by culture from their hosts, despite their common European identity. They left a small, predominantly rural economy and society which in the inter-war years had experienced an unprecedented level of development and prosperity – Latvia's golden age of independence – and, after several years of dislocation, homelessness and hardship, became in the main residents of industrial towns in the midlands and the north where life was generally hard and housing conditions poor.

In these towns, the EVWs began to reconstruct their lives, building not only new families but also a range of different forms of communal support based on their identity as Latvians, including national clubs, choirs and other cultural institutions, language classes, Lutheran churches, social events for children such as summer camps and, later, as the first generation population aged, welfare institutions to support the elderly. In addition, throughout the years of Soviet dominance of their homeland, the Latvian population in Britain organised in different ways to maintain contact with their friends and relatives in the Soviet Socialist Republic of Latvia and in support of its struggle for independence. In part, life cycle stage is an important indicator of the extent to which there has been both the establishment of contacts and the maintenance of distance between the Latvian incomers and the British population, as at different times over their lives in Britain they became more or less involved in both everyday life in the places where they lived and in the institutions and practices of the British national and local state and civil society. Time has played a further significant part as recent history – in the events surrounding the break-up of the former Soviet Union – saw the restitution of Latvian independence and allowed the now elderly Latvian women to become citizens of their own country once more.

Fitting In?

In the late 1940s, the dominant discourses of national identity in Britain were very different from those that now characterise discussions of belonging. Ideas about multiculturalism, about cultural integrity and about diversity and difference had no purchase at that time. Migrants to Britain in these first post-war years were not only officially designed 'aliens' but also regarded as such in the popular imagination. Their 'difference' was not celebrated nor seen as an interesting or valuable addition to British society but, rather, was regarded as a reason for suspicion. Correspondingly, the debates about migrant identity and belonging were set centrally within the notion of assimilation. Migrants were conceptualised as strangers, rather than as 'others', as in contemporary debates. It was their difference from the hegemonic norm – the version of white, middle class, middle England version of English identity that was most highly valued in the early post-war decades – that set them apart from the host society whose customs, manners and conventional practices they were expected to conform to as quickly and as closely as possible. It was their duty to start to 'fit in', rather than that of the host nation to accept and tolerate their difference and even to change itself as the population became more diverse. Thus, in the first months after the arrival of the EVWs, the Ministry of Labour sponsored a series of lectures on the 'British way of life' which, as Tannahill (1958, p 68) notes, 'almost inevitably sounded slightly smug or irrelevant to alien ears'. Worse, the maintenance of national languages and customs by EVWs was regarded with suspicion by British officials who attempted to discourage displays of national identity: an insensitive reaction to the plight of people who had lost their homeland and hence their nationality.

As I argued earlier, it was here – in their ability to 'fit in' – that the Latvians had one conspicuous and visible advantage compared with economic migrants who came to Britain from the Caribbean at much the same time – their skin colour. As the title of an early book examining the consequences of West Indian migration to Britain from 1947 onwards makes brutally clear, this latter group were not just strangers but *Dark Strangers* (Patterson 1965). They were immediately identifiable as a threat, embodied as dangerous through their mere presence in the towns and cities of post-war England, and so only too visible and vulnerable to racist discrimination because of their skin colour. (Reflecting more recent efforts to reclaim and subvert this label of stranger and transform images of belonging to Britain, the novelist Caryl Phillips (1997) called his edited anthology of writing by migrants in Britain *Extravagant Strangers*.) While Latvian EVWs may not have been citizens, being white gave them the significant advantage of a large degree of invisibility, at least in fleeting encounters in the street. However, accent, beliefs and cultural and political values meant that Latvians inevitably were strangers in post-war Britain.

As Ahmed (2000, p 4) has argued, drawing on the work of Bauman (1993, 1995), 'the figure of the stranger has been taken to represent all that was excluded or delegitimated in modernity with its belief in order, sameness and totality'. While this notion of a stranger is a useful way to understand the position of migrant groups in post-war Britain (and see Diken (1998)) it also disguises, as I have intimated, significant differences between people of different origins, in the reasons for their displacement from 'home' and in their location and position within British society. Within this general construction of 'strangers', there are important degrees of difference and so variations in the reception of migrants and in the extent to which they are tolerated. These relative and relational constructions of strangeness are political formations that are constructed through discourses and practices that construct some groups as less acceptable and less legitimate potential Britons than others. Practices of incorporation, of inclusion and exclusion, construct the boundaries of who belongs and who does not, both to local communities and to the nation itself. And as I showed in Chapter 4, young Latvian women had many characteristics that did indeed make them acceptable as potential Britons. But as I also argued in that chapter and in Chapter 5, the practices of the incoming group also affect the extent to which they desire to become and behave as potential Britons. Many Latvians preferred to think of themselves as Latvians, people in exile, reconstructing and holding fast to an imagined version of Latvian identity, deterritorialised and reinvented in Britain, and with little connection either to what was actually happening throughout the 1950s and 1960s in their homeland or to the changing political circumstances in Britain. The ways in which this cultural and political identity was created and maintained in post-war Britain that constructed Latvians as different from their hosts is the subject of this chapter.

Theorising community

In understanding the construction of an imagined version of Latvian identity in Britain the work of Benedict Anderson is particularly helpful. In his book *Imagined Communities*, first published in 1983 and later revised (Anderson 1983, 1991, p 6), Anderson argued that all modern nation states are an '"imagined political community" ... imagined because the members of even the smallest nation will never know most of their fellow members, meet them or even hear them, yet in the minds of each lives the image of their communion'. This communion, Anderson argues, is a feature of the modern era, made possible by technological change, especially the development of the printed word, and by education of the masses, enabling the majority of the population to consume the texts and maps that construct this imagined nationhood. Through maps, flags, buildings, monuments, the construction of common customs and myths of origin, through sports, culture and political rhetoric a dominant version of nationhood and belonging is created. Other theorists of national identity tend to emphasise the longevity of ideas of national identity, challenging Anderson's association of the rise of nationalism with modernity, and so have pointed to the continuing significance of pre-modern cultures and earlier ties between social groups and specific territories. Thus, writers within this perspective place greater emphasis than Anderson on the importance of long-standing ethno-symbolism in explaining how nationalism has such a profound hold on the popular imagination (Bell 2003), documenting the ways in which the historical past affects modern nation states, finding traces of premodern customs and myths even in modern urbanised societies. In both approaches, however, the nation state is recognised as a cultural construct, created and maintained through what has been termed 'the invention of tradition'

(Hobsbawm and Ranger 1983). Representation and discourse are therefore key constitutive features of nationalism. Thus, as Bell (2003, p 69) notes, whatever theoretical approach is adopted 'we are all constructivists is this sense'.

The meaning of nationalism or national identity and the boundaries of a nation state typically are constructed to be exclusive. Thus, there is a clear definition of who is included in the nation state and, conversely, who is not included, as well as (usually) clearly defined, albeit often contested, boundaries of its territorial extent. As Nairn (1977), Paxman (1998), Smith (1999) and others have shown, despite the assertion that a nation state is based on an idealised notion a 'deep horizontal comradeship' that exists 'regardless of the actual inequality that may prevail' (Anderson 1991, p 5), in fact the myths of identity, common origins and belonging act to exclude a range of 'others', who often might already live within the boundaries of the nation. These 'others' might be excluded or regarded as less acceptable on the basis of their class origins, their location in particular parts of the territory beyond the 'heartland' or because of their ethnicity.

The hegemonic construction of the British nation state, for example, is one that is based on an idealised version of 'middle England': a fundamentally decent and moderate place, an England of the south, of Shakespeare and rose-covered cottages in sleepy villages, a rural arcadia where English gentlefolk and middle class residents pursue a cultured life (Short 1991; Wright 1985). This respect for a largely middle class way of life is matched by a subservience to royalty and the upper class, reflected in a widespread disdain of 'trade' or industry (Wiener 1981) that excludes not only the 'nouveau riche' and immigrants but also the disreputable, non-respectable working class (Skeggs 1997), especially those living in the north of the country (Shields 1992), the Labour voting 'tribe-apart' (Barnett 1986, p 190) in Scotland and Wales and industrial northern Britain, as well as the Caribbean newcomers who were *de jure* British citizens but excluded by their ethnicity from belonging. As Gilroy (1987) has documented in his work on the place of black Britons in post-war society 'there ain't no black in the Union Jack'. Miles (1993) concurs with his argument, asserting more generally that 'the ideologies of racism and nationalism can be interdependent and overlapping, the idea of race serving as a criterion of simultaneous inclusion and exclusion so that the boundary of the imagined "nation" is equally a boundary of "race"' (Miles 1993, p 79). Thus, the white majority in the United Kingdom, or rather in England, is constructed as Anglo-Saxon with a common heritage.

This common heritage excludes not only minority and ethnic populations of colour but also the Celts, especially the Irish, who are constructed as racially inferior through a remarkably consistent set of negative stereotypes (Walter 2001), based on body images, apparent (lack of) intellect and cultural attributes. The Latvian migrants, in part, escaped the same sort of negative stereotyping if only because the British population was largely ignorant of the incomers' history and geography. But similar contradictory images of feckless scroungers and thieves of British jobs that are part of the long history of discriminatory attitudes towards migrants did play a part in their early reception in Britain. Tannahill (1958, p 70) quotes a study by Elizabeth Stadulis (1953) that documented some of the features of early hostility by British workers to the EVWs. They included a refusal to train EVWs in skilled tasks in case they became too competitive, threats of strikes and anti-EVW articles in trade union papers. Generally speaking, Stadulis found that the more skilled the union, the greater was the opposition to EVWs. There were various justifications of these hostile attitudes, including foreign workers' attitudes to women (left unspecified), that they were violent and used knives and that they were fascists (see below). But as I also argued earlier, the construction of by the British government of women workers from the Baltic as the opposite of Irish and Caribbean migrants – as clean rather than dirty, as sober hard-workers and potential mothers of British children rather than threateningly fecund – positioned them as the polar opposite of the other main migrant groups entering the UK at the same time. In that set of connections between disorder, pollution and dirt and working class women that have typified women in manual employment across the centuries (see, for example, Davidoff and Hall 1987), especially those working as domestics (Fuenmayer *et al* 1992; McClintock 1995), Latvian women, and the women EVWs from the other two Baltic states, were seen as the exception in 1940s Britain.

Early political disagreements

At a larger scale, this varied group of outsiders, the excluded residents – migrants, foreigners, strangers – play, as Cohen (1994, p 1) has argued, a key part in the discourses of national identity: 'a complex national and social identity is continuously constructed and reshaped in its (often antipathetic) interaction with outsiders, strangers, foreigners and aliens – the "others"'. Latvians, albeit welcomed by the Ministry of Labour, were nevertheless excluded from dominant notions of British nationality and nationalism by their ethnicity and language and, in the early years, their association, false or not, with fascism. In the late 1940s, the Latvians who had fled and who refused to return to the Soviet Union were regarded as traitors, as the Russians had been allies in the fight against the Germans. At the end of the war, there was a great emphasis in Britain on symbols of national unity and consensus (Addison 1975; Marwick 1968). National unity, as William Beveridge had announced in 1943, was the great moral achievement of the war years and, as the historian Kenneth O Morgan has argued, it was paralleled by widespread post-war support for social and cultural transformation. In place of 'the bitter aftermath and sense of class betrayal' that followed the end of the First World War, there was in 1945 'a genuine sense of unity rooted in the social and cultural realities of war-time' (Morgan 1990, p 3): realities from which the EVW populations inevitably had been excluded. Even if this national consensus proved in the event to be more fractured than its post-war architects envisioned, the long-standing hatred of Germans cast a long shadow over the decades. Morgan notes that, even in the 1980s, social workers found that children of German origin attending British schools sometimes were beaten up simply for their identity (p 5) and the anti-German chants of some British football 'supporters' are a continuing disgrace.

This anti-German sentiment, inevitably much stronger in the early 1950s than now, often tainted relations between the EVWs and the British population. The national origins of the Baltic EVWs were not clear to many Britons but they did know that they had come to Britain from Germany and refused to return to the

Soviet Union. It was to be a decade or more before the Soviet Union metamorphosed into an implacable Cold War enemy of the West and the strongly anti-communist Latvian community became regarded more sympathetically. By that time, the Rotarians, for example, were inviting membership applications from EVW men from the professional and business classes whom they regarded 'without exception victims of that Communism from which Rotary desires to save the world' (Stadulis 1952, pp 231–32). Meanwhile, in their first years in Britain the Latvian population, seeing little distinction between communism and socialism, were fiercely distrustful of Labour politicians and their post-war plans for socialist reforms. If they had any political affiliations at all in Britain, they became, in the main, strong supporters of the Conservative Party, despite their working class jobs and their residence in predominantly Labour voting constituencies. Labour's plans for social insurance, industrial modernisation and economic central planning seemed to the newly arrived Latvians to have too many suspicious echoes of the hated Soviet control of their own country during and after the war. This belief was supported by the fact that the leaders of some of the major British trade unions at the time were communists, including Arthur Horner of the Mineworkers, the industry to which some Latvian men had been allocated on arrival and in which many remained in employment.

Stories of the land and nature

Partly as a protective response to the reactions of the British public, especially in the immediate post-war years, and also as a way to build a collective sense of identity, the different EVW populations in Britain began to (re)construct stories about their origins as well as institutions for mutual support. As Bell (2003, p 64) argues, questions of personal and collective identity are a fundamental part of constructing a sense of belonging. 'To recognise oneself as a member of a particular nation ... and to be recognised by others as such, is a perquisite for the formation of the inside/outside, self/other, them/us boundaries that define the topography of nationalist sentiment and rhetoric.' A homeland, as well as an imagined community, is an essential part of national identity, and 'natural metaphors such as roots, soil, motherland and fatherland are employed to emphasise a sense of genealogical rootedness and exclusivity to a place' (Smith *et al* 1998, p 96). For Latvians in England, the cultural (re)construction of Latvian nationality, and their self-identification as different from the British population, drew strongly on the customs and practices during the inter-war period of Latvian independence, not only because this was the period in which they were young but also because of its symbolism as a 'golden era' in which positive images of the nation flourished. As Smith (1999, p 9) has argued, shared memories are integral to collective cultural identities and nationalism is given power through 'the myths, memories, traditions and symbols of ethnic heritage'. Bell suggests that the concept of collective memory should be used carefully and insists on a distinction between 'memory' which he argues is a socially framed property based on the experiences of individuals, and more general versions of nationalist story telling, which he suggests are better conceptualised as 'myth' than memory. Even if this distinction is accepted, for Latvians in Britain both collective memories and myth were key parts of the ways in which a sense of (still) belonging to Latvia was recreated in Britain.

Stories of loss and the journey across Europe at the end of the war, as well as stories of ancient origins and of lost golden ages in national traditions and histories are combined to recreate a particular version of 'belonging elsewhere' by Latvian exiles in Britain. The aesthetic construction of national identity in Latvia in the first decades of the twentieth century was strongly anti-urban and anti-modern, infused with a longing for an imagined traditional 'organic' society, free from the alienation of industrial capitalism. A strong sense of their genealogical connection to the land and its occupants was an important part of Latvian national identity. As Nash (2002, p 27) has argued: 'ideas of belonging, cultural identity and social relations [are often] based on ancestral connection, blood and primordial kinship.' Among diasporic populations, she suggests, questions of nationality, ethnicity and identity often meet in the pursuit of an essentialised ancestry and in genealogical research. Linke, too, in her work on Germanic notions of identity has argued that 'genealogical models appropriate images of nature – blood, soil and tree – as markers of descent, symbolizing the natural order of things' (Linke 1999, p 15). As I noted earlier, there was a long historical association between Latvia and Germany, in which German barons were important land holders in the pre-industrial era and in Latvia too the imagery of the 'natural' land is a key part of a sense of national identity: trees and the forest in particular are key symbols in Latvian myths and poetry, and in the shared sense of national identity. As Linke (1999) has also noted, the ideal of a sound and healthy body plays a key part in both the construction of national myths and in cultural activities in Germanic states or those with long connections to Germany. Indeed, the idea of the nation is often defined as a 'community of descent' in ways which link membership to a healthy body, to whiteness and to a particular type of racial aesthetic (Brubaker 1992; Linke 1999) (and as I noted earlier, Baltic people of German descent typically moved westwards during the war, nearer to the heartland). In Germanic cultures, a free and 'natural' body was strongly associated with the ideal of a natural premodern society. Nude bathing and sunbathing and other sports, for example, were prescribed as an antidote to the degenerative features of urban life, promoting not only physical but also racial fitness. 'Nudism was an attempt to regain, in the face of the ravages of industrialisation, physical and ideological spaces for the restoration of life in harmony with nature' (Will 1990, p 21).

In post-war Britain a somewhat similar impetus lay behind the Health and Beauty Movement to which many women belonged in the 1950s and 1960s, including one of the 25 women whom I interviewed. Similarly, in Latvian rituals reconstructed in Britain, the celebration of the passing of the seasons, the harvest and the midsummer solstice were celebrated communally by Latvians as an important reminder of the 'natural' world, and were often associated, metaphorically, with fertility rituals, as well marked by physical forms of celebration including traditional games and folk dancing, often in national costume. In Latvian poetry and folk narrative, the seasons and the land, especially the forest and its trees, play a significant part in the construction of national symbolism and identity, as well as in the preservation and rediscovery of Latvian culture by Latvians living elsewhere in Europe. The soil, its people and nature were intimately intertwined. Eksteins (2000, p 26) argues that the attachment to nature survived across the centuries not only in folk customs and oral traditions but also in family names. He notes that 'when the serfs were liberated and needed surnames, these were invariably taken from nature' and that the list of faculty at the agricultural college in Jelgava, where his mother went to school in the 1930s 'included the names Eglitis (little fir tree), Abolins (little apple), Krumins (little bush), Taurins (little butterfly), Briedis (stag), Gailis (rooster), Lapins (little leaf), Lacis (bear), Ozolins (little oak tree) and Rozkalns (rose hill). In poetry and in festivals, birth, marriage, spring, the rising sun, the white of the birch and the Baltic sand and snow are celebrated. Similarly, in their recollections of their childhood, the land and the seasons played a key role in the women's narratives. Beate, for example, spoke with longing about the seasons in Latvia, especially the beauty of the spring flowers after the severe winters and numerous other women talked about the land itself, especially the forest and the lakes, of how they missed the changing weather, especially the crisp snows of the Latvian countryside.

These lyrical celebrations of the land became typical in the poetry and drama written in the Latvian language between the mid-nineteenth century and before the Second World War: the works which would have been taught in school and were part of the 25 women's cultural heritage as well as a significant part of the increase in patriotism during the late nineteenth century. Before then Latvia was largely an oral culture, rich in folksongs, melodies and fairy tales, all of which influenced the remarkable establishment of a written culture during this period of 'national awakening' from the 1850s onwards. Urch (1938, p 185) suggested that 'it would be hard to find another nation of two million with such a record of lyrical poetry, drama and prose writing of high and passable quality in similar conditions and in such a brief period of time'. Until this period, the German colonisers had considered the Latvians inferior: 'their language a patois of kitchen and stable and their folk culture shallow' (Eksteins 2000, p 27). However, as Smith (1996, p 148) argued that from this time 'influenced by the Romantic movement's conception of the *Volk* and of a Lutheran religion which held that preaching such be conducted in a people's mother tongue, the Baltic German clergy and literati took a benevolent interest in the distinctive language and culture of the Latvian peasantry, particularly in their oral traditions, such as their folk songs (*dainas*) and folk tales, and in promoting the Latvian language' and a strong nationalist movement began to develop. The newly emerged intelligentsia called for 'seizing control of the past as well as the future' (Plakans 1995, p xvii) and so a nostalgic view of an earlier Eden, a simpler rural past that has been a continuous element in the imagining of Latvian identity, became important.

In the twentieth century, the pastoral tradition continued to dominate Latvian literature although the farmstead, rather than the land itself, became a central representation of Latvian ethnic identity. As Skultans argues, 'perhaps the most exuberantly romantic portrayal is to be found in Edvarts Virza's prose poem "Straumēni" [which] has as its focus a Zemgallian farmstead and its seasonal activities. It is a celebration of the rural idyll which has in the process transformed the ways in which Latvians perceive and remember their country childhoods' constructing a 'timeless and mythical bond between peasant and locality' (Skultans 1998, p 151). These memories of the farm and time spent in the countryside played a significant part in the narratives of the 25 women and, significantly, the residential retirement community near Catthorpe in the Leicestershire countryside where some of them now live is named after this poem. The timeless and symbolic elevation of the farmstead in Virza's poem, of course, conceals 'the painful history of serfdom and landlessness' (Skultans 1998, p 151) but, as Eksteins has suggested, 'Latvian literature [also] exudes longing and melancholy. Joy is never shrill, always quiet, because it cannot last. Beauty, too, is fleeting. Oppression, exile, pain and dreams that dissolve into illusions are standard themes' (Eksteins 2000, p 27). Despite the celebration of the land, the seasons and the farmhouse in oral and written culture and in memories, living was not easy in Latvia for most people. The climate is a hard one, with long winters and heavy rains, with frequent poor harvests, even famines, and the long history of conquest and domination is reflecting in the pain of exploitation and oppression. But as Anthony Smith argued in his work on nationalism, the tendency to historicise – to rediscover an ethnic past or a golden age – and to mythologise its beauty and benefits is a key element in the construction and maintenance of national myths of identity.

In the construction of a mythic 'golden age', certain places and periods become celebrated, even mythologised, and the pasts 'then become standards against which to measure the failings of the present generation and contemporary community' (Smith 1996, p 450). This tendency to reject the present, of course, is even stronger when it involves the rejection of what is still seen as an occupying power, as in Latvia at both the beginning and end of the twentieth century. Plakans (1995, p xiv) has also emphasised the continuing importance of the earlier 'golden age' of independence when links were established between 'the active intelligentsia, a school of literati and revolutionaries who were inspired by rising nationalism and socialism' in the last decade of the nineteenth and first decades of the twentieth century and especially in the establishment of an independent state between the First and Second World Wars. The modern study of Latvian folksongs, for example, which had long been part of the Latvian tradition of song festivals (the first national festival was held in June 1873), became established during these years and folk songs have remained a key element of the nationalist glue that holds together the diaspora population with those who remained in Latvia.

While the study of this literature, music and folklore largely disappeared in Latvia during the years of domination by the Soviet Union, it remained a significant part of the ideal image of Latvia among exiles and has been resurrected in Latvia since 1991, as prominent Latvian personalities and key moments in its history regain their significance in the recreation of images of Latvian identity. In the construction of this identity, symbols of the old rural economy such as bee-keeping and golden honey, as well as the golden amber which is also a national symbol, represent the various 'golden ages' in its history, whether in the myths of origin when Lāčplēsis, or the Bear-Slayer, who was found as a baby in the forests by a she-bear and sustained by her milk (Urch 1938, pp 23–25) or in the subsequent golden age of independence in the 1920s and 1930s. As Plakans (1995, p 137) argued, in these inter-war years, artistic creativity had a strongly nationalist tone. 'The best artists sought to articulate universal values and forms using the Latvian language and imagery and sounds from the Latvian natural world, the

Latvian past and Latvian traditional music.' An educational system with a specifically national Latvian content was put into place in the inter-war years when the women in this book were schoolgirls.[1]

In the sorts of reconstructed national myths and histories that characterised the emergence of Latvian nationalism, women typically are differently positioned to men, as well as in the debates about 'universal values' such as suffrage and citizenship that characterise the emergence of the modern nation state. As work on gendered images of the nation has shown (see, for example, Anthias and Yuval Davies 1992; Johnson 1995; Nash 1993; Radcliffe 1996) women tend to play a role in national symbolism and in images of the nation in a number of specific and paradoxical ways: as traditional, often static and unchanging representatives of home and family, as an image of the nation state itself and as an absence. The first two images or representations are sometimes combined as the nation itself is often portrayed as a fertile, home-based, typically rural, female figure, as a motherland symbolised by the natural association between fertility and femininity, between the land and its bounty. Allegorical figures of the nation as a woman draped with fruit or children are common images, for example, in art or on stamps, coins and notes. In Urch's survey of the land and people of Latvia published in 1938, for example, there is a striking image headed 'young ladies of Latvia' showing two young women waist-deep in a flowering meadow, emphasising their connection to nature. Alternatively, womanhood/the motherland is sometimes represented as culture, as a rational ethereal version of femininity above the (masculine) rush and tumble of everyday life, symbolising the purity of the nation state. This binary construction is reflected in the trope of war and death, sons and daughters of the nation in which men's association is with war and death, commemorated in national monuments and war memorials, whereas women are largely absent in these symbolic commemorations (Warner 1985), waiting in the home to welcome back wartime heroes and ready to re-establish family life. In Latvian cultural life, as well as other forms of representation, women are strongly associated with a version of a rural pacificity and fertility that played a key part both in the re-establishment of family life by Latvians in the 1950s, discussed in the preceding chapter, as well as in the celebration of Latvian customs and folklore in Britain discussed in this chapter.

Latvian nationalism

This sense of community, of an unbroken connection to a pre-industrial and pre-war past, primarily constructed around an idealised bucolic version of the folk customs and practices of the pre-war Latvian golden era, has been, from entry to Britain in the 1940s until the present, a crucial part of cementing ties between the 10,000 or so Latvians who came to Britain as EVWs. As Tannahill noted (1958, p 111), among all the different EVW groups, the Latvian community, in particular,

---

1 Almost three-quarters of children attended Latvian schools in the 1920s and 1930s. The constitution of 1922 had demanded that the cultural autonomy of minorities be protected and the other one-quarter of children were educated in Russian, German, Jewish, Polish, Lithuanian and Estonian language schools.

was strongly nationalistic and developed one of the most flourishing national organisations in this country: the Latvian Welfare Association that is still active today. This fervent attachment to an essentialised notion of Latvian identity that connected the scattered population existed despite the often multiple ethnic backgrounds of many Latvians. As I noted in the introductory chapters, the history of Latvia included numerous periods of domination by different states and this is reflected in its population. Ilona, for example, one of the women most active in the long post-war struggle against Soviet domination, told me that 'my grandfather was Russian and my grandmother Latvian from father's side and on my mother's side my grandmother was Swedish and my grandfather was German. So I am a liquorice all-sort'. However, Latvian nationalism was a potent source of community identification and Ilona had been educated in a Latvian-speaking school. From the late 1940s onwards, national social clubs sprang up in many towns and cities, especially in the north of England, organising a range of cultural activities, especially choirs and drama groups, as well as dances and other events that were an important way of building connections between Latvians during the 1950s and 1960s, as well as remembering and resisting the symbols of national heritage that were then being repressed by the Soviet Union. This is Jelena talking about those early decades in Britain when she lived in Hyde, near Manchester:

> Those were hard years, hard work and there was not much money to spare but we kept together with the Latvian society and there was an amateur theatre group and we joined that and the national dancing group and there was quite a Latvian society around Manchester. There were quite a lot of Latvians and there were concerts and dances maybe two or three times a year in our place in Christ Church Hall in Stockport.

Valda, who lived in the Catthorpe retirement community when I spoke to her but who had lived in Chesterfield throughout her married life, told a similar story:

> In Chesterfield, I was working shifts and he was on days. We had a social life. We had an international club. We used to have our own peoples. You know, there were quite a lot up there. We had our social nights and out evenings, gatherings, choirs and dances. I am not a singer. He is. We have still got a choir here (at Catthorpe). We didn't have a car but Peter had a motorbike so we used to go to Nottingham or Mansfield or somewhere, you know, where our people were. There's quite a lot, miners. We used to go to Bradford as well. And I danced in a folk group.

Several of the women to whom I talked had managed to hold onto small items of national costume right through the years of their journey and camp life in Germany – a small hat or a shawl, for example. Others had recreated their national costume when they joined folk groups in Britain. Most women, however, had lost all their belongings, including books, photographs and other personal mementoes and other than perhaps an identity card for the camps had few material objects to remind them of either home or the camps. In the early years, educational and social activities, including small libraries of books, Latvian newspaper published in London, choirs, dances, language classes, often organised through the Lutheran Church as well as through local associations, were an important way of cementing national ties. Plate 8.1 shows Latvian singers in the national dress at a song festival in Münster, Germany, in 1987.

Plate 8.1 Latvian singers in national dress

Source: Sinka, J (1988) *Latvia and Latvians*, Latvian Central Board, London. The photograph was taken during the Third World Latvian Song Festival, 2–8 August 1987 at Münster.

Through these communal activities the exiles were able to meet potential partners. Later, from about the mid-1950s onwards, they became an important part of socialising for their children, making them aware of the importance of their national origins and Latvian customs. For Latvian children growing up in Britain, summer camps, Sunday schools and language classes became a central part of constructing and maintaining community ties. Vida Skultans (2003) recalls that, as a Latvian child in London in the early 1950s, this entailed laborious journeys across the city to connect the pockets of Latvian activity.

As I documented in Chapter 6, all but one of the 25 women married and almost all of them became mothers. Their children were, with only one exception, brought up to speak Latvian at home, supported by Saturday language classes for children, many of whom were resentful about their attendance when their school friends were freer. However, as Lina emphasised, this practice has had long-term benefits in the post-independence period in the 1990s which many of the second generation now acknowledge:

> Oh yes, we always spoke Latvian at home and in Corby there was also a Saturday school for children to learn Latvian ... the children both went to learn Latvian and my older son, his Latvian is very good, reading and writing as well and the younger one, he speaks all right but his writing is not so good. Now that Latvia is free they are pleased that they can communicate with their relatives in Latvia.

Eva too emphasised the long-term benefits, even though her children resented their immersion in Latvian culture when they were young:

> We were always thinking about our country, how things are going, how they are suffering under communism and all that and we been telling the children about all that. And we have been dragging them to Saturday school in Coventry to learn history and folk dancing and that and they were dragged there with long faces. 'Why do we have to go, other children can play outside?' but once they were there, then they were quite jolly. You have to force them sometimes a bit, you can't just let them do want they want. They have to learn to do sometimes things they don't like because life is like that. You can't do in your life whatever you want. You could if you are lucky. They are so glad now, when Latvia was independent.

It also became clear that enjoyment, as well as resentment, was part of everyday family life and its association with Latvian cultural events. Many women told me of the happy summers they and their children had spent in the 1960s and early 1970s at rural camps which not only provided a cheap and healthy holiday but enabled these women to recreate for their children the sort of rural outdoor lives and traditions that had been a common part of their own childhoods. Indeed, these summer camps are still running, although reduced in number. As Valda, a resident in the Catthorpe community for retired Latvians told me: 'There are still two summer camps here – one for mixed marriages when they don't speak Latvian and another one for Latvian speakers.'

Political organisation and the meaning of 'home'

One of the most obvious grounds for distrust between the Latvian in-migrants and the British population lay in their political allegiances in the late 1940s and in the 1950s. For the native population, all Latvian EVWs, in their fervent distrust of Communism in general and the Soviet Union in particular and their history of what seemed like pro-German sympathies during the war in, for example, the formation of the Latvian Legion, were assumed to be fascists. The Latvians, in turn, regarded the British as naïve in their view of the Soviet Union, as well as feeling betrayed by them at the end of the war. As Agnese explained: 'We were full of hope, to have our country free. And we so depended on England, you have no idea, and of course no help came. So that's the sad part. We were still hoping when we came to England.' She agreed with the view of an anonymous EVW, originally from the middle classes, who reportedly told Tannahill (1958, p 100) in the early 1950s: 'You British don't understand the communists.' The general distrust of the Soviet Union among the EVW population in Britain took a public form in protest marches and the distribution of leaflets in several cities during the visit to the UK in April 1956 of Kruschev and Marshall Bulganin. Perhaps their distrust of both the Soviet Union and Britain was justified. Between 1949 and 1955, MI6, the British overseas intelligence service, apparently recruited numerous Latvians to spy on the Soviet Union. However, apparently the KGB had prior knowledge of the entire operation, capturing the Latvian spies and either killing or imprisoning them (Hiden and Salmon 1991, p 128). 1956, however, marked a watershed in the recognition of Soviet despotism by the Western powers. The year, which began with Russian tanks suppressing striking East Germans and Polish unrest, ended with the brutal suppression of the Hungarian rising, which saw 7,000 Hungarians and 3,000 Russian dead after three days of violence. It then became easier for the

Plate 8.2 Political postcards to commemorate the Soviet deportations in the 1940s

Drawn by Varis Zāns based on original drawing by Nikolajas Soikans

Drawn by Tenis Grasis

Latvians in Britain to mobilise support for their campaigns, even though Mr K, as the British press called Kruschev, had taken tea with the Queen in April that year.

A key part of the long campaign to regain Latvian independence has been the struggle to gain British recognition of the Soviet deportations from Latvia during and after the war (in 1941, 1944 and 1949) and several of the women to whom I talked showed me the letters they had written and the postcard campaigns (see Plate 8.2) that they had been involved in over many years.

Ilona, who had been active in Latvian political organising since the 1970s told me a little about the type of work in which she was involved:

> In 1970 I think or something like that, I started with the Latvian community and they elected me on a committee. I am now on a committee running Catthorpe (the retirement community in Leicestershire) and I do the information work. I am officially the information officer for the Latvian Welfare Foundation in Great Britain. And that's what I do. And erm, I collect material for the book which we are going to publish about our life and we are going to have an exhibition. We are going to have a global gathering in Latvia in August 2001. We are showing the Latvians in Latvia what we did in exile. For example every year I produce postcards like this one [see plate 8.2]. I produce this and people were disbelieving this about communism but I believe that communism kills. We talked about the crimes Hitler committed but not about the crimes that Stalin committed.

For these women, and many other Latvians, the years in England, as I noted earlier, were constructed as years of exile, dominated by recollections of the Second World War and suffused by the desire to return 'home', even though Latvia as a homeland no longer existed. As Giles (2002, p 28) has suggested, for people who have experienced dislocation and loss, such myths of belonging and of home are a key way 'to establish the coherence and sense of continuity that is the necessary foundation for the sense of shared belonging essential to any political solidarity'. In this longing for home, exiles may perhaps be distinguished from the more general category of immigrants, especially economic immigrants for whom the hope of financial gain and a better life is a strong motive and which may lead to a more positive identification with the new land. As Vieda Skultans, now a British academic who came to Britain from Latvia via Germany as a small child after the war, has argued: 'The word exile conveys many ambiguities. Dictionaries define it as an unwanted separation from a place one is no longer able to inhabit. As well as physical separation, war and loss, desire and longing serve to construct exile as a moral space characterised by absence. Exile is both backward and forward looking' (Skultans 2003, p 3). The moral space of absence for Latvian women was both a past home that had vanished and an imagined free Latvia that did not (yet) exist and this past and future yearning may have prevented their full participation in the institutions and customs of British life. Diana's comment captures this sense of loss and exile and also echoes Ilona's earlier comment in her puzzlement that English friends could not understand her anti-communist sentiments:

> Some-one – a visitor – said to me once 'you left for a better life'. It was as if someone had hit me. We left to save our lives. I was young and my life in front of me and suddenly it was all cut off. What I keep telling all my English friends, England is a very, very free country and they can't agree with me but I know what it means:

> freedom. You see there was always freedom here. You can think what you like and say what you like, and no one can interfere. But you see when the Russians were there you couldn't talk and still there were spies and when children went to school the teacher would say: 'What are your parents are talking about?'

Beate was still able to recall, with a flash of anger, a similar moment, clearly remembering her indignation when, during an inspection of the hospital where she worked in the late 1940s, one of the team asked her if she was happy. 'How can I be happy,' she replied, 'when I have lost everything? My home, my education, my future.'

Keeping contacts with home: the diasporic community and going 'home'

For Latvians in the UK, maintaining contacts with relatives and friends in Latvia during the post-war years raised complicated issues and anxieties about placing those still at 'home' in danger, as Elvira explains:

> In all the years before independence we were in touch with people but very little. It was more after Stalin's death but it was a long time before we could communicate. We didn't go before 1990 because it was dangerous for them, not so much for us but for them.

Many women, however, did write and send parcels from the 1960s onwards, although as they sometimes used false names or a different address they were often uncertain whether their letters and parcels arrived. As Mara told me, it sometimes placed Latvians in the UK in danger:

> There was a time when they (the Soviet authorities) wanted my husband to go back. It was a scary time for us in Golders Green. We had been in Sweden and I sent a parcel (to her husband's family still in Latvia) and they went to my sister in law and they made her write a letter to her brother and ask him to come back. My husband told the (British) police about it and they told us if someone came to the house, to give him a good lunch or supper and a lot to drink. So I did.

As relations between Britain and the Soviet Union became easier in the 1960s and 1970s, a few women began to ponder practicalities, as well as the morality, of travelling back to Latvia. Free travel was forbidden during these years and the only way to go to Latvia was on a tourist visa, travelling via Moscow to Riga. Once in Latvia, tourists were strictly chaperoned and were not permitted to visit any other towns or the countryside, where many of these women had spent parts of their childhood. It was also clear that many members of the British Latvian community disapproved of the decisions of those who did decide to visit, as Eva explains in an interesting comment on her first visit that slides into her views about the more recent relations between Latvians and Russians in the post-independence period, as well as a comment on the inter-war policy of separate schooling for minorities.

> Naturally we started to go to Latvia. I was there first time in 1978. ... I was already writing with my brother and something was, my inside, I wished to see my country, I wished to see Latvia. The Latvian society here wasn't very sympathetic

when somebody wanted to visit a communist country but me, this friend Agnes and my youngest son, we decided to go to Latvia and we were travelling by train. That was a marvellous experience and an awful experience.

The train went first to Moscow and then to Latvia and thank goodness I had this friend Agnes because she speaks perfect Russian. She is older than me. I can understand Russian a bit, I mean the year the Russians were there (in 1941) we had to learn at school and I wasn't so bad at school. And you hear, you know, we always been living together with Russians, Germans, these Baltic Germans been living there in generations in Latvia. They had their separate schools, the Russians and the Germans and the Jews but they all get along together. Why I am telling you this because the Russians have been claiming that we are unfair to them now. They say that is a dog's language, the Latvian language, they really, you know, put us down and they not going to learn, but they have to learn, if you are living in a county you have to learn the language. They been in Latvia for 50 years and they haven't because all the Latvians have to speak Russian. So my friend speak perfect Russian and that was good when the customs come on the train. But oh it was so awful, that was an emotional experience.

Many of the 25 women, however, decided not to visit their country as the conditions placed on where they might travel were so restrictive. As I documented in Chapters 6 and 7, they were both busy and financially hard up in the years when they were raising children.

Travel and decisions about citizenship

The re-establishment of an independent Latvia seemed a remote prospect during the long years of the Cold War and inevitably, as the years passed and hopes of Latvian independence receded, Latvians' involvement with the institutions and practices of daily life in Britain increased. Some accommodation with Britain became inevitable, especially as Latvians in Britain began to think about travel and building contacts with the wider Latvian diaspora in Canada, Australia and Sweden. Deciding to travel raised the difficult question of whether to take British citizenship. Although Latvians were able to travel to certain European countries on the travel papers they received in the 1940s, to go elsewhere, especially the United States, required a British passport and, in order to obtain one, the acquisition of citizenship. For some this decision was bound up with employment and business reasons rather than to facilitate travel. Elvira, for example, took citizenship when she became a teacher and Eva's husband did the same to make his business interests more secure. He had started a small business when he and Eva sold their guest house and, albeit with some reluctance, they took out British citizenship on the advice of his bank manager:

We took British citizenship, in what year? In the mid 1960s, I think. I know that the bank manager said to him a bit earlier, I think it would be nice that you took British citizenship but then my husband said no, he is not going to sell his citizenship but then we realised he had to take it and we started going abroad for holidays and things like that. ... It was much better. It is a bit silly now when I look back. I mean you can't change yourself, nobody is going to change you when you are British

> subject and there were so many privileges. And really in some ways and I mean, I feel, I say, this is now, England is home.

But Eva's acceptance that England had become home, again I think reluctantly, as her language reveals, was not a common view. Many of the EVW women to whom I talked continued to hope and work for Latvian independence, even though gradually over the decades most of them became British citizens for largely pragmatic reasons. A key reason in their decision to do so was the growth of travel opportunities elsewhere in Western Europe and more widely. There were two main reasons for travel: to be able to participate in the growing numbers of international Latvian festivals in Sweden and Germany or for reunions with friends and family members who had moved to the USA, Canada and Australia in the late 1940s, either directly from the displaced persons' camps or after being released from their contract labour in Great Britain. Thus, an irony of accepting British citizenship was that it resulted in a strengthening of the bonds within the Latvian diasporic community. Lina, with no need, is apologetic that travel was her reason for accepting British citizenship but her comments make clear how important song contests were in the construction of a pan-European Latvian identity:

> I took out citizenship in the 1970s as I wanted to travel. Not a very good reason. Before then we something called a travel document. I think for Germany you didn't need a visa but for some countries you did. Before then I wasn't going anywhere, I don't know why exactly. ...
>
> We went to Germany. Basically we went there because we had our European song festivals for people living in various countries in Europe. They were big events, really lovely. We have a very old song festival tradition. What happens is that many choirs get together and they sing the same songs. So you could have a choir of 500, even 1,000 and they sing together sometimes with an orchestra or without. It is lovely.

Sadly, she noted: 'We haven't got a choir at the moment as we are short of male voices.'

Agnese and her husband became British citizens in the late 1970s but, as she insisted, the decision did not dilute her attachment to her homeland:

> We took British citizenship, after 25 years and do you know we were cross-examined about why we were so late. But we always hoped to go home.

Old age

As these women moved into their retirement years, the strength of their identification with Latvia deepened. In part this was because, in retirement, they had more time to devote to community-based activities, especially if they had been in employment into their 60s. Identities, as post-modern theorists have argued, are multiple, fluid and mobile, and so context-dependent and changing over time. Thus, for the women who moved into professional or semi-professional employment, such as nursing, during their working lives, they had an identity that was separate from, if connected to, that of being a Latvian. In the years of post-retirement, however, nationality was reasserted as the dominant element in their sense of self, perhaps especially for the women who chose to move into a Latvian retirement 'village'. Thus, as Agnese explains:

> When I was still working I was friends with several English women. We used to go out after meetings, for example, and I still write to some of them. Work was important to me then, but now I live here (in a Latvian community home in Leicestershire), I feel I am a Latvian again. When I was at work I was still Latvian but there we were all nurses: English, Irish, Latvian or whatever – being a nurse was what mattered.

This sense of a workplace identity, however, was usually restricted to the women who had become nurses. For those who remained in the textile industry, employment had always been little more than a means to an end with little intrinsic meaning. It was their Latvian identity which gave meaning to these women's sense of themselves as Lizina who had worked in a Bolton mill throughout the 1950s and 1960s explains:

> I lived two lives even then. One was my working life – I went to work, earned my wages and that was that. As soon as I walked out of the workplace, I wasn't a worker or an English woman. I was a Latvian. I had my home, I had my family, we had Latvian books and papers, Latvian plays, Latvian choirs and so we had our own separate lives. Our social life was a Latvian life.

It was not only the women who chose to move into a Latvian community on retirement who felt a stronger connection to 'home' as they aged. Here is Vieda explaining the limited connections she maintained when she was married and how this has changed now:

> When they [her children] were small I used to sing them some lullabies or something in Latvian or some words and but otherwise no. But my husband though, when he was alive, there was a Latvian Embassy, no consulate then and every month he went to Queen's Terrace to buy me a Latvian book. We didn't belong to any Latvian networks. I didn't have the time and when my husband died I didn't have the time either. But only for the last fourteen years, I am now working for the Latvian welfare fund, and I am the London treasurer for five years or so and I am reading in for the blind people the cassette. ... It takes some time and it's something to do.

As Mara echoed:

> Now I am old and my friends now are Latvians. We do a lot of charity work. There is what you call it for the old people and for the children. We sell for the Christmas bazaar and money goes to Latvia.

However, the times had also changed, as well as these women's lives, with Gorbachev's policy of *perestroika* and *glasnost*. The prospect of Latvia regaining independence became more likely at the end of the 1980s and with it the restitution of Latvian nationality for Latvian exiles. At the beginning of the 1990s, as independence was recognised, the women who had never been 'home', unable to contemplate the restrictions imposed during the Soviet regime, had to face the difficult decision of whether to return. For them, Latvia had remained a 'real' home but an imagined one, the place from which they had originated, and so both familiar yet strange because of the long years of occupation. To return, whether in the 1970s as Eva had done, or in the post-independence years, meant going home as a guest, reliant on the hospitality of others. The sense of having become a stranger in a foreign land that was at the same time familiar and 'homely' is disconcerting, challenging the collective myths and memories that had become such a central part of the idea of home that had sustained and comforted the Latvian community in Britain through their long exile. Inevitably, return was emotional and overwhelming and at the same time disappointing as the beloved country seemed smaller and shabbier than in their memories. That familiar past that had been frozen through its reconstruction in myths, rituals and memories in Britain had disappeared. Furthermore, in some cases, feelings of resentment and jealousy among those who had been left behind resurfaced to spoil the reunion. As Beer (1989, p 3) has pointed out: 'The return of the native has often been an occasion of confusion, bloodshed and dismay as well as rejoicing'. Confusion, dismay and rejoicing were common parts of the mixed emotions described to me by those who returned. And even bloodshed was a possibility as one women told me that she and her husband had been advised to purchase a gun and keep it under their pillow if they used hotels in Riga as 'the city is now so lawless'.

This is Lina talking. She went back to Latvia for the first time since 1944 in 1990:

> The first time I went to Latvia was in 1990. I took part in the song festival in Riga. It was very moving. I still had a step-sister. I saw her that first time and her daughter and, of course, my own brother and sister. They had stayed. And step-sister had stayed with my step-father. I travelled to the rural area. I suppose it looked different because I was an adult. It seemed small but the countryside is beautiful.

In 1991, members of the Latvian diaspora were able to apply for Latvian citizenship and a passport, as Lina explains:

> I have a Latvian passport now. So I have two now. You could apply but there was a limit and now when you have to apply you have to give up your British passport. The rules have tightened up since then.

Agnese also made the same decision, as did her daughters:

> My daughters are British citizens but they have taken the Latvian citizenship as well now and we have dual citizenship. We could, you know register from 1991, and we did. We are Latvian patriots.

Agnese finally returned to Latvia in 1993 and, like Lina, her ostensible reason was to participate in a song festival. Her comments reveal the sense of regret that independence came too late for her generation as well as her continued resentment of the Russian dominance of her country:

> We finally went in 1993 for the first time, there was a song festival and the choir from here [the Catthorpe residential community] sang in the festival. But we are too old to go back. My husband's parents had a big farm in northern Latvia but it has been sold for coppers, hundreds of pounds to some wheeler-dealer and he can't even get it back. The house, it is ruined, not looked after and probably dropping and orchard has been cut down and it is really in a poor state. He can get some land round about but not the house and it is too late. I am 74 and my husband is 76, even

> 10 years ago we were too old to start and we have no knowledge of farming. My husband's leanings are not that way, not to farming or even to gardening. It is difficult ... and we have nowhere to live, there are so many Russians living in our country. Our people still live in these communal, like a flat, in Riga, three rooms, a family lives in each room and uses the kitchen and toilet.

Diana also felt too old to return, even for a brief visit. Regaining her Latvian passport, however, gave her great pleasure and was both a key part of her 80th birthday celebrations and a justification of her decision not to accept British citizenship:

> We never took British citizenship, nothing again. For my 80th birthday I had a big present. I had a Latvian passport. Now I know it doesn't give me anything but the Russians took it away and I obey all the laws and what I have to do in England but somehow I am too old to change.

Having a passport meant that travel to Latvia became easier, but the decision to return was less straightforward and many women told me of the difficulty they had in deciding whether to go back or not. Here is Diana explaining why she decided not to return:

> It is completely different though, Latvia now. It is not the Latvia I remember. Everything has changed. In 1991 or 1992 both my sisters went but I haven't been. I am too scared I might have heart attack. Both my children have been and grandchildren. But I sometimes think I am too old. The house we had, my father liked to garden and there was flowers and fruit trees but when they went there it was different. There was nothing and the house looked dilapidated. They could hardly recognise the place. Just before we left my father planted a new garden with apples and pears and cherries and there was nothing. I want to remember as it was. Maybe it is cowardly but ... maybe for you it looks sentimental or childish but for us ...

Although Diana had never returned to Latvia her recollections of her country are similar to those of women who have visited. Guilt, ambivalence, sadness about the poor state of the land and its infrastructure and a sense of loss are threaded through their memories, as well as the emotional drain imposed by return. Ilona's reactions are typical:

> I first went back in 1992. In 1991 my cousin came here. We parted as schoolgirls and we meet as old ladies. I went in 1993 and 1994 and then just last year. I went back to my home village. I left the stones of the mill to go to produce another mill. It hadn't been looked after. The land is there and the potteries and I am having compensation for the potteries. ... When I first went back it was tears, tears, tears, one big cry. Even last year I felt I was walking back into the past. Nothing is changed. I went where I used to walk to school and looked at the houses and they are all drab, nobody around. People peering through the curtains as you walk by. And do you know, I couldn't remember a thing and I arrived by the school and I asked myself what are you looking for, because you don't really belong there any more. I was in my teens, 18 and I go back as a 70 year old. It is a long time away. I haven't got a Latvian passport. I have a British one. I am a British citizen but I have a little slip that says I am a Latvian citizen but I haven't got a passport yet, no. I think I shall or I can't vote there.

But compare this with Elvira's more pragmatic comment:

> I don't have a Latvian passport that would just be sentimental. We can't travel on it. I still feel Latvian. I am Latvian but I also feel very much for England. My life has been here. Two of my daughters are here and one is in Canada.

Ilona's ambivalence is matched by Vieda's guilt at having left and her ambivalence about returning as she explains below in a long quote that illustrates both her sense of loss, framed in typical bucolic images of the golden inter-war years, but also her gratitude for her life in Britain:

> But now since it is independent I always go to Latvia every year. Because I still have one school friend from the same village. I regularly visit to Latvia every year. First year when I went back I felt like a traitor, I felt very bad, because it was so bad there, everything. I remember as a child the big fields, barley or flax, all beautiful, growing and clean because Latvia came up from 1918 to 1940, for twenty years I think her status was just behind Sweden, it was very high, we had the first hydraulic station and all the things, it was hard working and it was good those years were good and I remember it like that. Those years were good not that I had particularly good but that besides the point but when I went back it was such a contrast. It was dreadful, dreadful. ... First time when I went back, I felt, I don't know. I just cried all the time, for two weeks I cried it was so stupid but I don't know it was kind of ...

I asked why she felt like a traitor, and she replied:

> Well look, I left it and I know it was very, very hard, sometimes really, really difficult, all those walks and digging potatoes from a field and sleeping in the woods and so but it was, while you are young you do that and you survive you know. And then when I went back I thought well I survived and I live reasonably well and two children and so on even though husband has gone and I live different life from them there. And it's so down on a ground level, you know, that I felt guilty, why I should have stayed you know and done, lived all what they lived. It's a bit of patriotism I think and when I go I still feel, many people who lived in a way, many people who live here in England or in America, Australia and so go back and go back but I could not do that. I think I will never be able to do it for I always feel I should have been there when was the times were bad.

Other women echoed this comment with pain in their voices. After decades of being strangers in Britain, it was hard to accept that in Latvia too their identity was also that of a stranger, even an intruder who should have been there during the difficult years but instead had chosen to leave.

Rethinking home

It became clear to these women that a more complicated, a complex and contested, notion of 'home' and belonging had been forged by the historical circumstances that had separated them from their country and its occupants during the war. Estrangement and the absence as well as presence of a shared history and a sense of national belonging both united and divided Latvians who had left and those who had stayed. The Latvian language, as used locally, had changed during their absence and some of them found it hard to make themselves understood, even though before their visit they had assumed that they were still fluent in their first language. A number of women also found the open hostility in shops and in the streets, for example, between the indigenous population and the large Russian minority that was disenfranchised on the regaining of independence (Smith *et al* 1998), hard to cope with. Almost all of the 25 women to whom I talked knew, like Vieda, that they would never be able to return permanently:

> I am too old now. I am 70 and anyway all my things are here now, my son and daughter and my grandchild. I see them, they come all the time to see me and so and even though you are born you belong to two places. I think all displaced people, one sort of part you are Latvian but in a practical sense and for other things I am British and I feel that here I have to play my part and I am very much interested what is going on here, with the politics and everything because I live here and England has been good to me, even if it was hard time. But you forget those hard times and England is my home and I could not go back. But I visit and there I make some good friends there, in Riga. When I grew up I was too poor and anyway was no opportunity but now I try to see every corner of Latvia: the flowers, the stars at night in the autumn, the blue sky and the stars, it is so, it is so beautiful. We have forest and forest and lakes and rivers.

Although a sense of this dual or hybrid identity, or perhaps to phrase it less positively, of being out of place in both countries, dominated many of the comments, Mara, who was amongst the oldest of the 25 women, had a much stronger sense of herself as still Latvian, in part, perhaps, because she had been able to repossess family property:

> 1991 Latvia was free again and after that I go twice a year. We got a house back. It had been nationalised. We had a lovely house on the outskirts of Riga and a lot of land around. The Russians took it and built a block. It had belonged to my father-in-law. My sister-in-law got it back. She got some money from leasing the land. The block is not worth anything. It was built 50 years ago and never repaired. It has 8 little flats or rooms, flatlets really, and my sister-in-law now has 4 of them and we have a flat there too, on the ground floor. My husband never went as he was already ill. He died in 1992 but his ashes are in Latvia.

In response to a question about her sense of identity, whether she felt Latvian or British, Mara replied :

> Latvian. I still feel as a foreigner. I don't know. I don't know why. I was 25 when I came out of Latvia and even now, even my children when I have to speak English to them they say you don't feel like my mother when I speak a different language to them.

For Lina return was marked by feelings of loss but also of resentment:

> I go back now for holidays. I suppose I am scared to return permanently. I don't want to give up everything here and start again over there. I don't feel up to it, sort of thing. You asked if I am Latvian or British or a bit of both? A bit of both, I think. Well, it's quite funny I have an accent when I speak English but sometimes people in Latvia say you have an accent. And I am quite annoyed. How dare they? But then in a way I suppose we are different. For 50 years we have lived apart. We have lived in the West and they have lived under the communist regime so I think quite a few things may be different or may have changed over the years.

Agnese also told me that going home was not straightforward. In this case the feelings of resentment were among the population that had stayed not those who returned:

> Some of our people resent us. They think we are millionaires. ... They can't believe it, that it's been so hard. Men working in the mines, the steel industry, textiles, or farms and they don't believe it that we came to England with nothing.

This lack of understanding of the struggles to make a living and keep alive a spirit of national belonging made it hard sometimes for relations to be re-established between Latvians 'here' and 'there', after the long years of separation. The pain of finding that the long years had made these women strangers in their own country, the grief of finding themselves once again a refugee and exile but this second time in their own land was an unexpected and unwelcome result after the long years of yearning for home.

Although this sense of not being at home in one's home is a common response of return migrants (Smith 1996) it was perhaps particularly poignant for these women as it coincided with the re-establishment of the Latvian 'homeland' as an independent nation state. But because 'home' had been recreated through myth and memory in the imagination of the Latvian diaspora as an idealised place, it also became a place to which it was impossible to return, an imagined place of origin rather than a 'real' geographical locality. Disappointment, then, was inevitable as the lived experiences that had constituted home for these women were so long ago and the country had undergone such significant changes. But despite these difficulties, despite the apparent lack of empathy between those who had stayed behind and those who had not, and the feeling that independence had come too late for the women who had left in 1944, Lina feels that the establishment and long persistence of a sense of community among Latvians in Britain was still worth it:

> All those years you know – 50 years. I think to begin with for many years we were all waiting for the independence to come and to go back. And now, as the independence came so late, we're no longer planning to go back but we still feel as Latvian and now those people who take part in the Latvian community here, you know in the welfare work, all our funds go to Latvia now for education, for orphans, for big families, ill people or for pensions. So we send lots of funds over there now to help to rebuild the country. Also having a Latvia passport I feel I can take part in the elections. I feel that I want to be part of that as well. I have always voted in Britain too, so it's a bit of both.

Thus, in her concluding comment, Lina captures the notion of hybridity that informs contemporary theorising. Yet for many women, this 'betweenness' – 'a bit of both', as Marta termed it – is not a celebration of diversity, nor a successful transition or translation between two different societies but rather the sense of a hard life, often informed and infused by the sense of great loss that leaving Latvia in 1944 brought to these women.

These women had not chosen to be nomads, or travellers; they were exiles, longing for home and refusing to transgress the stubborn boundaries of their self-identification as, above all, Latvian. Not all migrants are implicated in the creation of a new form of globalised identity as contemporary theorists sometimes too uncritically assert. As Ahmed (2000, p 86) argues: 'There is no necessary link between forms of travel, migration and movement and the transgression and destabilisation of identity.' In certain versions of post-modern theory this link is perhaps too easily assumed, rather than critically assessed, albeit in invaluable attempts to combat contemporary fundamentalist and racist movements based on essentialist notions of an unchanging identity. Diana's stoical summation of her life perhaps best captures the mutual sense among these migrant women that their lives had been transformed by material circumstances that they were powerless to resist:

> We have never been rich but we have managed. I can't say I am happy but you have to live through it.

Reclaiming and reconstituting their Latvian identity in exile was part of the mechanism of 'living through it'. By 1990 and with the prospect of Latvia regaining her independence, their long exile and the continued belief in their separate, unique Latvian identity seemed vindicated, even though independence came a little too late for most of these women. Interestingly, their strong sense of identity has been passed on to their children, some of whom are now, in their middle age, actively involved in Latvia's future.

CHAPTER 9

CONCLUSIONS: MEMORY, IDENTITY AND TRANSLATION

The lives of the 25 women in this book bring together some of the most significant events of the second half of the twentieth century, as well as a range of dominant ideologies and key theoretical debates. The great political movements of fascism and communism, the Nazi domination of Germany and Stalin's grip on the Soviet Union, are reflected in the experiences of dislocation, loss and exile that were the consequence of their own and their families' decisions to leave Latvia in 1944. In Britain, post-war ideals about gender, femininity and domesticity and their eventual (partial) disruption were the background to their decisions as adult women, as technological and local, national and increasingly global social, economic and political changes altered the structure of opportunities for ordinary working families with relatives scattered across the world. Living standards rose during the 1950s and 1960s. Later, the quite extraordinary changes in technologies that transformed space and time enabled these women to build new contacts with distant friends and relatives as the decades in Britain passed. Then, in later life, the radical transformation and disintegration of the Soviet Union brought independence back to Latvia and allowed these women to reclaim their Latvian citizenship, completing their transformation from citizens to exiles to British citizens and, finally, once again as citizens of their own homeland.

Their lives also provide a useful illustration of and challenge to some of the key contemporary debates that currently fascinate professional social scientists and historians as well as an educated public: about the long shadow of the Second World War and the quite remarkable interest that is still evident in all its aspects, about the significance of migration, about the impact of loss on identity, about gender relations and the changing status and roles of women and men, about the meaning of citizenship and its significance in an increasingly globalised world that paradoxically has been increasingly riven in recent years by nationalist movements and sectarian claims. I am not arguing that the lives of these women can be 'read off' from these grand historical forces. As Brah (1996, p 124) has argued in the context of her work on more recent migratory movements from South Asia: 'Each 'I' is a unique constellation of shared collective meanings. Thus the relationship between personal biography and collective history is complex and contradictory ... [and] the specificity of a person's life experience ... [does] not simply mirror group experience.' For these women, the type of work to which they initially were allocated, their first job in the open labour market, where they lived, whether they married and had children or not, as well as the more random blows of fate and accident that left one woman a young widow, another childless and yet another as a victim of domestic abuse differentiated their lives. And yet, as they themselves recognised and enunciated, the events of the Second World

War and the long aftermath united them and produced lives of recognisable similarity. As Vieda Skultans (1998, p 8) has suggested, for Latvians, whether those who became part of the diaspora or those who remained in place after 1945, the past 50 years have involved living with the recognition of 'the engulfment of personal narratives by the collective narrative of history'.

Her claim is reflected in these women's narratives: their dominant view was of their own powerlessness in the face of the brute force of historical events that had shaped their lives before they had any agency as adult women. As Eva argued:

> We just had to get on and do our best; our ambitions were for our children, not for ourselves. Our own lives seem unimportant.

Her words were, unknowingly, echoed by those of Agnese who said in a comment on Latvia regaining her independence:

> It was too late for us – we don't belong in either place. Our lives have been but also should be forgotten. What matters is the future and our children.

I disagree with both of them: the lives of these women should not be forgotten. Instead, their memories and narratives provide an invaluable contribution to knowledge about the ambivalences and ambiguities of diasporic identities, as well as new insights into British immigration and labour market policies in the immediate post-war years. As the previous chapters have demonstrated their voices are extraordinarily strong and fascinating.

The interconnections of class, gender and ethnicity

As well as the intrinsic interest in lives straddling and affected by such large historical events, I believe that the now largely forgotten history of the Latvian population's recruitment to and residence in Britain is also significant for a number of interconnected reasons. These reasons are theoretical and conceptual as well as policy related and add to our understanding not only of the late 1940s and the 1950s but also to contemporary issues and dilemmas. First, their lives show how the category of economic migrants is a complex one, and one that repays disaggregation, looking at the commonalities and differences between peoples who migrate for economic reasons or who are officially placed into this category, as well as similarities and differences based on their class background and ethnic origins. As I have shown, Latvian European Voluntary Workers (EVWs) continued to see themselves as refugees, as political exiles rather than as economic migrants and this identification had a powerful impact on the decisions they made in later years. I have also shown, however, that despite the catch-all category of economic migrant, the EVWs from the Baltic were initially constructed in both official discourse and in their own view as different from and superior to other economic migrants – especially Irish and Caribbean migrants to the UK – in the same early post-war years. This superiority was based on both their class and ethnic background, as well as their religion. This they were seen as more 'eligible' because of their class position, their skin colour and their Protestantism, that distinguished them not only from Caribbean migrants but also from Irish and from Polish and other peoples from Catholic or Slav countries. This apparent superiority was in part reflected in their recruitment and early allocation to particular forms of employment in Britain and in the movement of some women into nursing, as well as in their future lives as wives, mothers and as members of an imagined Latvian community in exile that led to their differentiation and separation from the lives of other working women living in the same neighbourhoods. Their narrative constructions of self and their memories also reveal that this sense of themselves as Latvian was a powerful challenge to the initial hopes of the government of the time that EVW women from 'superior' backgrounds would quickly be assimilated into a hegemonic version of Englishness, would adopt dominant societal norms and begin to breed future Britons once their brief years as 'volunteers' in the labour market were completed and so conform not only to idealised notions of femininity in the 1950s, but would also marry British men. As I have shown, these hopes were confounded.

A second axis of differentiation between migrants is that of gender. It has become more common in studies of migration and dislocation to emphasise the significance of gender and its relationship to both patterns of movement and reconstructed lives. The narrative reconstructions of the lives of these Latvian women and, indeed, of the expanding body of work about women migrants living in diasporic communities, reveal some of the weaknesses in conventional distinctions in the literatures of migration. A focus on the specificity of the schemes challenges assumptions about women as dependants and also permits the particularities of gendered experiences to be unravelled. Addressing women's lives tends to lead analysts to place more emphasis on questions about domesticity, to look at women's roles within the home and the local community as well as their lives as migrant labourers than is sometimes the case when male migrants are the focus. The specificity of this particular study with its location in the 1940s and 1950s permits a challenge to be mounted to conventional associations between femininity and domesticity that sometimes dominates histories of these decades. Almost all of these women were paid labourers for considerable periods of their lives, including when their children were young. Family support – typically from older relatives who were allowed to come to Britain once the initial EVWs were more economically secure – and from within the wider Latvian community – permitted these women to combine employment and motherhood, relying on both paid and reciprocal forms of exchange for childcare, cleaning and laundry, for example. The lives of these women show the interconnections between the formal and informal relations of labour that were common in migrant communities in Britain.

However, although these women came to Britain as 'workers' and remained in employment, they also placed great store in family life, both reconstructing an idealised version of patriarchal family relations common in their girlhood, as well as sharing in the development of a more privatised form of family life that was becoming common in 1950s Britain. As life became easier and the home more comfortable, men and women perhaps had more shared leisure, although for women, the combination of paid work and the continued responsibility for almost all of the domestic labour in the home, meant that a 'double shift' was typical. Most Latvian men, like British men in the 1950s, seldom saw domestic labour as their responsibility, although a number of them cared for their children when their wives were doing shift work. But, for these women, communal solidarity as well as domestic privatisation and privation was a key part of their lives outside the labour market. Indeed, for most women it was their Latvian identity that was most significant in their construction of their own sense of identity in Britain as Latvian exiles and their participation in communal cultural and political activities probably far exceeded the levels of participation in similar events by the indigenous white working class. It might also be, however, that the example of a working mother produced independent and ambitious children, perhaps especially among the daughters of these women, who were untrammelled by the dominant view that a woman's place was in the home. British feminist theorist, Juliet Mitchell, has suggested that women of her generation who were children of British women who were employed during the war, were perhaps encouraged by their mothers' example to seek independence through labour market participation.[1] A future project based on interviews with the second generation might profitably explore the connections between mothers' and daughters' lives.

Migrant Identities

The particular circumstances of these white, alien, European immigrants also provide a challenge to more conventional narratives of immigration within the UK, allowing the complex interconnections between class position, 'race' and ethnicity, age, gender and nationality to be addressed through a new empirical lens, and so providing not only a more sophisticated understanding of historical patterns of movement but also new insights into contemporary migration flows. An understanding of the position of these white female migrants in the late 1940s and 1950s unsettles some of the taken-for-granted binary associations between migration and identity, disrupting not only the black/white binary distinction but also showing the complexities of the associations between whiteness and migrant identities in Britain. In the strongly gendered and racialised construction of British identity in the 1940s and 1950s, indigenous white men and women were assumed to occupy different spheres. White women were identified by their domesticity, constructed as good mothers in the home (and perhaps in combination with a little job for pin money) and white men proved their worth as breadwinners. Black men were the 'other' (Webster 1998) in British society in these years, constructed both as an economic and a sexual threat to the masculine superiority of British men, and feared and desired by men and women alike. Migrant women underpinned these distinctions and social constructions by their largely unseen presence, almost invisible as private domestic labourers in the home and largely ignored by most analysts of workplace change, although their relative significance as paid domestic workers in the post-war period has been documented. But 'race' divided these women. Bronwen Walter (2001, pp 108–09), for example, has argued that whereas 'white migrant women were permitted to

1 Remarks during a plenary address to the annual conference of the International Association of Feminist Economists, St Hilda's College, Oxford, 5 August 2004.

work inside the homes of indigenous English women ... black women were not seen as suitable for this work. Instead they were distanced from the personal lives of white English people and given public domestic work, such as hospital cleaning'.

But as I have shown here, this oversimplifies the story. White Latvian women also worked in the public arena as cleaners and domestics. Furthermore, both Baltic and Irish women were an important element in the labour supply of the textile industry in the late 1940s, alongside indigenous, but working class, white women. Thus, the connections between ethnicity, colour, gender and national identity were more complex in the immediate post-war years than some of the histories of this period allow. As the comparisons between Latvian and Irish women also make clear, 'whiteness' is itself a multiple category that repays disaggregation. In her study of Irish women in Britain, Walter (2001, p 272) pertinently noted that too many of the admittedly pioneering studies of whiteness that were published in the 1990s assumed whiteness was a singular category, failing to recognise 'the heterogeneity of its constituent parts'. Thus, in studies as diverse as Vron Ware's (1992) assessment of the place of white women in Imperial India and Ruth Frankenberg's (1993) work on white women in the USA in the twentieth century, there is no consideration of differences between white women based on their ethnicity. In case studies of British society, whiteness is also too often unproblematically assumed to confer either an Englishness or a middle class identity with its associated privileges, or both (see, for example, Bonnett 1996; Jeater 1992; Mirza 1992). These assumptions and associations tend to lead to the invisibility of white migrants and sometimes to the neglect of their specific problems. Paradoxically, it also results in, as Wendy Webster (1998) argued in her study of women's lives in the same post-war decades, a lack of acknowledgment of the shared circumstances of both white and black migrants in the 1940s. Although Latvians, often middle class and urban by background and forced to move because of the traumas of war, might deny the extent to which they share experiences with, for example, Polish women of rural origins, let alone migrants from the Caribbean, it is clear that in the 1940s they occupied similar locations in the labour market. But the differences between these three groups – EVWs, Irish and Caribbean migrants – were also significant as whiteness is a heterogeneous category, as marked by differences and fractured by power differentials as any other social division. Despite their white skins, Irish and Latvian women in Britain in the 1950s and 1960s lived different lives, even though both groups of women were migrant workers.

What this case study so clearly illustrates is the complexity and specificity of social relations and the interconnections and relationships between the key social divisions or categories of social scientists. It shows how ethnicity, gender and class relations overlay, cross cut and intersect each other so that a singular explanation, based on just one of these divisions is insufficient. Approaches that emphasise the relationality or intersectionality of social divisions, as well as their variety, have now become common within the social sciences (see, for example, Glucksmann 2000; McDowell 2004; Massey 2004). And the specificity of both time and space are a key part of these approaches. Social relations are both complex and particular taking different forms as circumstances change over time and between different places, where the histories of, for example, employment, class relations, local politics and policies construct a varied set of opportunities in different places. I hope that this book has adequately demonstrated the key significance of geography: that place matters too. Location – place of birth, of exile, place of work both in the sense of the town, city or village where work is undertaken as well as its sectoral location within a specific industry with the associated conditions of work and rates of pay – has influenced these women's opportunities, their circle of friends and acquaintances, their access to local resources and their sense of themselves as women, as Latvian, as members of the working class, as northerners or southerners.

The significance of place

Place brings particularity to people's experiences, grounding them in specific relations of power that operate across a range of spatial scales and which both enable and constrain the lives of the inhabitants. As I have shown, regional and local variations in the nature of the labour and housing markets, in the class structure and in beliefs about what is appropriate for 'people like us' influence the ways in which decisions about work and family life are made. In their early years in the UK, Latvian women, as soon as they were permitted to do so, moved jobs and homes to be closer to the people with whom they felt a sense of solidarity and could build networks of communal support, often in towns and cities in the midlands or the north of England. Regional differences and uneven development was a marked part of the geography of post-war Britain (Walby 1986) and the standard of living in many places shocked some of the young women when they first arrived. The poor sanitation and inadequate heating of many British homes was remarked on by many of the women, as well as the inadequate diets of the working class. Despite the hardships they themselves had suffered during their journey across Europe and time spent in the camps, they commented adversely on the conditions under which they had to live in the first five or so years in Great Britain. In these largely working class towns and neighbourhoods, the Latvian women did their best to reconstruct a version of 'home'. Through their long involvement in paid work, they lived everyday lives that challenged the dominant belief that women's place was in the home and yet, as I argued above, through their deep commitment to a traditional form of patriarchal family life, these women also conformed to the strong belief in 1950s Britain in domesticity and femininity. In both arenas, their lives had certain similarities to those of indigenous working class women, especially those living in the industrial and mill towns of Lancashire and Yorkshire. These women were not in the vanguard of challenges to women's roles and typical gender relations based on male dominance – that came from middle class women. Instead, through their conformity, they rebuilt lives committed to what might be seen as conservative views of the place of the family, the state and the nation. Through their adherence to hard work in the public arena of the workplace and in the private arena of the home they attempted to rebuild lives shattered by exile and loss in their teens and early 20s in ways that kept them, as they still do, largely out of view in 1950s and

1960s Britain and which were centred on a sense of continuous membership of the Latvian nation.

Thus place, in a different way, in a metaphorical sense of belonging or not belonging, as being insiders or outsiders, of displacement and (re)placement, defines the lives of migrant peoples. It is clear that the narratives of these Latvian women provide a sceptical redress to those contemporary theories of hybrid and mobile identities that suggest that identity is fluid and mobile, based on the intersectionality of key social and spatial divisions that helps to create among migrants and the indigenous populations of the places in which they settle a new sense of themselves as neither/or, but instead a new form of hybrid identity that is forged through the translation of original identities. Instead, these Latvian women, through their insistence on the singular significance of their Latvian nationality and their long commitment to an imaginary version of Latvia, remained committed to an essentialised version of who they were and remain. In this sense, too, their lives and beliefs also challenge claims that it is primarily the discriminatory attitudes and practices by the indigenous population that construct migrants as 'outsiders'. These Latvian migrants determinedly clung to their sense of themselves as different and had almost no interest in official acceptance by the British state. It was the tenacity of their belief that Latvia would once again achieve recognition as an independent nation state that sustained these women throughout their long lives in Britain.

In their middle years, quite clearly other aspects of their everyday life also took on a significance in their sense of themselves as, for example, paid workers and as mothers, but their Latvian identity and their participation in communal activities and events was maintained throughout these busy years and in retirement gained a new significance. Nevertheless, formal recognition as British citizens enabled some of them to travel in their middle age and provided a way of participating in the life of a Latvian diasporic population spread across Europe as well as in the USA, Canada and Australia. To adopt Avtar's Brah's (1996, p 8) vivid description of the lives of migrants in Britain, however reluctantly these Latvian women became part of the 'entanglements of dispersion with those of staying put'. This notion of entanglement seems to me to capture the ways in which Latvian women's lives in Britain were constructed with its overtones of reluctance and being trapped by historical circumstances over which they had little or no control. Although access to British citizenship did eventually become important for many EVWs, the history of their entry to the UK and its comparison with that of the almost concurrent entry of migrants from the Caribbean reveals the relative insignificance of formal citizenship rights in ensuring decent and equal treatment in comparison with the significance of skin colour and an idealised Enlightenment version of European identity. Despite being citizens, it was the latter group who were treated as despised outsiders. Skin colour has continued to have a malignant resonance right through the post-war history of immigration policy until the present day and is still reflected in contemporary policy decisions and dilemmas.

As Kathleen Paul has argued 'the decade between the passing of the 1948 British Nationality Act and the 1962 Commonwealth Immigrants Act constitutes a critical period in the politics of citizenship in post-war Britain' (Paul 1997, p 131). At the end of the Second World War, the aim was to maintain Britain's position at the centre of the Commonwealth through the export of white Britons to the 'periphery'. Thus, out-migration, combined with the demands of the post-war construction programme, created labour shortages within Britain which initially, at least, were met through the importing of 'suitable migrants': people of white European origins from Ireland and from among the displaced people of Europe. In this way, the British State attempted, for a brief period and unsuccessfully, to evade the implications of its colonial history and the post-colonial consequences. But the EVW schemes were insufficient in scale to prop up the notion of a white Britain and/or of a European conception of Britishness. The EVW schemes were a short-lived and unrepeatable phase in British immigration policies, formulated to meet an immediate crisis in 1945. As the labour shortages in Britain eased and as the numbers of people stranded in camps for displaced persons in Germany declined as other countries offered more generous terms including a more certain prospect of resettlement, the flow of migration to Britain began to decline. Continuing trade union opposition to EVWs probably also hastened the decline.

The EVW schemes clearly illustrate the limits of the notion of assimilation that was so influential in both academic and policy discussions of immigration policy in the early post-war years. As I have documented here, migrants – however 'suitable' they may appear – cannot be corralled into an official version of British identity but persist in building and rebuilding 'other' identities – albeit ones that were unthreatening to the white British population. These EVWs from the Baltic States and from elsewhere, as well as the considerable numbers of Polish servicemen who were demobilised in the UK, neither threatened nor challenged idealised images of Britishness, but neither would they submit to it and adopt the identity of a 'proper' English man or woman. Instead, their deep commitment to their own ethnic identity, their relatively small numbers, their skin colour and their strong Protestant work ethic based on an ideal of self-help and individual effort allowed them to recreate imagined versions of essentialised European identities without disruption from racist reactions. Instead, it was the almost concurrent migration of British citizens from the Caribbean, and the later movements from the Indian subcontinent, whose larger numbers and visible difference that was to disrupt the older version of a white, European Britishness that the governments of the post-war decades had assumed was immutable. Even though these Caribbean and Asian economic migrants and refugees were in the main citizens of the UK, they were constructed as less suitable for assimilation and as parents of future Britons because of their skin colour. Consequently, from 1947 onwards 'by highlighting skin colour as a distinguishing feature rather than nationality as a binding fact, the policy-making elite's terms of reference implicitly identified the UK indigenous population and the colonial migrant population as opposites' (Paul 1992, p 135).

European in-migrants, whether Irish or not, as a consequence of pigmentation, were able to avoid this construction as the 'other', although people of Irish origin quite clearly suffered from stereotypical labelling as inferior in all sorts of ways. For EVWs, a complex and interconnected set of factors meant that they avoided 'othering' and discriminatory treatment to a large extent. The combination of their European heritage and skin colour, the (limited) post-war sympathy for refugees and displaced persons, as well as political prisoners, together with a general level of ignorance of Baltic and other north and eastern European traditions among the British population, meant that the first group of post-war labour migrants remained largely invisible within Britain. This invisibility, combined with their relatively small numbers and their desire to remain unassimilated, allowed them to organise their own communal institutions without harassment from the population at large or from the State.

Although the EVW population doubled the number of aliens resident in Britain at the end of the war, the discriminatory policies of controlled migration lay not in numbers but in the post-war construction of black migrants as inferior. The overt racism of British society from this time has a long and undistinguished history and has been mirrored in official immigration policy throughout the second half of the twentieth century and into the new millennium. The liberal and open provisions of the 1948 Act were replaced 14 years later by the 1962 Act which replaced the open borders of Britain by a policy of control and policing. In the 40 years since then, immigration controls have been intensified and the liberal policy of uncontrolled migration seems but a distant dream. At present the vexed distinctions between the status of different migrants (between refugees and economic migrants), between *de jure* rights of British citizenship and membership of a more fluid European community, between skin colour and class position, between the former colonies and post-Soviet states, are again on the political agenda as a right wing Labour Home Secretary attempts to restrict rights of entry to the UK, despite labour shortages in key sectors and to balance the maintenance of rigid borders with a humanitarian commitment to those seeking asylum (White Paper 2002 legislation that came into force in November 2004). The expansion of the European Union in 2004 to include the three Baltic States, among others, once again raises difficult but interesting questions about the associations between white European identity and the status of economic migrants.

Oral histories and memories

Talking to EVWs and attempting to reconstruct their lives also raises important questions about methods and ethics in carrying out historical and social science research. Doing the sort of work reported here based on interviews and the establishment of a relationships of personal trust between respondents and interviewers places a burden of responsibility on the researcher in a role that is similar to a cross between being a detective, a translator, an inquisitive stranger and a sympathetic friend. Personal attributes such as age, class and ethnicity all take on a significance in the encounter between researcher and the researched. As a geographer, I hesitate to draw parallels between my methods and those of anthropologists who, in their commitment to the ethnographic method, often spend months if not years among their 'informants'. As Agar has argued, and many other anthropologists since, 'ethnography is really quite an arrogant enterprise ... an ethnographer moves in among a group of strangers to study and describe their belief, document their social life, write about their subsistence strategies and generally explore their territory right down to their recipes for the evening meal (Agar 1980, p 41). While I partially concur with Agar, and I am conscious that I too wanted to know many personal details of these women's long lives, times have changed and the unthinking authority of the arrogant observer in Agar's description has been challenged. The sort of qualitative case-study research described here is, I hope, more of a partnership in which the relationship between the participants is less authoritarian and more tentative than in the past and the version of the stories told to me about loss, dislocation and rebuilding lives and communities is accepted as just a version of what happened told to a particular listener at a particular time rather than 'the truth'. I should like to place the approach that I adopted within feminist debates about the relationship between researchers and respondents, in ideas about a more dispersed form of authority based on listening and collaboration (Gluck and Patai 1991) in which texts become dialogical or polyphonic (Clifford and Marcus 1986), rather than the singular voice of the author. I am sure readers were quick to hear the strong voices and views of the women to whom I talked.

As I mentioned at the start of the book, these women reformed my initial research agenda for me by their insistence on the significance of their exile and their refusal to accept that their long lives in Britain were as important as the events in their own land that shaped their identities as Latvians throughout their lives but especially at the key moments in their teens and in their retirement to which they themselves attributed greatest significance. And while I did send a version of an early draft of an academic article to the women whom I interviewed they did not read this entire manuscript before it was published. Further, as I promised when I started the work, I have changed their names here, randomly assigning a name that I hope is acceptable to each woman, if she recognises herself but not, of course, altering any of the events of her life. It is clear, then, that claims about collaboration mutual influence cannot, and should not, disguise the influence and responsibilities of the author, who chooses, selects, interprets and re-presents what she has heard, and, of course, partially determines the stories that she is told through the sorts of questions posed and through the relationship that is forged with her 'informants'.

As Judith Stacey (1988) argued almost two decades ago, feminist researchers cannot avoid difficult ethical questions about exploitation. Researchers who collect people's life stories are inevitably confronted by complex and difficult memories that may enrich their work and cause pain both to the teller and the recipient. As Stacey suggests, this results in 'conflicts of interest and emotion between the ethnographer as authentic related person (ie participant) and as exploiting researcher (ie observer)', conflicts that 'are an inescapable feature of ethnographic method' (Stacey 1988, p 26). For Stacey it was constructing the life history of someone who had died during her research that brought this awareness. In this study, I found it difficult to ask about and record stories of deportations, of hunger and hardship and especially rape, and hard to know how to write about these experiences in ways that captured the feelings without being voyeuristic. As Janet Liebman Jacobs (2004, p 233), a feminist sociologist who has written about wartime memories and memorial sites in Eastern Europe, has argued, it is hard to avoid concluding that 'such studies invite a kind of observational voyeurism, especially when gender is the focus of analysis'. Writing about the racialised and gendered gaze that constructed EVW women in particular ways once again constructs these women as objects, even if the perspective is both critical and sympathetic. As well as the ethnographer/writer and the women EVWs whose stories I collected, a third set of individuals enter the equation: you – the readers of this book who may be more or less familiar with the events that shaped the lives of young Latvian women from 1944 onwards and who will read this book in different ways. You too have reactions to and make judgments about what you have read here (McDowell 1994) and these will vary depending on your social position, personal characteristics, political opinions and prior knowledge of the period.

An act of translation

In collecting and interpreting life histories and writing this account, then, I hope that I have managed to tread a line between scholarly observer and empathetic listener, caught up in the immediacy of the stories retold but also able to set them in their theoretical and historical context. I feel that the best description of the role that I have played is that of a translator as I traced, talked to and began to reconstruct the lives of these 25 women whose vivid voices illuminate the arguments made here about the connections between migration, memory and identity. This book and the research that informs it is an act of translation in the sense that I have attempted to render familiar, or at least place within a set of academic debates that facilitate the interpretation of the lives of young European women caught up in the events of the Second World War. Their lives were transformed by the war and so have been radically different from the lives of women of my own generation, born as the Second World War ended. But there are certain parallels with, as well as remarkable differences from, the lives of women of my own mother's generation, especially the working class 'native' women who continued to work in hospitals, factories and mills in the post-war period rather than retiring to their homes to conform to the hegemonic notions of good mothering.

In this process of rendering the lives of others familiar, or perhaps accessible is a better word, to general readers, to academic specialists and perhaps to other women who came to Britain as part of the EVW schemes or as economic migrants in a later period, I hope that I have successfully translated one system of meaning – the oral histories graciously recalled and patiently retold to me by 25 Latvian women – into another – an academic argument – without altering its coherence or radically transforming its meaning. By placing the lives of individual women in their historical context and through comparisons between the 25 oral histories and with other sources, the events experienced by individual women become part of a larger story about loss, regret and dislocation and about rebuilding lives in a different place, and illuminating a small part of the history of the Second World War as well as knowledge about the history of immigration in Britain that is relatively unknown.

I hope too something of the strangeness, the particularity, remains, of the ways in which these women's lives have been significantly different from those of many women in Britain today. One of the pleasures of writing feminist history is the ability to explore the rich diversity of the lives of 'ordinary' women who, in fact and not surprisingly, turn out to be far more than ordinary, trying to capture something of the complexity of the relationships between gender, class position and ethnicity that mark everyday lives in contemporary Britain. One of the women involved in this work suggested that she was part of a forgotten generation and others too suggested that their experiences should be forgotten. I hope our collaboration means that this verdict has to be revised. These women's lives are part of a remarkable history of wartime dislocation and post-war reconstruction and too little is known, both in Latvia and in the UK, of the young women who came to Britain after the war to contribute to the efforts of rebuilding and eventually relative affluence. It is clear that many of these women have had hard lives, often working in low status and poorly paid jobs and too many of them came late in claiming their share of post-war affluence. Yet they have participated in post-war British social change and economic growth with remarkable energy, bringing a great deal of pleasure to numerous people, in a range of family, communal and cultural events that kept alight a notion of what it meant to be Latvian in exile throughout the second half of the twentieth century. If independence was late in coming for these women, it has been nonetheless valued and most of the women to whom I talked have managed to visit their homeland in the last decade, even though none of them has returned to live there. Their lives have been ones of a steadfast commitment to their national origins and of exile, characterised above all by hard work and a stoical determination to survive for the sake of their children whom they protected from the experiences of loss and dislocation that defined their own lives. There is no doubt that the remarkable stories of these women's journeys from wartime Latvia to early post-war Britain, and subsequently their lives as workers and as family providers over the following decades provide new insights into some of the most significant events of the twentieth century.

BIBLIOGRAPHY

Abella, I and Troper, H (1983) *None is Too Many: Canada and the Jews of Europe, 1933–1948*, New York: Random House

Adamczyk, W (2004) *When God Looked the Other Way: an Odyssey of War, Exile and Redemption*, Chicago: University of Chicago Press

Addison, P (1975) *The Road to 1945*, London: Cape

Addison, P (1985) *Now the War is Over: a Social History of Britain 1945–1951*, London: Cape

Agar, M (1980) *The Professional Stranger: an Informal Introduction to Ethnography*, New York: Academic Press

Ahmed, S (2000) *Strange Encounters: Embodied Others in Post–Coloniality*, London: Routledge

Aly, G (1995) *Endlösung: Völkerverschiebung und der Mord an den Europäischen Juden* Frankfurt: S Fischer

Anderson, B (1983) *Imagined Communities*, London: Verso (revised edition 1991)

Anthias, F and Yuval-Davis, N (1989) *Woman–Nation–State*, London: Macmillan

Anthias, F and Yuval-Davis, N (1992) *Racialised Boundaries: Race, Nation, Gender, Colour and Class and the Anti–Racist Struggle*, London: Routledge

Ball, C (1986) 'Women, rape and war: patriarchal functions and ideologies' *Atlantis* 12, 83–91

Barnett, C (1986) *The Audit of War: the Illusion and Reality of Britain as a Great Power*, London: Macmillan

Bauman, Z (1993) *Postmodern Ethics*, Oxford: Blackwell

Bauman, Z (1995) *Life in Fragments: Essays in Postmodern Morality*, Oxford: Blackwell

Beer, G (1989) *Can the Native Return?* The Hilda Hulme Memorial Lecture, London: University of London Press

Beevor, A (2001) *Berlin: the Downfall, 1945*, London: Viking

Bell, D (2003) 'Mythscapes: memory, mythology and national identity' *British Journal of Sociology* 54, 63–81

Benton, P (1984) *Baltic Countdown*, London: Centaur

Beveridge, WM (1942) *Social Insurance and Allied Services*, Cmnd 4606, London: HMSO

Beveridge, WM (1943) *The Pillars of Security and Other Wartime Essays and Addresses*, London: Allen and Unwin

Biddiscombe, P (2001) 'Dangerous Liaisons: The Anti–Fraternisation Movement in the US Occupation Zones of Germany and Austria, 1945–1948' *Journal of Social History*, Spring

Blackstone, T (1971) *A Fair Start: the Provision of Pre–School Education*, London: Allen Lane

Bloxham, D (2001) 'A survey of Jewish labour in the Nazi system' *The Journal of Holocaust Education* 10(3)

Bonnett, A (1996) '"White studies": the problems and projects of a new research agenda' *Theory, Culture and Society* 13, 145–55

Bonnett, A (1997) 'Geography, "race" and whiteness: invisible traditions and current challenges' *Area* 29, 193–99

Bonnett, A (2000) *White Identities: Historical and International Perspectives*, Harlow: Prentice Hall

Bourdieu, P (1979} 'Symbolic power' *Critique of Anthropology* 4, 77–85

Bourdieu, P (1986) *Distinction: A Social Critique of the Judgement of Taste*, London: Routledge

Bourdieu, P (1987) 'What makes a social class? On the theoretical and practical significance of groups' *Berkeley Journal of Sociology* 8, 1–17

Bourdieu, P (1989) 'Social space and symbolic power' *Sociological Theory* 7, 14–25

Bourke, J (1994) *Working Class Cultures in Britain, 1890–1960: Gender, Class and Ethnicity*, London: Routledge

Bowlby, J (1952) *Maternal Care and Mental Health*, Geneva: World Health Organisation

Boyd, M (1997) *'Migration Policy, Female Dependency, and Family Membership: Canada and Germany'*, in Evans, P and Werkele, G (eds), *Women and the Canadian Welfare State*, Toronto: Toronto University Press

Bradley, H (1989) *Men's Work, Women's Work: a Sociological History of the Sexual Division of Labour*, Cambridge: Polity

Braidotti, R (1994) *Nomadic Subjects*, New York: Columbia University Press

Brah, A (1996) *Cartographies of Diaspora*, London: Routledge

Braziel, J and Manur, A (eds) (2003) *Theorizing diaspora: a reader*, Oxford: Blackwell

Brooke, S (2001) 'Gender and working class identity in Britain during the 1950s', *Journal of Social History* 37

Broomhill, R and Sharp, R (1999) Restructuring our lives: engendering debates about social and economic policies in south Australia in Spoehr, J (ed), *Beyond the Contract State: Policies for Economic and Social Renewal in South Australia*, Adelaide: Wakefield Press

Browning, C (2000) *Nazi Policy, Jewish Workers, German Killers*, Cambridge: Cambridge University Press

Brownmiller, S (1975) *Against Our Will: Men, Women and Rape*, New York: Simon and Schuster

Brubaker, R (1992) *Citizen and Nationhood in France and Germany*, Cambridge, Mass: Harvard University Press

Bruce, J (1982) *After the War*, Don Mills, Ontario: Fitzhenry and Whiteside

Buhler, E (1998) 'Economy, state or culture? Explaining regional differences in gender inequality in Swiss employment' *European Urban and Regional Studies* 5, 27–39

Burawoy, M, Blum, J, George, S, Gilie, Z, Gowan, T, Haney, L, Klawiter, M, Lopez, S, O'Riain, S and Thayer, M (2000) *Global Ethnography: Forces, Connections and Imaginations in a Postmodern World*, Berkely and London: University of California Press

Butler, J (1992) 'Contingent foundations: feminism and the question of "postmodernism"', in Butler, J and Scott, J (eds), *Feminists Theorise the Political*, London: Routledge

Cabinet Papers (1946) *CAB 129/7 CP (49) 71*, 20 February

Cairncross, A (1985) *Years of Recovery: British Economic Policy*, 1945–51, London: Methuen

Card, C (1996) 'Rape as a weapon of war', *Hypatia* 11, 5–18

Cass, B (1998} 'The social policy context', in Smyth, P and Cass, B (eds), *Contesting the Australian Way: States, Markets and Civil Society*, Cambridge: Cambridge University Press

Castles, S and Miller, MJ (2003) *The Age of Migration: International Population Movements in the Modern World*, London: Palgrave Macmillan, 3rd edn

Cesarani, D (1992) *Justice Delayed: How Britain Became a Refuge for Nazi War Criminals*, London: Heinemann

Charlesworth, A (1994) 'Contesting places of memory: the case of Auschwitz' *Environment and Planning D: Society and Space* 12, 579–93

Chesser, E (1956) *The Sexual, Marital and Family Relationships of the English Woman*, London: Hutchinson

Chivallon, C (2001) 'Bristol and the eruption of memory: making the slave trading past visible' *Social and Cultural Geography* 2, 347–63

Clark, D (ed) (1992) *Marriage, Domestic Life and Social Change: Writings for Jacqueline Burgoyne 1944–88*, London: Routledge

Clarke, P (1996) *Hope and Glory: Britain 1900–1990*, London: Allen Lane

Cleaver, H (2003) 'We were war victims too, say Germans' *The Observer*, 3 August p 19

Clifford, J and Marcus, G (eds) (1986) *Writing Culture: the Poetics and Politics of Ethnography*, Cambridge: Cambridge University Press

Clifford, J (1997) *Routes: Travel and Translation in the Late Twentieth Century*, London and Cambridge, Mass: Harvard University Press

Cohen, R (1994) *Frontiers of Identity: the British and Others*, London: Longman

Commission of the Historians of Latvia (2000) *The Issues of the Holocaust Research in Latvia*, Vol II, report of a conference 16–17 October, Riga

Connell, R W (1987) *Gender and Power*, Cambridge: Polity Press

Connerton, P (1989) *How Societies Remember*, Cambridge: Cambridge University Press

Costello, J (1985) *Love, Sex and War: Changing Values 1939–1945*, London: Heinemann

Cowan, J, Dembour, M-B and Wilson, R (2001) *Culture and Rights: Anthropological Perspectives*, Cambridge: Cambridge University Press

Cowley, J (2004) '"This is not the country it was when Labour returned to power in 1997": the NS essay', *New Statesman* 29 March, 26–30

Curtis, L (1984) *Nothing but the same old story: the roots of anti–Irish racism*, London: Information on Ireland

Daly, M and Lewis, J (2000) 'The concept of social care and the analysis of contemporary welfare states', *British Journal of Sociology* 51, 281–98

David, M (1980) *The State, Family and Education*, London: Routledge and Kegan Paul

Davidoff, L and Hall, C (1987) *Family Fortunes: Men and Women of the English Middle Class*, London: Hutchinson

Davies, A (1992) *Leisure, Gender and Poverty: Working Class Culture in Salford and Manchester, 1900–1939*, Buckingham: Open University Press

DEW (Deutsche Edelstahlwerke) end of 1943 *Undated report*, B A (Bundesarchiv Koblenz) 10 III/134 c, fols 111–12

Diken, B (1998) *Strangers: Ambivalence and Social theory*, Aldershot: Ashgate

Dohse, K (1988) *Ausländische Arbeiter and bürgerliche Staat*, Hain: Konistein/Taunus

Dummett, A and Nicol, A (1990) *Subjects, Citizens, Aliens and Others: Nationality and Immigration Law*, London: Weidenfeld and Nicolson

Duncan, J (2002) 'Embodying colonialism? Domination and resistance in the nineteenth-century Ceylonese coffee plantations' *Journal of Historical Geography* 28, 317–38

Duncan, S (1995) 'Theorising European gender systems' *European Journal of Social Policy* 5, 263–84

Duncan, S and Edwards, R (eds) (1997) *Single Mothers in an International Context: Mothers or Workers?* London: UCL Press

Duncan, S and Edwards, R (1999) *Lone Mothers, Paid Work and Gendered Moral Rationalities*, London: Macmillan

Duncan, S, Edwards, R, Reynolds, T and Alldred, P (2003) 'Motherhood, paid work and partnering: values and theories' *Work, Employment and Society* 17, 309–30

Duncan, S and Smith, D (2002) 'Geographies of family formations: spatial differences and gender cultures in Britain' *Transactions of the Institute of British Geographers* 27, 471–93

Dyer, R (1988) '"White" ' *Screen* 29 (4), 44–65

Dyer, R (1997) *White*, London: Routledge

Eksteins, M (2000) *Walking since Daybreak: a Story of Eastern Europe, World War II and the Heart of the Twentieth Century*, Basingstoke: Macmillan

Elliott, J (1991) 'Demographic trends in domestic life, 1945–87' in Clark, D (ed) *Marriage, Domestic Life and Social Change*, London: Routledge

Elliott, MR (1982) *Pawns of Yalta: Soviet Refugees and America's Role in their Repatriation*, Urbana: University of Illinois Press

Elson, D and Pearson, R (1981) '"Nimble fingers make cheap workers": an analysis of women's employment in Third World export manufacturing' *Feminist Review* 7, 87–107

Esping-Andersen, G (1990) *The Three Worlds of Welfare Capitalism*, Princeton: Princeton University Press

Esping-Andersen, G (ed) (1996) *Welfare States in Transition: National Adaptations in Global Economies*, London: Sage

Ezergailis, A (1996) *The Holocaust in Latvia*, 1941–1944, Riga: The Historical Institute of Latvia

Ezergailis, A (ed) (1997) *The Latvian Legion: Heroes, Nazis or Victims?* Riga: Historical Institute of Latvia

Fanon, F (1967) *Black Skin, White Masks*, New York: Grove Press

Fielding, S, Thompson, P and Tiratsoo, N (1995) *'England Arise!' The Labour Party and Popular Politics in 1940s Britain*, Manchester: Manchester University Press

Finch, J (1993) *The Classing Gaze: Sexuality, Class and Surveillance*, St Leonards, NSW, Australia: Allen and Unwin

Finch, J and Mason, J (1993) *Negotiating Family Responsibilities*, London: Routledge

Fortier, A-M (2000) *Migrant Belongings: Memory, Space, Identity*, Oxford: Berg

Fosberg, G (1998) 'Regional variation in the gender contract: gendered relations in labour markets, local policies and everyday life in Swedish regions' *Innovation* 11, 121–210

Foucault, M (1994) *Discipline and Punish: the Birth of the Prison*, New York: Vintage

Fowler, D (1995) *The First Teenagers: The Lifestyle of Young Wage-Earners in Interwar Britain*, London: Woburn

Frankenberg, R (1993) *White Women, Race Matters: the Social Construction of Whiteness*, Minnesota: University of Minneapolis Press

Franz, B (2003) 'Bosnian refugee women in (re)settlement: gender relations and social mobility' *Feminist Review*, no 73, 86–103

Freud, S (1909) 'Notes upon a case of obsessional neurosis' (the 'Rat Man') in *The Pelican Freud Library* Vol 9, translated and edited by Strachey, A and Strachey, J, London, 1973–1985

Friedan, B (1963) *The Feminine Mystique*, London: Victor Gollanz

Fryer, P (1984) *Staying Power: the History of Black People in Britain*, London: Pluto Press

Fuenmayer, J, Haug, K and Ward, F (eds) (1992) *Dirt and Domesticity: Constructions of the Feminine*, New York: Whitney Museum of American Art

Garfield, S (2004) *Our Hidden Lives: the Everyday Diaries of a Forgotten Britain*, London: Ebury

Giles, J (2002) 'Narratives of class, gender and modernity in women's memories of the mid-twentieth century' *Signs* 28, 21– 48

Gilroy, P (1987) *There Ain't No Black in the Union Jack*, London: Routledge

Gilroy, P (1993) *The Black Atlantic: Modernity and Double Consciousness*, Cambridge Mass: Harvard University Press

Glick Schiller, N (1999) 'Transmigrants and nation-states: something old and something new in the US immigrant experience' in *The Handbook of International Migration*, New York: Russell Sage Foundation

Gluck, S and Patai, D (eds) (1991) *Women's Words: the Feminist Practice of Oral History*, London: Routledge

Glucksmann, M (1990) *Women Assemble: Women Workers and the New Industries in Inter-War Britain*, London: Routledge

Glucksmann, M (1995) 'Why "work"?: gender and the "total social organisation of labour"', *Gender, Work and Organisation* 2, 63–75

Glucksmann, M (2000) *Cottons and Casuals*, Durham: sociologypress

Gorer, G (1955) *Exploring English Character*, London: Cresset Press

Government Social Survey (1948) *Women and Industry*, London: Central Office of Information

Graham, B (1998) *Modern Europe: Place, Culture and Identity*, London: Arnold

Grass, G (2002) *Im Krebsgang*, Gottingen: Steidl Verlag (published in English 2003 *Crabwalk* London: Faber and Faber)

Gray, JG (1970) *The Warriors: Reflections on Men in Battle*, New York: Harper and Row

Greer, G (1985) *Sex and Destiny: the Politics of Human Fertility*, London: Picador

Greer, G (1992) *Change: Women, Ageing and the Menopause*, Harmondsworth: Penguin

Gregson, N and Lowe, M (1995) *Servicing the Middle Classes: Class, Gender and Waged Domestic Labour in Contemporary Britain*, London: Routledge

Greico, E and Boyd, M (1998) *Women and Migration: Incorporating Gender into International Migration Theory*, Center for the Study of Population, Florida State University WPS 98–139

Griffiths, M (1995) *Feminisms and the Self: the Web of Identity*. London: Routledge

Grossman, A (1997) A question of silence: the rape of German women by occupation soldiers in Moeller, R (ed) *West Germany Under Construction*, Ann Arbor: University of Michigan Press

Grunts, M (1980) *Latvians in Exile in the Free World, 1940–1980* self-published booklet, available in the West Room, University Library, Cambridge

Gupta, A (1992) 'The song of the nonaligned world: transnational identities and the reinscription of space in late capitalism' *Cultural Anthropology* 13, 63–79

Halbwachs, M (1925) *Les Cadres Sociaux de la Memoire Paris* (*On collective memory*) (Chicago, Chicago University Press 1992) (trans and ed Lewis Coser)

Hall, S (1990) 'Cultural identity and diaspora' in Rutherford, J (ed) *Identity: Community, Culture, Difference*, London: Lawrence and Wishart (reprinted in McDowell, L (ed) (1997) Undoing Place? London: Arnold)

Hall, S (1992) 'New ethnicities' in Donald, J and Rattansi, A (eds) *'Race', Culture and Difference*, London: Sage

Hanson, S and Pratt, G (1995) *Gender, Work and Space*, London: Routledge

Haraway, D (1991) 'Race' in *Primate Visions: gender, race and nature in the world of modern science* London: Routledge

Hart, N (1989) 'Gender and the rise and fall of class politics' *New Left Review* 175 May–June, 24–46

Harvey, B (1994) *The Fifties: a Woman's Oral History*, New York: HarperCollins

Harvey, D (1989) *The Condition of Postmodernity*, Oxford: Blackwell

Hennessy, P (1992) *Never Again: Britain 1945–1951* London: Vintage

Herbert, U (1990) *A History of Foreign Labour in Germany, 1880–1980: Seasonal Workers, Forced Labourers, Guest Workers*, Ann Arbor: University of Michigan Press (originally published in German in 1986 as *Geschichte der Ausländerbeschäftigung in Deutschland, 1880 bis 1980*)

Herbert, U (1997) *Hitler's Foreign Workers: Enforced Labour in Germany under the Third Reich*, Cambridge: Cambridge University Press (originally published in 1985 in German as *Fremdarbeiter: politik und praxis des 'Ausländer-Einstatzes' in der kreigswirtschaft des dritten reiches*)

Heron, L (ed) (1985) *Truth, Dare or Promise: Girls Growing Up in the Fifties*, London: Virago

Hiden, J and Salmon, P (1991) *The Baltic Nations and Europe: Estonia, Latvia and Lithuania in the Twentieth Century*, London: Longman

Hillel, M (1983) *L'Occupation Francaise en Allemagne, 1945–1949* Montrand: Saint-Armand

Himmelweit, S and Sigala, M (2004) *Choice and the relationship between identities and behaviour for mothers with pre-school children*, paper given at an ESRC Seminar, LSE, 28 May (available at www.lse.ac.uk/worklife)

Hirsch, M and Smith, V (2002) 'Feminism and cultural memory: an introduction' *Signs: Journal of Women in Culture and Society* 28, 1–19

Hobsbawm, E (1994) *The Age of Extremes: the Short Twentieth Century, 1914–1991*, London: Michael Joseph

Hobsbawm, E and Ranger, T (1983) *The Invention of Tradition*, Cambridge: Cambridge University Press

Hoggart R (1957) *The Uses of Literacy*, London: Chatto and Windus (reprinted in 1992, London: Penguin)

Holcomb, B (1998) 'Gender and heritage interpretation' in Uzzell, D and Ballantyne, R (eds) *Contemporary Issues in Heritage and Environmental Interpretation* London: HMSO

Holloway, S (1998} 'Local childcare cultures: moral geographies of mothering and the social organisation of pre-school education', *Gender, Place and Culture* 5, 29–53

Holloway, S (1999} 'Mother and worker: the negotiation of motherhood and paid employment in two urban neighbourhoods' *Urban Geography* 20, 438–60

hooks, b (1991) *Yearning: Race, Gender and Cultural Politics*, London: Turnaround Books

Hopkins, H (1963) *The New Look: A Social History of the Forties and Fifties in Britain*, London: Secker and Warburg

Hulme, K (1954) *The Wild Place*, London: Frederick Muller (originally published in 1953, Boston: Little Brown)

Hulme, K (1956) *The Nun's Story*, London: Frederick Muller

Humphries, J (1977) 'Class struggle and the persistence of the working class family' *Cambridge Journal of Economics* 1, 241–58

Hunt, A (1968) *A Survey of Women's Employment*, London: Government Social Survey

Index on Censorship (2002) Germany: Bertelmann's Nazi past, *Index on Censorship* 9 October, available at www.indexonline.org (accessed on 7 April 2004)

Iwaskiw, WR (1996) *Estonia, Lavia and Lithuania: Country studies*, Washington DC: Library of Congress

Jackson, B (1968) *Working Class Community*, London: Routledge

Jacobs, JL (2004) 'Women, genocide and memory: the ethics of feminist ethnography in Holocaust research' *Gender and Society* 18, 223–38

Jarvis, H, Pratt, A and Cheng-Chong, P (2001) *The Secret Life of Cities: the Social Reproduction of Everyday Life*, London: Prentice Hall

Jeater, D (1992) 'Roast beef and reggae music: the passing of whiteness' *New Formations* 18, 107–21

Jephcott, P (1942) *Girls Growing Up*, London: Faber and Faber

Jephcott, P (1948) *Rising Twenty*, London: Faber and Faber

Jephcott, P (1954) *Some Young People*, London: George Allen and Unwin

Jephcott, P, Seea, N and Smith, J (1962) *Married Women Working*, London: Allen and Unwin

Johnson, N (1995) 'Cast in stone: monuments, geography and nationalism' *Environment and Planning D: Society and Space* 13, 51–65

Joshi, H (1989) 'The changing form of women's economic dependency' in Joshi, H (ed) *The Changing Population of Britain*, Oxford: Blackwell

Joshi, S and Carter, B (1984) 'The role of Labour in the creation of a racist Britain' *Race and Class* 25, 53–70
Kandiyoti, D (1988) 'Bargaining with patriarchy' *Gender and Society* 2, 274–90
Kaplan, C (1996) *Questions of Travel: Postmodern Discourses of Displacement*, Durham, NC and London: Duke University Press
Karay, F (1996) *Death Comes in Yellow: Skarżysko–Kamienna Slave labour camp*, Amsterdam: Harwood
Kay D and Miles R (1992) *Refugees or Migrant Workers? European Volunteer Workers in Britain, 1946–1951* London: Routledge
Kearney, R (ed) (1990) *Migrations: the Irish at Home and Abroad*, Dublin: Wolfhound Press
Kerr, M (1958) *The People of Ship Street*, London: Routledge and Kegan Paul
King, N (2000) *Memory, Narrative, Identity: Remembering the Self*, Edinburgh: Edinburgh University Press
Klein, V (1965) *Britain's Married Women Workers*, London: Routledge and Kegan Paul
Kofman, E (2000) 'The invisibility of skilled female migrants and gender relations in studies of skilled migration in Europe', *International Journal of Population Geography* 6, 45–59
Kuhn, A (1995) *Family Secrets: Acts of Memory and Imagination*, London: Verso
Landzelius, M (2003) 'Commemorative (dis)rembering: erasing heritage, spatializing disinheritance', *Environment and Planning D: Society and Space* 21, 195–221
Lansmanis, A (1967) 'Latvia' in Rutkis, J (ed) *Latvia: Country and People*, Stockholm: LN5
Langhamer, C (2000) *Women's Leisure in England, 1920–60*, Manchester: Manchester University Press
Law, C (1994) 'Employment and industrial structure' in Obelkevich, J and Catterall, P (eds) *Understanding Postwar British Society*, London: Routledge
Lefebvre, H (1991) *The Production of Space*, Oxford: Blackwell
Lewis, J (1992) *Women in Britain since 1945*, Oxford: Blackwell
Lewis, P (1978) *The Fifties*, London: Heinemann
Liddington, J and Norris, J (1978) *One Hand Tied Behind Us: the Rise of the Women's Suffrage Movement*, London: Virago
Linke, U (1999) *Blood and Nation: the European Aesthetics of Race*, Philadelphia: University of Pennsylvania Press
Low, S and Lawrence-Zuniga, D (2003) (eds) *The Anthropology of Space and Place: Locating Culture*, Oxford: Blackwell
McClintock, A (1995) *Imperial Leather: Race, Gender and Sexuality in the Colonial Context*, London: Routledge
McClintock, A, Muft, A and Shohat, E (eds) (1997) *Dangerous Liaisons: Gender, Nation and Postcolonial Perspectives*, Minneapolis and London: University of Minnesota Press
McDowell, D (1989) 'Negotiating between tenses: witnessing slavery after freedom – Dessa Rose' in McDowell, D and Rampersad, R (eds) *Slavery and the Literary Imagination*, Baltimore: Johns Hopkins University Press
McDowell, L (1983) 'Towards and understanding of the gender division of urban space', *Environment and Planning D: Society and Space* 1, 59–72

McDowell, L (1991) 'Life without father and Ford: the new gender order of postFordism' *Transactions of the Institute of British Geographers* 14, 400–19

McDowell, L (1994) 'Polyphony or commodified cacophony: making sense of other worlds and pedagogic authority', *Area* 26, 241–48

McDowell, L (1999) *Gender, Identity and Place,* Cambridge: Polity Press

McDowell, L (2001) 'Father and Ford revisited: gender, class and employment change in the new millennium' *Transactions of the Institute of British Geographers* 24, 448–64

McDowell, L (2004) Work, workfare, work/life balance and an ethics of care *Progress in Human Geography* 28, 15–31

McDowell, L and Massey, D (1984} 'A woman's place?' in Massey, D and Allen, J (eds) *Geography Matters!* Cambridge: Cambridge University Press

McKibbin, R (1998) *Classes and Cultures: England 1918–1951,* Oxford: Oxford University Press

MacLaughlin, J (ed) (1997) *Location and Dislocation in Contemporary Irish Society,* Cork: Cork University Press

Maitland, S (ed) (1988) *Very Heaven: Looking Back at the 1960s,* London: Virago

Malcolm, N (1998) *Kosovo: A Short History,* Basingstoke: Macmillan

Marrus, MR (1985) *The Unwanted: European Refugees in the Twentieth Century,* Oxford: Oxford University Press

Marwick, A (1968) *Britain in the Century of Total War,* London: Bodley Head

Mason, J (1996) 'Gender, care and sensibility in family and kin relationships' in Holland, J and Adkins, L (eds) *Sex, sensibility and the gendered body,* Basingstoke: Macmillan

Massey, D (1998) 'Theories of international migration: a review and appraisal' *Population and Development Review* 19, 431–66

Massey, D (1984) *Spatial Divisions of Labour,* Basingstoke: Macmillan

Miles, R (1993) *Racism after 'Race Relations',* London: Routledge

Ministry of Labour and National Service (1949) *Minutes of Regional Controllers' Conference,* 13 April, file LAB8/1731

Mirza, HS (1992) *Young, Female and Black,* London: Routledge

Mitchison, N (1947) *You May Well Ask: a Memoir 1920–1940,* London: Victor Gollancz

Morgan, KO (1990) *The People's Peace: British History 1945–1990,* Oxford: Oxford University Press

Morokvasic, M (1984) 'Birds of passage are also women', *International Migration Review* 18 (4) 886–907

Morkovasic, M (1991) 'Fortress Europe and migrant women' *Feminist Review* no 30, 74– 92

Myrdal, A and Klein, V (1956) *Women's Two Roles: Home and Work,* London: Routledge and Kegan Paul

Naimark, NM (1995) *The Russians in German: a History of the Soviet Zone of Occupation, 1945–1949,* Cambridge Mass and London: Harvard University Press

Nairn, I (1977) *The Break Up of Britain,* London: New Left Books

Nash, C (1993) 'Remapping and renaming: new cartographies of identity, gender and landscape in Ireland' *Feminist Review* 44, 39–57

Nash, C (2002) 'Genealogical identities' *Environment and Planning D: Society and Space* 20, 27–52

Nead, L (1988) *Myths of Sexuality: Representations of Women in Victorian Britain*, Oxford: Blackwell

Nesaule, A (1995) *A Woman in Amber: Healing the Trauma of War and Exile*, London: Penguin

Nollendorfs, V (ed) (2002) *Museum of the occupation of Latvia, 1940–1991: Latvia under the rule of the Soviet Union and National Socialist Germany*, Riga

Oakley, A (1974) *The Sociology of Housework*, London: Martin Robertson

Oakley, A (1974b) *Housewife*, London: Allen Lane

Obelkevich, J (1994) 'Consumption' Obelkevich, J and Catterall, P (eds) *Understanding Post-War British Society*, London: Routledge

Ogersby, B (1998) *Youth in Britain since 1945*, Oxford: Blackwell

Okin, S (1989) *Justice, Gender and the Family*, New York: Basic Books

Ong, A (1999) *Flexible Citizenship: the Cultural Logics of Transnationality*, Durham, NC and London: Duke University Press

Oram, A (1992) 'Repressed and thwarted, or bearer of the new world? The spinster in inter-war feminist discourses *Women's History Review* 1, 3

O'Reilly, J and Spee, C (1998) 'The future regulation of work and welfare: time for a revised social and gender contract?' *European Journal of Industrial Relations* 4, 259–81

Parliamentary Papers (1947) Economic Survey for 1947 Cmnd 7046, London: HMSO

Pateman, C (1988) *The Sexual Contract*, Cambridge: Polity Press

Patterson, S (1965) *Dark Strangers*, Harmondsworth: Penguin

Paul, K (1992) 'The politics of citizenship in post-war Britain' *Contemporary Record* 6, 452–73

Paul, K (1995) 'British "subjects" and British "stock": Labour's post-war imperialism' *Journal of British Studies* 34, 233–76

Paul, K (1997) *Whitewashing Britain: Race and Citizenship in the Post-War Era*, Ithaca: Cornell University Press

Paxman, J (1998) *English: a Portrait of a People*, London: Michael Joseph

Pessar, P (1999) 'Engendering migration studies. The case of new immigrants in the United States' *American Behavioural Scientist* 42(4), 577–600

Peterson, E (1990) *The Many Faces of Defeat: the German People's Experience in 1945*, New York: P Lang

Pfahlmann, H (1968) *Fremdarbeiter und Kriegsefangene in der deutschen Kriegswirtschaft 1939–1945*, Darmstadt: Wher and Wissen

Pfau-Effinger, B (2000) 'Gender cultures: gender arrangements and social change in the European context' in Duncan, S and Pfau-Effinger, B (eds) *Gender, Economy and Culture in the European Union*, London: Routledge

Phillips, A (1987) *Divided Loyalties: Dilemmas of Sex and Class*, London: Virago

Phillips, C (ed) (1997) *Extravagant Strangers: a Literature of Belonging*, London: Faber and Faber

Phizacklea, A (ed) (1983) *One Way Ticket: Migration and Female Labour*, London: Routledge

Phizacklea, A. (2003) 'Transnationalism, gender and global workers', in Morokvasic, M Erel, U and Shinozaki, K (eds) *Crossing Borders and Shifting Boundaries: Gender on the Move*, Berlin: Leske and Budrich Opladen

Pinch, S (1984) 'Inequality in pre-school provision: a geographic perspective' in Kirby, A, Knox, P and Pinch, S (eds) *Public Service Provision and Urban Development*, London: Croom Helm

Plakans, A (1995) *The Latvians: a Short History*, Stanford Ca: Hoover Institution Press

Portes, A (1999) 'Conclusion: towards a new world: the origins and effects of transnatioanl activities' *Ethnic and Racial Studies* 22, 2

Portes, A, Guarnizo, L and Landolt, P (1999) 'The study of transnationalism: pitfalls and promises of an emergent research field' *Ethnic and Racial Studies* 22, 2

Pressley, A (1999) *The Best of Times: Growing Up in Britain in the 1950s*, London: Michael O'Mara Books Ltd

Priestley, JB (1956) *All About Ourselves and Other Essays*, London: Heinemann

Priestley, JB (1973) *The English*, London: Heinemann

Rabinow, P (1982) 'Ordonnance, discipline, regulation: some reflections on urbanism' *Humanities in Society*, 5, 267–78

Rabinow, P (1989) *French Modern: Norms and Forms of Disciplinary Pathos*, Cambridge, Mass: MIT Press

Radcliffe, S (1996) 'Gendered nations: nostalgia, development and territory in Ecuador' *Gender, Identity and Place* 3, 5–21

Reith Committee Report (1946) *Final Report, New Towns Committee*, Cmnd 6876, London: HMSO

Rex, J and Tomlinson, S (1979) *Colonial Immigrants in a British City*, London: Routledge and Kegan Paul

Rich, A (1977) *Of Woman Born: Motherhood as Experience and Institution*, London: Virago

Richards, M and Elliot, B (1991) 'Sex and marriage in the 1960s and 1970s' in Clark, D (ed) *Marriage, Domestic Life and Social Change*, London: Routledge

Riley, D (1983) *War in the Nursery: Theories of the Child and Mother*, London: Virago

Roberts, E (1984) *A Woman's Place: an Oral History of Working Class Women, 1890–1940*, Oxford: Blackwell

Roberts, E (1995) *Women and Families: an Oral History 1940–1970*, Oxford: Blackwell

Roberts, M (199)1 *Living in a Man-Made World*, London: Routledge

Roediger, D (1991) *The Wages of Whiteness: Race and the Making of the American Working Class*, London: Verso

Rollett, C and Parker J (1972) 'Population and family' in Halsey, AH (ed) *Trends in British Society Since 1900*, London: Macmillan

Ross, K (1994) *Fast Cars, Clean Bodies: Decolonization and the Reordering of French Culture*, Cambridge Mass and London: MIT Press

Rowbotham, S (1989) *The Past Is Before Us: Feminism in Action Since the 1960s*, London: Pandora

Rowntree, BS and Lavers, GR (1951) *English Life and Leisure: A social study*, London: Longmans

Royal Commission on Equal Pay (1946) *Report* Cmnd 6937, London: HMSO

Royal Commission on Marriage and Divorce (RCMD) (1956) *Report* Cmnd 9678, London: HMSO

Royle, E (1994) 'Trends in post–war British social history' in Obelkevich, J and Catterall, P (eds) *Understanding Post-War British Society*, London: Routledge

Runnymede Trust (2002) *Cohesion, Community and Citizenship*, London: Runnymede Trust

Sage, L (2000) *Bad Blood*, London: Fourth Estate

Said, E (1978) *Orientalism*, New York: Random House

Schmidt, U (2001) Discussing slave labourers in Nazi Germany: topography of research or politics of memory? Report of a *Conference on Slave Labourers in German–occupied Europe during the Second World War*, Institute for Social Movements, Bochum, 26–28 March, report available at www.kent.ac.uk/history/staff/material/schmidt/labourers.htm (accessed on 7 April 2004)

Seabrook, J (1982) *Working Class Childhood*, London: Gollancz

Shields, R (1992) *Places on the Margin: Alternative Geographies of Modernity*, London: Routledge

Short, J (1991) *Imagined Country: Society, Culture and Environment*, London: Routledge

Skeggs, B 1997 *Formations of Class and Gender: Becoming Respectable*, London: Sage

Skeggs, B 2004 *Class, Self, Culture*, London: Routledge

Skultans, V (1998) *The Testimony of Lives: narrative and memory in post-Soviet Latvia*, London: Routledge

Skultans, V (1999) 'Remembering time and place: a case study in Latvian narrative, *Oral History* 26, 55–63

Skultans, V (2003) *Narratives of displacement and identity*, draft paper available from the author at the University of Bristol, Bristol, UK

Slater, E and Woodside, M (1951) *Patterns of Marriage*, Heinemann, London

Smith, AD (1986) *The Ethnic Origins of Nations*, Oxford: Blackwell

Smith, AD (1991) *National Identity*, Harmondsworth: Penguin

Smith AD (1996) 'Culture, community and territory: the politics of ethnicity and nationalism' *International Affairs* 72, 448– 69

Smith, AD (1999) *Myths and Memories of the Nation*, Oxford: Oxford University Press

Smith, CD (1996) *Strangers at Home: Essays on the Long-Term Impact of Living Overseas and Coming 'Home' to a Strange Land*, New York: Aletheia Publications

Smith, G (1987) *When Jim Crow met John Bull: Black American Soldiers in World War II Britain*, London: Tauris

Smith, GE (ed) (1996) *The Nationalities Question in the Post–Soviet States*, London: Longman (revised edition, first published 1990)

Smith, GE (1999) *The Post–Soviet States: mapping the politics of transition*, London: Arnold

Smith, GE, Law, V, Wilson, A, Bohr, A and Allworth, E (1998) *Nation Building in the Post-Soviet Borderlands: the Politics of National Identities*, Cambridge: Cambridge University Press

Smith JH (1961) 'Managers and married women workers' *British Journal of Sociology* 12, 12–22

Spring Rice, M (1939) *Working Class Wives: their Health and Conditions* Harmondsworth: Penguin

Stacey, J (1988) 'Can there be a feminist ethnography?' *Women's Studies International Forum* 11, 21–27

Stadulis, E (1953) 'The resettlement of displaced persons' *Population Studies* 3, 207–37

Steedman, C (1986) *Landscape for a Good Woman: a Story of Two Lives*, London: Virago

Summerfield, P (1984) *Women Workers in the Second World War: Production and Patriarchy in Conflict*, London: Croom Helm

Summerfield, P (1989) *Women Workers in the Second World War*, London: Routledge

Summerfield, P (1994) 'Women in Britain since 1945: companionate marriage and the double burden' in Obelkevich, J and Catterall, P (eds) *Understanding Post-War British Society*, London: Routledge

Summerfield, P (1998} *Reconstructing Women's Wartime Lives: Discourse and Subjectivity in Oral Histories of the Second World War*, Manchester: Manchester University Press

Swirsky, R (1999) 'Migration and dislocation: echoes of loss within Jewish women's narratives' in Brah, A, Hickman, M and Mac an Ghaill, M (eds) *Thinking Identities: Ethnicity, Racism and Culture*, Basingstoke: Macmillan

Tannahill, JA (1958) *European Volunteer Workers in Britain*, Manchester: Manchester University Press

Thane, P (1991) 'Towards equal opportunities? Women in Britain since 1945' in Gourvish, T and O'Day, A (eds) *Britain Since 1945*, London: Macmillan

Thomas, G (1948) *The Social Survey*, London: Allen and Unwin

Tolstoy, N (1979) *Victims of Yalta*, London: Corgi (revised edition)

Tunbridge, J and Ashworth, G (1996) *Dissonant Heritage: the Management of the Past as a Resource inConflict*, Chichester, Sussex: John Wiley

Urch, R (1938) *Latvia: Country and People*, London: Allen and Unwin

Uzzell, D and Ballantyne, R (1998) 'Heritage that hurts: interpretation in a postmodern world' in Uzzell, D and Ballantyne, R (eds) *Contemporary Issues in Heritage and Environmental Interpretation*, London: The Stationery Office

Vernant, J (1953) *The Refugee in the post war world*, London: Allen and Unwin

Vertovec, S (1999) 'Conceiving and studying transnationalism' *Ethnic and Racial Studies* 22, 447–62

Vickers, J (1993) *Women and War*, London: Zed Books

Von Krockow, C (1991) *The Hour of the Women*, London: Faber and Faber (translated by K Winston; originally published in German in 1988 as Die Stunde der Frauen, Stuttgart: Deutsche Verlags)

Walby, S (1986) *Patriarchy at Work: Patriarchal and Capitalist relations in Employment*, Cambridge: Polity

Walby, S (1997) *Gender Transformations*, London: Routledge

Walter, B (2001) *Outsiders Inside: Whiteness, Place and Irish Women*, London: Routledge

Ware, V (1992) *Beyond the Pale: White Women, Racism and History*, London: Verso

Warner, M (1985) Monuments and Maidens: the Allegory of the Female Form, London: Picador

Webster, W (1998) *Imagining Home: Gender, 'Race' and National Identity, 1945–64* London: UCL Press

Webster, W (2000) 'Defining Boundaries: European volunteer worker women in Britain and narratives of community' *Women's History Review* 9, 257–276

Westergaard, J and Resler, H (1976) *Class in a Capitalist Society: a Study of Contemporary Britain*, Harmondsworth: Penguin

White, H (1973) *Metahistory: the Historical Imagination in Nineteenth Century Europe*, Baltimore: John Hopkins University Press

White, H (1980) 'The value of narrativity in the representation of reality', *Critical Inquiry* 7, 5–27

Whiteside, N (1999) 'Towards a modern labour market? State policy and the transformation of employment' in Conekin, B, Mort F and Waters C.(eds) *Moments of Modernity: Reconstructing Britain 1945–1964*, London: Rivers Oram Press

Whittaker, E (1995) 'Some anthropological reflections on ethnography, war, ethnicity and other matters' in Whittaker, E (ed) *Baltic Odyssey*, Calgary, Alberta: University of Calgary Press

Whittaker, E (ed) (1995) *A Baltic Odyssey: War and Survival*, Calgary, Alberta: University of Calgary Press

Wiener, M (1981) *English Culture and the Decline of the Industrial Spirit*, 1850–1981, Cambridge: Cambridge University Press

Will, W van der (1990) 'The body and the body politic as symptom and metaphor in the transition of German culture to National Socialism' in Taylor, B and van der Will, W (eds) *The Nazification of Art*, New York: The Winchester Press

Williams, R (1961) *The Long Revolution*, London: Chatto and Windus

Williams, R (1980) *Problems of Materialism and Culture*, London: Verso

Wilson, E (1977) *Women and the Welfare State*, Andover: Tavistock

Wilson, E (1980) *Only Halfway to Paradise: Women in Post-war Britain, 1945–1968*, London: Tavistock

Winship, J (1987) *Inside Women's Magazines*, London: Pandora

Wright, P (1985) *On Living in an Old Country*, London: Verso

Wyman, M (1998) *DPs: Europe's Displaced Persons, 1945–1951*, Ithaca and London: Cornell University Press (originally published in 1988)

INDEX